The Swiss Alps

1   (overleaf) *Engelberg*

The
SWISS ALPS

Vivian H. Green

B. T. BATSFORD LTD
LONDON

For my Mother

First published 1961

Made and printed in Great Britain
by William Clowes and Sons Ltd, London and Beccles, for the publishers
B. T. BATSFORD LTD
4 Fitzhardinge Street, Portman Square, London W.1

PREFACE

I AM WELL AWARE that this essay contains many imperfections and omissions. I can only make the plea that I have written a book of this kind because I find nowhere as satisfying as the Swiss Alps for spiritual and physical refreshment. I am neither a climber nor a sportsman, but I hope that what I have written may help others to appreciate and understand the beauty and the people of the Swiss Alps.

I have mentioned my indebtedness to particular books during the course of this work; but I must stress what I owe to the writings of two lovers of the Swiss mountains, Sir Arnold Lunn and Sir Gavin de Beer. Sir Gavin de Beer's *Travellers in Switzerland* (O.U.P., 1948) has proved an inexhaustible and rewarding quarry. I must also mention my debt, among more recent publications, to Claire Engel's *History of Mountaineering in the Alps* (1950), Hubert Walker's *Walking in the Alps* (1951), Cecil J. Allen's *Switzerland's Amazing Railways* (1953), Hugh Merrick's *The Great Motor Highways of the Alps* (1958) and Heinrich Harrer's *The White Spider* (1959).

Finally it gives me great pleasure to thank my friend Mr H. H. Brown, the companion of many journeys, for his invaluable help in reading the manuscript, and for providing, as always, the most useful of comments and suggestions.

VIVIAN H. GREEN

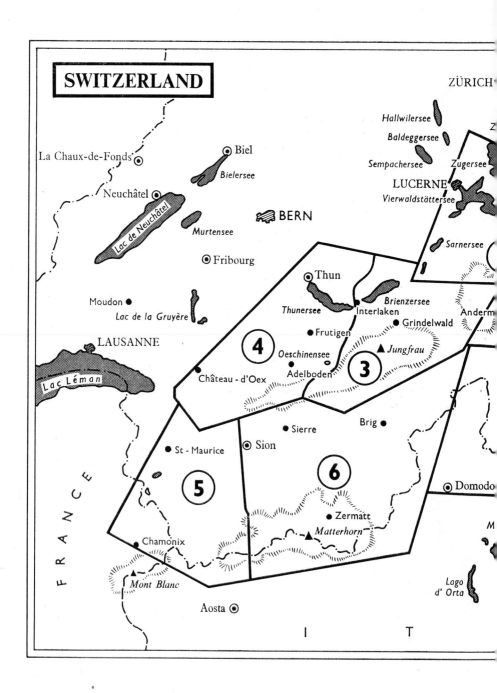

ACKNOWLEDGMENT

The Author and Publishers wish to thank the following for permission to reproduce the illustrations appearing in this book:

Bavaria-Verlag, Munich, for figs. 1, 46, 47 and 51–5.
Beringer and Pampaluchi, Zurich, for figs. 6, 7, 9–11, 13, 19, 21, 23–5, 30, 33, 36, 38 and 43.
J. Allan Cash, F.R.P.S., for figs. 12, 15, 32, 41 and 44.
Robert Löbl, Bad Tölz, for figs. 8, 14, 16, 17, 22, 26–8, 31, 34, 37, 39 and 49.
Herbert Maeder, St. Gallen, for figs. 2–5, 40 and 45.
Paul Popper, Ltd., for fig. 48.
Toni Schneiders, Lindau-Schachen, for fig. 42.
The Swiss National Tourist Office, for figs. 20, 29 and 50.

Figs. 18 and 35 are from photographs by the Author.

For permission to include extracts from copyright works, they also wish to thank:

Basil Blackwell and Mott Ltd, *The Matterhorn* by Guido Rey.
Elek Books Ltd, *Swiss Life and Landscape* by Emil Egli.
Rupert Hart-Davis Ltd, *The White Spider*, Heinrich Harrer.
Longmans, Green & Co Ltd, *Human Personality* by F. W. H. Myers;
    A Playground of Europe by Leslie Stephen.
Sidgwick and Jackson Ltd, *Early Travellers in the Alps* by Sir Gavin de Beer.

CONTENTS

LIST OF MAPS

LIST OF ILLUSTRATIONS

I

INTRODUCTION

THE SWISS ALPS form only a part, and that the least populous, of Switzerland; but the mountain lands are the cradle of the Swiss nation. Its wealth comes from highly-specialised industries and world-wide business connections, and three-fifths of its people are located in the plain. This plain or high plateau, resulting from the contraction of the mountain ranges of the Juras and the Alps, is a long and narrow corridor, stretching from the blue waters of the lake of Geneva to the lake of Constance and the German frontier, some 150 miles long and 30 miles wide. Here are the important towns, Basle, Berne, Zürich, and the majority of the factories. Here too is farmland rich in fruit and corn; as many as three-fifths of the milk cattle live on the plain. Yet the plain is tied to the mountains out of whose sight the plainsman rarely lives. Both are indeed complementary to each other, but the experience of history suggests that the Alps fostered communal feeling and freedom as well as courage and toughness. Switzerland was born in the mountains.

This is a commonplace of history for the Swiss child. The three mountain cantons, Uri, Schwyz and Unterwalden, bordering the lake of Lucerne, embodied a tradition of political independence in their opposition to Austrian overlordship and were the nucleus of the Swiss confederation. They entered into an alliance, whether this was a repetition of an earlier understanding or not is a matter of no great importance, in August, 1291, on a green meadow, the Rütli, just above the lake of Lucerne and under the shadow of the mountains. The Rütli has remained for the Swiss a centre of political and national pilgrimage. Yet acute discernment rather than political senti-ment caused General Guisan to call his commanders together at this historic spot on July 25th, 1940, to tell them that his country had decided to resist any violation of its neutrality. Less than a fortnight previously he had told the Swiss Federal Council that his army would abandon the plain if Switzer-land were invaded and concentrate all its force in the defence of an Alpine redoubt, flanked by the fortifications of Sargans, St. Moritz and the St. Gotthard Pass. The expected crisis did not materialise, but the decision had shown the ultimate political significance of the Alps. 'Here,' as a Valaisan peasant explained to the eighteenth-century English traveller, Archdeacon

Coxe, waving his hands towards the snow-clad peaks, 'are our fortifications.' Whether in the conditions of twentieth-century warfare, the defence of an Alpine redoubt could be more than a serious delaying action is doubtful; but the gesture had been historic. 'The very soul of Switzerland,' as André Siegfried has observed, 'fell back on its original hearth.'

Historically the Swiss nation was formed by a process of agglomeration and association. The three original cantons, Uri, Schwyz and Unterwalden, were joined by the other cantons as mutual interest dictated opposition to the control exerted by their Hapsburg overlords; Lucerne in 1332, Zürich in 1351, Berne in 1353. Apart from the cantons which made up the Swiss Confederation, there were for long many territories, great and small, in alliance with it or ruled jointly by it. The history of the Anglo-Saxon kingdoms of England is less complex than that of the Swiss Confederation before the end of the eighteenth century. It was not until the Napoleonic wars were over that the cantons of Valais and Geneva became full members of the Confederation; nor indeed until the nineteenth century that Switzerland achieved effective political unity. Cantonal feeling had for centuries been the determinant political force. It still remains exceptionally strong, though now submerged in a genuine national patriotism.

In spite of the economic and political power exerted by the urban patriciates of Berne and Zürich, the Alpine communities were the core of what was for so long an amorphous association. Why they were so is a question not susceptible of a simple answer. In part, at least, it was, and is, a question of character. The Alpine peoples were fashioned by a continuous struggle against nature, early snow and heavy rain, stony soil and the threat of avalanche. They had a struggle to be self-sufficient and to make both ends meet. The peasant, his wife and his children gathering in every wisp of hay as a darkening sky over the mountains foretells the coming storm epitomise the long and constant conflict with forces which they could not enslave. They emerged tougher and more independent-minded than the plainsman. From the economic point of view the plain is essential, as M. Siegfried has observed, 'to the whole but psychologically it is the mountains.' 'Enclosed spaces,' he has written, 'formed by nature herself and sketched in at least by heights are necessary to ensure the stability of a local way of life, and to protect them from the covetous attacks of neighbours.'

But this is not the only reason why the Alps form the heart of Switzerland. A way of life developed in the Alpine valleys sustained by a love of freedom and the need of co-operation. The Alps have few of the castellated dwellings which in other countries recall the domination of a powerful feudal aristocracy. Here and there they survive, the splendidly-situated castle of Tarasp perched on its hill commanding a view of the lower Engadine, the red and black shuttered windows of the castles of Spiez and Oberhofen looking over

2 *Girls of the Lower Engadine*

the placid waters of the lake of the Thun, and the over-photographed silhouette of Chillon near Montreux; but these ruins are rare. Most of the castles disappeared long ago either in the continuous wars against the Hapsburgs and their agents or in upsurges of local feeling against oppressive landlords. The large Swiss towns still have a patriciate of birth who once dominated their councils but the countryside has been long free of dominance by wealth, privilege or power. Within the peasant communities wealthier farmers have exerted on occasions more than their just influence, and have sought to restrict the membership of the *Burgerschaft*; but since the ending of the middle ages the Alpine communities experienced a marked degree of self-determination, often strengthened by their comparative isolation.

Economic and political factors obliged the peasants to co-operate. Every Swiss citizen has the right to serve on the local council or *Gemeindrat* of the commune in which he lives. The commune controls most of the local activities and collects taxes. Inevitably the more affluent peasants have tended to dominate the communes, but even so the stress and strain of life in the Alps have brought rich and poor together in a common effort. They were both materially interested, as they still are, in rights of pasture and wood-felling, of hay harvest and of water-courses. The word 'alp' means indeed the rich grass slopes just above the tree line and below the bare rock of the mountain where immemorially the peasant sends his cattle to graze in the summer. The cows leave the lower pastures for the alps in June, returning to the fields in the valley towards the end of September, the date depending upon the weather. Their return here, as in Austria, is a matter of some ceremony. The leader, wearing a resounding bell, and many of her followers. have their heads decorated with greenery, flowers and ribbons; one such cow that I saw near Steffisburg had a garland of roses and even rouged cheeks. No more sophisticated animal ever came down from the mountains. The right to graze cows on the alps thus constitutes a precious privilege. In some valleys it may be restricted to those who own certain property or to members of the *Burgerschaft*. In some cantons the law provides that new-comers to the district have the right to be admitted to the *Burgerschaft* on a money payment after they have lived there for a certain length of time. The communes have the responsibility of appointing the local herdsmen or *Senns* who will accompany the cattle to the high alps and live with them until they come down in the autumn. During the summer the various owners of the cows will visit the high pastures for a test of their cows' milk-producing capacity. The average of the official records taken on these occasions will determine how much of the cheese made on the alps will be ultimately distributed to them. Such co-operation provides ample opportunity for conflict and jealousy. Quarrels over grazing rights as over water-courses have given rise to fierce litigation and armed conflict. But it has

19

Sheep caught in the Alps by an early snowfall
The shepherd and his flock

afforded also a lesson in communal living which has by the experience of centuries fostered a truly democratic way of life. The people of the Alps, diverse in character as in religion, yet possess an independence of spirit, a love of liberty which wins admiration if the taciturn aloofness and dour self-sufficiency associated with it are occasionally daunting. The Alpine peasants remain proud of their local traditions and suspicious of innovation.

Their natural conservatism has certainly been challenged by the mechanical ingenuity of twentieth-century civilisation, nor is it possible to say for how long these Alpine communities can resist current fashion, diffused by the building of roads in the remote valleys and by the contacts provided by radio and the foreign tourist. The increasing mobility of the population may itself provide a more dangerous challenge. In 1860 58·7% of the Swiss lived in the communes in which they had been born and a further 27·7% who no longer dwelt in their native village still inhabited their original canton. In 1947, and the process has quickened since that date, only 31·3% lived in the commune of their birth while 33·1% dwelt in their original canton, and 30·4%, by comparison with 9% in 1860, had moved to other cantons. The Swiss depend for manual labour for the building of their new roads and for the construction of their vast new dams (as indeed for service in their hotels) on foreign workers, more especially Italians, who bring with them an alien culture, evanescent perhaps but eroding the centuries-old customs of the Alps.

Outwardly communal life seems moderately unaffected. The cinema and the dance hall are very much on its periphery, if they are there at all. The young men are noticeably free from habits customary to their continental and American counterparts. Their dress is sober, workmanlike, unexciting, even drab; not for them, unless they are Italians employed in the locality, tight jeans and fanciful colours, not even the black leather jerkin of their French contemporaries. Alpine conservatism is, however, on the defensive. The middle-aged and elderly woman of the Val d'Hérens in the Valais continue to wear every day their long black skirts, black boots, red and white bodice, and the somewhat witch-like black hats, which have for centuries been the valley's dress; but the young women prefer the cosmetics, the nylon stockings and blouses of the towns. Who, envisaging the heavy black boots and the somewhat unhygienic long skirts treasured by tradition, can blame them? Local costume, still worn on festive occasions, is becoming increasingly archaic and appears less spontaneously than, for instance, it does in the Austrian Tyrol. The movement away from the villages to the towns, stimulated by the higher wages offered by the factories of the plain, must lead to a steady modification of Alpine traditionalism. In the Grisons where Romansch, recognised since 1938 as a fourth national language, has long been spoken, strong efforts have been made to protect and promote it, but the ultimate success of these attempts is doubtful.

Yet although the Alpine customs may be challenged and the Alpine communities may be invaded by extra-mural habits of mind and behaviour, the traditional way of life is too deeply imbedded to be overturned at the first clarion of rock-and-roll. The family is still the determinant unit in the commune. The commune itself is in-bred, often giving the impression to the outsider of a closed community which he could never after long years of residence effectively penetrate or even properly understand. Family and communal life have a basic social solidarity. The timbered chalets give the impression of a life lived, not as in Italy on the streets and in the piazza, but in the homes, warmed in winter against the deep, crisp snow by wood-burning stoves, the subtle smell of the burning pine perfuming the cold air. The family from the oldest to the youngest tossing the hay under the warmth of the summer sun, or taking turns to watch the cattle in late autumn, bear witness to the strength of the home in Swiss life. All in all, the tenacity of communal life appears greater than in some other countries. In England village life steadily evaports not merely because of the magnetism of urban entertainment and industry but partly at least because it had for so long been closely associated with the paternalism of the local squire and parson, the one now often non-existent, the other no longer a potent factor in social life. In the Alps communal feeling runs deeper and flows more strongly.

There is then something in the notion that the real Switzerland, *Ur Schweiz*, consists of the mountainous cantons and the further it is from the Alps the less authentically and intrinsically Swiss is a community bound to be. In truth, however, in modern Switzerland, the plainsman is as vital to the Alpine peasant as is the peasant to the man of the plains. Here is that 'unity in diversity' which so effectively describes not merely the Swiss nation but the Swiss Alps.

The Swiss Alps cannot be pictured as a homogeneous entity. They vary in their peoples, in their structure, in their language and in their religion. The Confederation recognises four languages, Romansch spoken by 1·1%, in the Grisons, Italian spoken by 3·9%, principally in Ticino, French, spoken by 20·9%, mainly in south-western Switzerland, in the Jura mountains, around the lake of Geneva and in the Valais, and German spoken in northern and central Switzerland including the Bernese Oberland, by 73·9% of the population. These linguistic distinctions, which apparently constitute no barrier to national unity, do not in fact give a correct impression of the real diversity. In many Alpine valleys the peasants still speak a dialect of their own which to the traveller with a moderate knowledge of German may well be as unintelligible as Turkish or Arabic. Until recent times, and perhaps even now, a man in one valley might find it difficult to understand the dialect of the man from the neighbouring district. The possession of four common tongues does not eliminate the secretive independence of an Alpine dialect.

Religion provides a similar kaleidoscopic pattern. The division of Switzerland into Protestant and Roman Catholic areas was mainly a matter of historical accident, conditioned by geographical factors. As soon as the traveller crosses the Brünig Pass from the Bernese Oberland into Unterwalden, he passes from Protestant to Roman Catholic territory, though both districts are German speaking. In the Grisons, one principal valley, that of the Vorder Rhein, has remained strongly Roman Catholic, while the Engadine and the Val Bregaglia which stretches beyond it to the Swiss–Italian frontier have kept the Protestant faith. Here Roman Catholicism begins at the Italian customs office. There was a time when Swiss politics were more affected by religious controversy than cantonal rivalry or economic conflict, and as late as 1846 the country was brought to the brink of civil war by religious differences. In the twentieth century the *odium theologicum* has no place in the national life, partly because of the extent to which the spirit of toleration has grown and partly, at least in Protestant Switzerland, by the way in which the influence of the churches has itself diminished. In Roman Catholic Switzerland there is a plethora of clerical collars, but the Protestant clergy are at least far less obvious, though no doubt in the cities well-informed.

The Alps themselves are as various in shape and structure as the language and religion of the peoples who live among them. The Swiss Alps do not in fact form a separate geographical unit but constitute a part of the range of mountains which intrudes into France, Italy and Austria, albeit they are the backbone of Switzerland. The technical language of the geologist is beyond my understanding, but in simple fashion the Alps can be said to have come into existence as a result of great volcanic upheavals which shot them through the waters which so many aeons ago covered the continent. The crust of the floor over which this great prehistoric sea flowed was made in the first instance of the shells of marine creatures; exposed to the air it formed sedimentary rock, a phrase which includes both soft chalk and hard dolomite limestone. Below this layer there was crystalline rock which had solidified and which constitutes granite. Millions of years ago the troubled crust below the waters heaved and folded, and the great mountains rose above the sea to become subject to the various erosive forces of water, extremes of heat and cold and the slow solvents in nature's laboratory. Naturally the mountains became themselves subject to climatic changes and to chemical action. On some the layers of sedimentary rock were removed, disclosing the crystalline surface beneath. Many of the high Alpine peaks, Monte Rosa among them, are composed of this, but there are others, and the Eiger in the Bernese Oberland is the highest example, still made of the original sedimentary rock.

This primitive eruption was followed by others. There was a second folding, criss-crossing the first and dislocating the crust which had been formed after it had occurred. Water scooped out the valleys, many of which became filled with great glaciers of ice. The mountains were slowly sculptured by time. The process of geological change is indeed continuous, but man's own life is so brief that this is rarely perceptible. Few things give so great an impression of the primeval and the permanent as the precipitous cliffs of the high Alps.

The Swiss Alps consist of two principal ranges. The first of these is usually known as the Pennine Alps, which stretch from Mont Blanc to the Lepontine Alps, the Simplon Pass constituting a rough dividing line between the Pennine and the Lepontine chains. The only road over the range is that of the Great St. Bernard, but there are many high mountain passes. The Swiss or northern side of the Pennine Alps is pierced by a number of extremely beautiful, deep, lateral valleys, the Val de Bagnes, the Val Ferret, the Val d'Hérens, the Val d'Anniviers, the Turtmanntal, and the depressions which lead to Zermatt and Saas-Fee. The Pennine Alps are separated from the other range, that of the Bernese Alps, by a broad but steep-sided valley down which the waters of the River Rhone flow towards the lake of Geneva. The Bernese Alps present a steep, southern slope to the Rhone valley, penetrated here and there by short glens, but their northernmost flanks are intersected by fertile, green vales, penetrating to the foot of the snow-covered mountains and extending from west to east as well as from north to south.

The Bernese Alps are divided by a deep geological fault, which stretches from Brig to Gletsch and by way of the Furka Pass to Andermatt and the Schöllenen Gorge. This gap provides a cross-roads of communication and many passes radiate from Andermatt, to the north the Oberalp which takes the traveller to Disentis and the Grisons, to the east the St. Gotthard over which traffic moves to Ticino and the Italian lakes; and to the south the Furka opens the way to Brig and the Rhone valley or via the Grimsel Pass to the Bernese Oberland.

Within this area there is an infinite variety of scene. The southerly flanks are turned towards the Italian lakes where the spring comes so much earlier than in the north. Here maize, figs and almonds flourish in the warm, moist air while chestnuts clothe the mountain slopes. In the villages the houses are built of stone and cluster around an Italianate church, seeming far-removed from their northern neighbours, though only separated by a few miles and the height of a pass. The sun is often brilliant but the rain when it comes is torrential. On the northern side of the Alps the rainfall is ample and the mist pervasive. The chalets are timbered and the streams rush through woods of larch and pine.

The mountainous country is poor and unproductive. The sunny climate of the Rhone valley supports vines. Rye and potatoes grow at 4,000 feet in the Grisons, but the Alpine farms are primarily pastoral. The green hillsides are patched with the bronze of ripening grain. Here and there sheep graze but the king, or rather the queen, of the Swiss Alps is certainly the cow. Its annual migration to the high pastures has been already mentioned. The cowherd who passes his summer among the animals on the high alps may appear superficially to grow more bovine. On the other hand, the cows who spend so much of their time in human company, stall-fed in the winter months, their tails tied to a string attached to the rafters to ensure cleanliness, seem the more human. The Alpine cow is a charming creature, friendly, gentle, curious, unafraid. The music of distant cow bells, filtering through woods or over meadows, is a pleasing reminder of the fundamentally domestic character of Alpine civilisation. In closer proximity its incessant tintinnabulation can prove irritating, though in a world seldom free from the noise of the car and the cursed aeroplane, who shall complain if his rest is disturbed by the unmenacing clanging of cow bells?

In some sense the cow can claim to be almost the oldest inhabitant of the Alpine world. The Roman classical writer, Columella, wrote of Alpine stock sent down to help rear cattle in Italy. The small brown and grey cows of central and eastern Switzerland may be the descendants of the shorthorn herds of the neolithic lake dwellers. The Romans introduced into Helvetia, as they called Switzerland, a rather larger cow with a short head, the descendants of which are still said to flourish in the Val d'Hérens. The large brown cow most often found in Schwyz, Zug and Lucerne is very likely a cross between the Roman and native shorthorn. The cow is the backbone or the foundation, use what word you will, of Alpine economy. The peasant is continually exercised by the problem of finding its provender. In the summer the communes arrange for the cattle to live on the alps. They may even be obliged to ration the number of cows the peasant farmers send up to the high pastures to safeguard the hay fields. The sowing of new grasses has done something to solve the problem of winter feeding; but the life of the Alpine village still revolves around its domestic animals, the cow, and, to a lesser degree the sheep, the friendly goat and the pig.

Alpine economy is even in the twentieth century inevitably austere. It will be affected, perhaps disastrously, by the climatic extravagances of Alpine weather; it will be liable to interruption by avalanche tracks, by swollen water-courses, and by too late or too early snow. It is chastened by the rocky character of the soil. Until recent times the peasant was obliged to grow all his own crops. Many a smallholder is still relatively self-sufficient, owning his chalet, some cattle, goats and poultry, and selling milk and potatoes to procure the other necessities of life. Even now there are places where the old women spin the farm wool during the snowy months to provide the family with cloth. The snow makes for late planting and the harvest is hardly gleaned before the onset of winter.

The unproductive character of Alpine agriculture has provided a challenge which the Swiss has not failed to meet. His readiness to fight for others, to act as a mercenary soldier, which gave the Swiss such a military reputation towards the close of the middle ages, arose not only from the lucrative rewards of such service but from the need to survive. The conditions of his life fostered local independence, a respect for tradition and communal co-operation.

The remoteness and isolation of life in the Alps before the development of modern communications must not be overstressed. If Alpine farming has never enabled the peasant to do much more than eke out a bare livelihood, the communications which the Alpine passes provided enriched the communities through which the travellers journeyed. All the Swiss rivers have their sources in the Alps. The Rhine, for instance, flowing in two streams, the Vorder Rhein and the Hinter Rhein, mingling together at Reichenau, surges past Chur towards the lake of Constance. The Aar tumbles down the Haslital, through the lakes of Brienz and Thun to Berne where it bends north-eastwards to discharge itself into the Rhine. The Reuss, a swift torrent in the Schöllenen Gorge, gathers strength as it flows towards the lake of Lucerne, on its way too to join the Rhine. The Engadine is watered by the Inn before it enters Austrian territory. The river valleys, steep and stony at their higher levels, gave the opportunity for the building of the roads and the railways which make it possible for the traveller to cross the Alps from Germany to Italy and from France to Austria.

Where the valleys were obstructed by the mountains, men early made use of the high-altitude passes. Roman legionaries certainly tramped over the Great St. Bernard. When the St. Gotthard was opened in the twelfth or thirteenth century, it introduced a new element into Swiss politics, for supervision of the routes leading to the rich cities of the south was a matter of moment to all concerned, more especially for the cantons through which the road passed. There were tolls and trade to provide a rich reward. Sooner or later the communes realised that it was not enough to control a pass. They must also administer the regions adjacent to it. If all this is past history, it is still true that Alpine communications retain their economic significance. The roads and the railways carry an immense amount of traffic, while the advent of the motor car in summer and of the winter sports addict has brought prosperity to many an Alpine village.

For the majority of people the Swiss Alps signify less the life of the people who live under the shadow of the mountains than the tourists who make their transitory mark during the summer and winter months. Tourism is undoubtedly a significant aspect of Swiss economy but considerable as is its franc-earning capacity, it does less to balance the Swiss trade than insurance, banking and watchmaking. From the point of view of Swiss economy tourism may be ultimately less important than the dams built in the high mountains to provide the plains with power. It is indeed only during the past century that the tourist has become a significant factor in the economy and life of the Swiss Alps.

The peasants who lived by the mountains were for centuries comparatively uninterested in them. If they spoke of them, they were on the whole content to give them direct, unimaginative, self-explanatory names, Rothorn or Red Peak, Weisshorn or White Peak, Schwarzhorn or Black Peak, Matterhorn or Peak of the Meadows. It was the foreign climbers who furnished the mountain peaks with more fanciful nomenclature. Nor did the peasant bother to climb them. This was partly because Alpine folklore undoubtedly endowed many of the mountains with sinister legends and characteristics. They were peopled with demons and spirits and fairy cities. In his classic *Scrambles Among the Alps* Edward Whymper mentioned that the peasants in the valleys spoke of a ruined city on the summit of the Matterhorn where the spirits dwelt; 'and if you laughed they gravely shook their heads; told you to look yourself to see the castles and the walls, and warned one against rash approach, lest the infuriated demons from their impregnable heights might hurl down vengeance for one's derision.' There is indeed an eerie quality, not easily described, about the mountains, more especially when mist enshrouds the rocks and cloaks the tops of the pine trees. *Variabile et mutabile semper*, the mountain displays the facets of its character sometimes by a silence only broken by odd untraceable little sounds, sometimes by a fury of menacing noise when thunder, wind and rushing avalanche reveal the full extent of the orchestra which it commands. It is easy to understand why they should be called the Eiger or the Ogre, the Jungfrau or the Young Lady.

The mountains were long thought to be the homes of fiery dragons, even by respectable students. The early eighteenth-century traveller Johann Scheuchzer saw the stone with healing properties which the dragon had dropped in its flight from the Rigi to Pilatus. Another writer, Christopher Schorer, vouched that he had observed an object like a snake with the wings of a bat fly from a cave on Pilatus, while in the Grisons Bartholomeo Alegro saw a dragon with a red hairy head like a cat, fiery eyes, scaly legs, a snake's tongue and a long, furry tail. The peasant could see no reason for penetrating a fastness known to be barren and harsh, and suspected of harbouring demons and evil spirits.

Apart from legend there was the certainty that the mountains could be devastatingly cruel and destructive. Many valleys and villages, the Val Bedretto and the Val Tremola near the St. Gotthard Pass in particular, have felt the full force of the dreaded avalanche. With a great roar the mass of

26

snow glissades like a sea of spray, seethes, foams, carries rock, debris and mud, in a relentless trail of destruction. Not all avalanches are of the same character. When there is heavy snowfall in winter and the new snow fails to adhere to the old, it plunges below with a great roar, accompanied by a terrific blast of wind which can uproot trees and sweep houses before it. Avalanches of old snow which may carry away the subsoil occur when the temperature rises in the winter or in the spring. Such avalanches are less destructive because they follow a regular and known track. More than 8,000 avalanches of this kind occur in the late winter and early spring. Some occur so regularly that they have been given names, like the Bristen avalanche from the Bristenstock, near Amsteg in the Reuss valley and the Spreit which falls near the little village of Guttannen in the Haslital. No wonder then that the peasant for long either ignored or dreaded the mountains around him. They were a potential source of danger, and he could not conceive that they might be a source of profit unless they contained buried treasure, for which, indeed, he often believed the early climbers to be searching (unless they were spies). His aesthetic sensibilities were not aroused.

Nor indeed were the early travellers who crossed the Alps more attracted by the scenery through which they passed. In his fascinating book *Early Travellers in the Alps* Sir Gavin de Beer lists no less than 68 passes mentioned or described by sixteenth-century writers. He points out the growing interest in the Alpine regions at the time of the Reformation, finding expression in the first books written about the Alps, by Aegidius Tschudi, Johann Stumpf of Zürich and Jonas Simler. These early travellers were children of the Renaissance world, disliking the discomforts and perils of Alpine travel, averse to the bare majesty of the mountain peaks, but eager to describe the territory they were exploring. This was the background to Simler's description of the Valais, published in 1574 and to Ulrich Campbell's book on the Grisons; a few years later Thomas Schöpf first described the mountains of the Bernese Oberland. Jonas Simler's description of Alpine travel could hardly be regarded as an inducement to visit the Alps. The paths, he said, were so narrow and precipitous that the traveller often suffered from vertigo. Where there was ice on the track, he was advised to wear iron shoes with a sharp spike and to carry a stick with a sharp point. Where there was snow, he ought to wear a kind of snow shoe, which Simler described as a lattice-work of cord stretched on a hoop. Cold or frost-bitten feet should be placed in icy water gradually warmed. The tired traveller must never be tempted to rest in the snow lest he never wake.

Scientific interest or mere curiosity was for long the chief stimulus to interest in the Swiss Alps. Among the more curious of Alpine travellers was the Englishman Thomas Coryat, or the 'Odcombian Legge-stretcher' as he called himself, who travelled over Europe, including a crossing of the

Splügen Pass, with a single shirt and a pair of shoes (which he later hung up in the church of his native place, Odcombe, near Yeovil). In the eighteenth century, Johan Sulzer, realising the need for improved maps and more scientific observation, was interested in noting whether the earth's magnetic effect on the compass needle diminished with altitude, while Gottlieb Grüner was perhaps the first scholar to make a specialised study of glacial action founded on his knowledge of the glaciers of the Bernese Oberland.

An illustration of the growing interest in the Swiss Alps which can still be seen in the Glacier Garden at Lucerne was the first relief map of the Alps made by General Pfyffer, a member of a well-known Lucerne family. This map, the earliest accurately triangulated map of the Alps, took the general 19 years to complete. Archdeacon Coxe who called on him in 1776 described its construction: 'The composition is principally a mastic of charcoal, lime, clay, a little pitch, with a thin coat of wax, and is so hard as to be trod upon without receiving the least damage.' The general told him that he had himself 'raised the plans upon the spots, taken the elevations of the mountains, and laid them down in their several proportions. In the prosecution of this laborious performance, he has been twice arrested for a spy; and in the more heavily-populated cantons has frequently been forced to work by moon-light, in order to avoid the jealousy of the peasants, who think their liberty would be endangered, should so exact a plan be taken of their country. As he is obliged to remain some time upon the tops of the Alps, where no provision can be procured, he generally carries with him a few she-goats, whose milk supplies him with nourishment. . . . When he has finished any particular part, he sends for the peasants and chasseurs who reside near the spot, and bids them examine accurately each mountain; whether it corresponds, as far as the smallness of the scale will admit, with its natural appearance.' The indefatigable General Pfyffer was in the tradition of a long line of distinguished scientific successors: de Saussaure who ascended Mont Blanc in 1787, Louis Agassiz, Bonney and John Tyndall whose present-day successors may be found manning the observatory on the Jungfraujoch. In his eagerness to collect data on the progression of glaciers, the British geologist, J. D. Forbes, together with the Swiss naturalist, Louis Agassiz, camped in 1841 in the most primitive conditions for three weeks on the Unteraar Glacier in the vicinity of the Grimsel Pass. 'During several weeks, when not compelled by stress of weather to seek a more hospitable shelter, we remained in a sort of bivouac under a huge stone on the moraine of that noble glacier.' In his endeavours to further his research in geology the Swiss scientist, Joseph Hugi, who began climbing in 1828, made unsuccessful attempts on the Schreckhorn, the Finsteraarhorn and the Eiger. He also wrote a book detailing the equipment necessary for the mountaineer.

A new spirit was, however, beginning to show itself. For almost the first time mountain scenery began to be appreciated. The physiologist, Albrecht Haller, published in 1729 a poem *Die Alpen*, the fruit of a youthful walk in the mountains, which glorifies the dweller in the Alps in his struggle with the forces of nature and depicts the mountain lands as the last remnant of a fast-disappearing happiness. The mountains were no longer 'considerable protuberances' obstructive to travellers and economically valueless, but were at last seen to have a majestic beauty of their own. In Rousseau's *La Nouvelle Héloise* his leading character passes through the Valais. 'There is something magical and supernatural in hill landscape which entrances the mind and the senses; one forgets everything, one forgets one's own being; one ceases to know where one stands.' 'Had you been with me,' the Abbé Murith wrote to de Saussure after climbing the snow peak, Mont Vélan, which overlooks the Glacier de Valsorey at the head of the Val de Bagnes, 'you would have enjoyed the most splendid spectacle of mountains and glaciers you can imagine; you would have been able to gaze on a wide circle of peaks of different heights, from Turin to the Little St. Bernard, from the St. Bernard to the Lake of Geneva, from Vevey to the St. Gotthard, from the St. Gotthard to Turin.' The Alps were soon indeed to be a part of the romantic movement. The rushing waterfalls, the mossy rocks, the dark forests, the snow-covered summits entranced the travellers who came to Switzerland after the Napoleonic Wars, though few as yet penetrated far above the snow line.

It was this remote and in many ways medieval world which the bustling Victorian was to invade in considerable force, whether for health and recreation or for the new-found joy of conquering the peaks. The passion for the building of English churches in Swiss villages was no greater than the desire to climb the virgin heights. The search for information indeed provided the chief impetus. The first President of the British Alpine Club, John Ball, went equipped with thermometers, a pocket clinometer, a compass, an opera glass and measuring tapes and advised other climbers to take a 'flask with strong cold tea, to be diluted with water or snow, a tin box for plants, a geological hammer of a form available for occasional use as an ice-axe.' The irascible John Tyndall was equally irritated by what he regarded as Forbes' inaccurate theories on glaciation and Leslie Stephen's facetious attitude to mountain climbing. Later Coolidge often made his ascents to confirm points of alpine history. Mountain climbing was still frequently didactic and scientific in purpose.

Soon, however, climbers began to climb for climbing's sake. The experience of the view, breath-taking as it might well be, was only a fraction of the reward. In his book on *The Matterhorn*, Guido Rey wrote that he 'saw the mountains as none had ever painted them, as no book had ever described them to me; full of new wonders that no fairy-tale had ever shown me even in dreams. I knew sensations that nothing had ever afforded me till then—the instinctive pleasure of rising above the plain, the delight of great exertion, and of complete repose that followed. The bread I ate so hungrily up there had a sweet savour hitherto unknown to me, and I tasted the fresh ineffable joy of reaching the highest point—the summit; the spot where the mountain ceases to rise and man's soul to yearn. It is an almost perfect form of spiritual satisfaction, such as is perhaps attained by the philosopher who has at last discovered a truth that contents and rests his mind.' The climber, A. F. Mummery wrote later, 'delights in the fun and jollity of the struggle. The gaunt, bare slabs, the square precipitous steps, and the black bulging ice of the gully are the very breath of life of his being. I do not pretend to be able to analyse this feeling still less to make it clear to unbelievers. It must be felt to be understood, but it is potent to happiness and sends the blood tingling through the veins, destroying every trace of cynicism and striking at the very roots of pessimistic philosophy.' The mountains became endowed for many with a religious or semi-mystical meaning. 'The great mountains,' Lord Conway of Allington wrote after viewing the place where a friend of his had been killed while climbing, 'did not seem inimical, as the Cervin used to be. No! They put on an aspect of higher dignity. They withdrew themselves again into the other world to which years ago they seemed to belong.' The Alpinists had indeed discovered a new world, and were not slow to revel in their discovery. The Swiss climbers had been first in the field. Johann and Hieronymus Meyer, accompanied by chamois hunters, reached the summit of the Jungfrau in 1811, having made their way there from the Grimsel Pass. The naturalist Oswald Heer climbed the highest mountains in the Engadine, the Piz Palü and the Piz Linard, in 1835. The Finsteraarhorn had been conquered in 1829, the Wetterhorn in 1844. The Swiss forestry expert, Coaz, made the top of the Piz Bernina in 1850. But the Swiss climbers' very familiarity with the mountains, tinged indeed by sentimentality and patriotic feeling, discouraged the sense of high adventure and even of mystical exaltation, characteristic of so many British climbers of the Victorian epoch.

The great age of mountaineering began in the middle of the nineteenth century, affording a new means of recreation which proved especially attractive to the more athletic and academically-minded of the British upper middle classes. The British Alpine Club was founded in 1857. Within four years some 281 members had joined, of whom some 80 were lawyers, 34 were parsons and 22 dons or schoolmasters. *The Alpine Journal*, established under the editorship of H. B. George in 1863, was designed as a 'record of mountain adventure and scientific observation.' The Swiss Alpine Club was started in 1863 and by the turn of the century had 6,000 members and 44 sections. During the next ten years Austrian, German, Italian and French clubs of a similar character had been founded.

Within the next 20 years summit after summit fell to alpinists, the majority of whom were of British nationality. In 1856 Ames made the first ascent of the Allalin and the Laquinhorn in the Saas valley. A Viennese doctor, Sigismond Pörges, climbed the Mönch in 1857, but next year an impecunious Englishman, Charles Barrington, reached the top of the Eiger. The same year, the Rev. J. L. Davies first climbed the Dom, so-named by the Abbé Berchtold of Zermatt, the highest mountain completely on Swiss soil. Leslie Stephen made the first successful ascent of the Bietschhorn in 1859, adding the Blümlisalp to his triumphs the next year. The same year Frank Walker, accompanied by his son, Horace, and his daughter, Lucy, climbed the Balmhorn. The scientist John Tyndall conquered the Weisshorn in 1861. Three years later, Leslie Stephen and F. C. Grove climbed the Zinal Rothorn, while the next year after many attempts the Matterhorn fell to Whymper and his companions. If a new world had opened, a new vocabulary was in process of development, of pitons and crampons, of chimneys and arêtes, and the virgin territory of the great mountains was being fast explored, conquered and mapped. 'I thought of Englishmen in battle,' Tyndall wrote of his ascent of the Weisshorn, 'of the qualities which had made them famous; it was mainly the quality of not knowing when to yield, of fighting for duty even after they had ceased to be animated by hope. Such thoughts helped to lift me over the rocks.' When the Rev. Frederick Hardy reached the top of the Lyskamm in 1889, he described how he and his companions sang the National Anthem, 'and we sang with uncovered heads, the noble old anthem fills our English hearts with happy thoughts of home, and Fatherland, and of the bright eyes that will sparkle, and the warm hearts that will rejoice, at our success.'

These early climbers were pioneers in mountain climbing, lacking the technical knowledge and equipment available to their successors. As there were no mountain huts, they had to make use of uncomfortable high-altitude bivouacs. Their iron-shod boots were far from efficient. Their ice-axes differed little from ordinary axes. The long smooth pole, the alpenstock, upon which they placed such reliance, was sometimes positively dangerous. They knew little about the use of the rope. Gradually experience brought an improvement in climbing conditions. The mountains were accurately mapped and equipped with huts. Within a quarter of a century the Swiss Alpine Club had erected 38 huts, the earliest being the Grünhorn hut on the Tödi (1863), the Trift hut near the Dammastock (1864) and the Matterhorn hut (1865). When Leslie Stephen crossed the high mountain passes in the Oberland, much time was invariably spent in cutting steps in the snow and ice. Soon it began to be realised that it was better to climb a rock ridge than attempt a snow slope. Ice-axes were improved in shape and effectiveness. Guides ceased to recommend the habit of making a sitting glissade down a snow slope and the use of ladders, once much used for crossing deep crevasses, was discontinued. Greatly improved use was made of ropes, especially of the double rope, the texture of which changed from manilla or hemp to silk, and from silk to nylon. Steel pitons were carried to be wedged in rock fissures with hammers or specially adapted ice-axes.

This strange migration was greeted by the mountain Swiss with interest, and, as its financial effects gradually made themselves felt, with articulate enthusiasm. The peasants in the more remote valleys at first disliked this alien intrusion, hardly believing it possible that any man could climb a mountain without substantial material reward; but for the guides it meant a new and lucrative source of income which they were not slow to exploit. The earliest guides were often no more than incompetent amateurs. Peter Damatter, who escorted Professor Forbes up the St. Théodule Pass in 1842, instead of taking with him a rope and an iron-pointed stick, took only an umbrella and when he came to the glacier asked Forbes to lend him his stick. It was said of two other guides that they had refused to proceed unless the travellers they were accompanying would go in front and cut the steps in the ice. But a profession was in course of development which would soon produce men of the greatest skill and toughness, men like Christian Almer, Melchior and Jacob Anderegg, Auguste Balmat, François Devouassoud, Alexander Burgener, Christian Klucker, and Franz Lochmatlter, without whose assistance the ascents could never have been made. As the demand for guides grew, so did their fees. Alfred Wills, who made a famous climb of the Wetterhorn in 1854, told young Coolidge when he asked for his advice about guides that they, 'like most other commodities, have risen in the market. . . . The usual thing at present for a Chamouni guide who goes a tour with men who are going to climb is 8 fr. (about 7s.) a day when nothing exceptional is done, and a good deal more for *grands courses.*'

The advent of the tourist opened a new era in the life of the Alpine villages. What hotels or inns there were had so far offered only the simplest accommodation. When Leslie Stephen was staying at Zinal in the summer of 1864, preparatory to his ascent of the Zinal Rothorn, he found his host, M. Epinay, an excellent cook, but 'Macdonald and Grove had to sleep in two cupboards opening out of the coffee-room, whilst I occupied a bed . . . in the coffee-room itself. . . . The room boasted of one of the few decent sofas in Switzerland. It is true that it was only four feet long, and terminated by two lofty barriers; but it was soft and had cushions—an unprecedented luxury, so far as my Alpine knowledge extends.' Fourteen years later when Mrs. Warwick Cole visited Zermatt, she thought herself fortunate to 'secure a bedroom in a little wooden inn belonging to the village doctor,

32

Herr Lauber, which was then the only house for the reception of travellers.
... It was tolerably comfortable, but unfortunately the floors looked as if
they had never been washed since the house was built.' When T. W.
Hinchliff sought accommodation at Ayer in the Val d'Anniviers in 1857 he
found that all he could get was a single gloomy room in which there were
two beds and a mattress, the mattress occupied by a young shepherd and one
of the beds by an old lady and her niece. The surviving hotel register at the
Hotel Bella Tola at St. Luc, situated in the same valley, tells of the agonies
endured by early travellers at other inns in the district.

But things were changing rapidly. New hotels were being built in every
resort, sometimes even in the most remote spots. In 1850 Ulrich Melchior
said that the new inn at Saas-Fee, the Monte Rosa, had pleasant, comfortable,
clean rooms and plentiful food at low cost. Whether Melchior's standards
were low or the new innkeeper found it difficult to maintain his own, this
was not Alfred Wills' experience two years later. 'The fleas,' he wrote of a
visit in 1852, 'were intolerable. Their size, and the fierceness of their appetite
exceeding anything of the kind I ever knew; and when a cold or wet day
drove one near the fire, their attacks became unendurable.' Two years later
he found the fleas and the cuisine greatly improved, though he was obliged to
add that 'the only day that we escaped the plague of garlic was a day when
they apologised for the absence of the cook, who was gone to act as guide
over the mountains. We found great cause to rue his safe return.' Frederic
Harrison found no inn nor even a chalet where he could get a glass of milk
at Mürren in 1852–4, but a small hotel had opened the very next year.
In 1852 John Ruskin remarked that there was a new inn at Airolo, 'not a
fashionable hotel, but small, clean and Swiss.' A new hotel had been opened
at Evolène in the Val d'Hérens by 1858, though Wills found that the landlord was indifferent to his needs and ready only to supply black bread and
salted mutton. Edwin Godkin and his wife were the first guests at the hotel
established on the Belalp in 1861.

The growth and development of the Swiss hotel industry was a highly
important factor in the country's economy. With surprising quickness the
Swiss made themselves experts in hotel management, suiting themselves to
their customers' needs, making their food palatable, their beds comfortable,
their service clean and efficient. There was indeed a debit as well as a credit
side to all this. The countryside has not been spoiled but certainly marred by
the immense buildings, designed at one of the periods of the world's worst
taste, to house the teeming tourists of Victorian Europe. They constitute a
legacy which the Swiss themselves must regret since they are in the twentieth
century impossible to modernise effectively, difficult to staff and expensive
to run (and to stay at). Two world wars disastrously affected their economy,
and the number of hotels held by the Swiss banks is a secret known only to

their directors. Yet the majority of them survived, retained their efficiency, their staff (though many are often not Swiss nationals) and their reputation for cleanliness and good food. I have had poor meals in Swiss hotels; and culinary standards are perhaps a little lower than they once were. Cream is too sparingly used and the cuisine rarely achieves the imaginative excellence of the good hotel or restaurant in France. The standards of the Swiss hotel industry still, however, remain high. In the 1930s some 62,400 people were employed in it. There are special schools for training hotel personnel at Lausanne and Lucerne, and for those engaged in restaurants at Zürich. The Swiss makes a genuine effort to please his customer. The British would be well-advised to take some hints, for the cleanliness of the linen, the spotless table-cloths placed on the table in the simplest restaurant, the absence of the horrid paper napkin, the china, the cutlery, the décor are in nearly every respect superior to those of the ordinary English tea room, hotel and restaurant. It may be that the British are fundamentally dirtier than the Swiss (and certainly more dishonest, for what English station waiting-room could provide illustrated papers without fear of loss or what English farmer would leave his lighter tools such as scythes and rakes at the side of the road without losing them?), but cleanliness is sometimes a response to a clean environment. How some of the hotels survive is a problem, but if it is rare, if by no means unknown, to find a new hotel being built—I saw one in 1960 in course of construction at Merligen on the lake of Thun—it is also unusual to find a hotel being pulled down or converted into flats. The architectural demerits of the great hotels are less noticeable in resorts like Interlaken and Montreux which are fundamentally as Victorian or Edwardian as Leamington or Torquay, and in the Alpine villages the scenery is sufficiently grandiose to dwarf and absorb them. The Swiss hotelier, skilled in offering courtesy and service, has often been steeled to a shrewdness, almost Scotch in its perception of where lies the profit. I am told of a hotel proprietor in the Engadine who to save postage on his letters to England regularly sends them in a much delayed bunch to his daughter in London to post. Yet for better or worse the Swiss hotels have become part of the Swiss Alps. And in general how much for better. There are nearly always hot water, comfortable beds, immaculate rooms, well-cooked food and efficient service, and I am of insufficiently adventurous a nature to wish to exchange the remoter and unconventional, even in certain respects more picturesque, parts of the world for these pleasures.

The Swiss tourist industry came into being not merely in response to the needs of a comparatively small group of climbers and their relatives, but to cope with the demands of a new travelling public, stimulated by the building of railways, coming from all parts of the world, even if the Victorian British were more especially drawn to the Alps. Already by the middle of the

34

nineteenth century the stream was beginning to become a flood. In 1856 a
Swiss traveller could comment acidly on the presence of a 'smart set' at
Interlaken: 'The fragrance of the trees is swamped by the odour of Eau de
Mille fleurs and patchouli and . . . the wasp-like waists of the ladies spoil
one's taste for the Jungfrau.' Soon John Addington Symonds was to deplore
the 'troops of tourists' who came up from Interlaken to lunch at Mürren
and then went 'noisily away again.' In 1875 Anne Ritchie commented that
'All Cambridge seems to be about.' These quotations give an impression of
the social milieu of the Victorian tourist to Switzerland. They were at least
at the start predominantly representative of the upper middle classes, schoolmasters, dons, clergy, doctors and lawyers. They were able in Switzerland
as in the then far-flung British empire to create a little bit of England on
foreign soil. In the mid-nineteenth century this took the form of building a
small Anglican church, usually with a spire, sufficiently reminiscent of
England (and sufficiently Evangelical) to suit the religious needs of the
Victorian families. No major Swiss resort, and many very inconspicuous
and remote ones, was without its Anglican church. Where this was lacking,
the English tourists improvised a hotel lounge for their Sunday services,
sometimes to the discomfort of the other guests. Leslie Stephen wrote
disapprovingly of 'that variety of English clergyman which travels in
dazzling white ties and forces church services upon you by violence in remote
country inns,' and in 1883 J. V. Widmann commented despairingly on
the six Englishwomen who were practising their service for the Sunday
on the hotel piano when he was staying at Evolène. 'Nothing,' he wrote, 'is
so appalling as when religion, which should blossom as a hidden flower within the quiet of a modest soul, takes on a form which imposes itself on society.
And how utterly devoid of taste is this chant by six untalented and completely
unmusical Englishwomen!'

But the flood-gates were opening still wider. Leslie Stephen was irritated
to find at St. Moritz cockneys and Cook's tourists as well as kings. Thomas
Bonney, the Cambridge geologist, recalled that he had seen one of Thomas
Cook's parties at Chamonix in 1875. 'It was an irregular procession of
incongruities, headed by an elderly clergyman in a top hat who "pegged" the
footpath with his alpenstock at every step as if that were a ceremonial
performance.' Actually Cook's excursions to Switzerland were already
eleven years old. Thomas Cook, whose entry into the excursion world had
been stimulated by his enthusiasm for the cause of temperance, wrote from
Paris in August 1863, that 'France and Switzerland now present to me new
and almost unlimited fields of tourist labour.' Five hundred people responded
to Cook's first advertisement of Swiss tours, and his first conducted trip took
his party to Geneva, Chamonix, Martigny, Sion, Leuk, the Gemmi Pass,
Kandersteg, Interlaken, Brienz, the Brünig Pass, Sarnen, Lucerne, Berne,

Neuchâtel and Lausanne. Another of the early tourist agents, John Frame, was also an ardent supporter of temperance and demanded strict abstinence from alcohol by his clients. Dean and Dawson, now associated with Thomas Cook, started with a factory outing from Stockport to Paris in 1871. The Polytechnic had originated a year earlier from a holiday home at Brighton for poor members of the London Polytechnic. In 1892 Sir Henry Lunn began his career as a tourist agent with a special trip to Rome. A multitude of other firms, many founded since 1945, have been established in their wake to 'conduct' the tourist to the Swiss Alps in the company of thousands of his fellows.

The development of winter sports opened a new field to the tourist, and stimulated the prosperity of those resorts which now enjoyed two seasons. It has been said that the first Swiss ski tour was done by two Norwegians who skied from Muotathal, north of the Gulf of Uri in the lake of Lucerne, to Klöntal near Glarus over the Pragel Pass. The first skiers entered the Zermatt valley six years later, in 1898, and in 1902 Dr. Hermann Seiler opened a ski-course for guides there. The British were certainly the pioneers in the development of winter sports. They were, as Sir Arnold Lunn has stressed, the first to introduce skiing into the Bernese Oberland (Knocker at Meiringen in 1890, Gerald Fox at Grindelwald in 1891) and they did much to shape the sport of competitive skiing. Sir Arnold himself and his fellow sportsmen at Mürren were responsible for drafting the rules for downhill ski-racing and for inventing the modern slalom, in January 1922. A year previously, almost to the day, the first national championship to be decided on the result of a downhill race took place on the Kleine Scheidegg. The non-sportsmen, among whom I must include myself, are apt to associate the cult of winter sports with young men in shaggy pullovers and young women in tight skiing trousers laughing heartily in the purlieus of Victoria station on a foggy winter morning; but if the British were the first to put winter sports on the map, they soon became a pastime in which all including the native Swiss could eagerly take part. The brilliance of the winter sun, the frosted snow, the translucence of the atmosphere, the exhilaration involved in the sport itself, the high degree of skill which it called for, all explain its popularity. The winter tourist contributed something more than his money to the high Alpine resorts. The long, often tedious winter days, broken only by drinks in the inn and the Swiss card game of 'Jass,' were enriched by a new, pleasant and fascinating diversion.

The twentieth century, more especially since the ending of the Second World War, has seen the complete democratisation of continental travel. For those who prefer foreign lands to remain foreign, and to be insulated from social contacts they would not ordinarily wish to make in their home country, the impact of this revolutionary process can have appalling con-

5 *A Band Festival in Lavin, Lower Engadi*

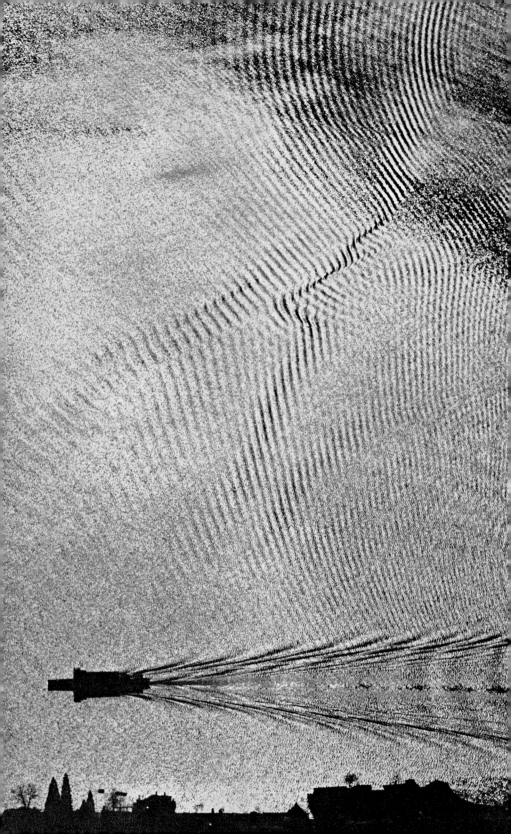

sequences. The wiser and more sophisticated traveller to the Alps will select the early summer and autumn, making sure, however, that no period of his stay coincides with the school holidays. He will find the roads freer of traffic, the hotels less expensive, the colours of the foliage more delicate and splendid. The Swiss hotelier to-day caters for a different social class than did his Victorian grandfather; but his clientele may be as ready to spend money and as genuinely appreciative of scenery. And in the last resort, albeit I say it reluctantly, should the beauties of the Alps be reserved for an élite? For the élite can still, if it will take a little trouble, find in the Swiss Alps the remote and the beautiful, the tranquil and the unspoiled, undisturbed by the bustling and deserving proletariat.

Against the majesty and beauty of the Alps the tourist is a transitory and ephemeral phenomenon. The daily life of the peasant follows a routine which is fundamentally untouched by those who stay near his home. When the snow begins to fall, usually in November, in the high Alpine villages, the long winter begins. The cattle will now remain in their stalls of heavy logs, padded with moss, until the spring. The women will spin and knit while their menfolk clean the stables, shovelling the manure down a trap-door into a pit or cellar. Later in the season a yellow spray of rich dung will enrich the fields and suffuse the atmosphere. In the winter months the men will fell the timber and let it slide down the icy slopes. During the long evenings they will sit smoking their cheroots or the hooked pipes decorated with tassels of chamois hair. The snow falls, creating a silent, white world. 'The wind has fallen,' wrote the historian of the Renaissance, John Addington Symonds, who came to live at Davos in 1877. 'Later on, the snow-flakes flutter silently and sparely through the lifeless air. The most distant landscape is blotted out. After sunset the clouds have settled down upon the hills, and the snow comes in thick, impenetrable fleeces.... Next morning there is a foot and a half of finely powdered snow, and still the snow is falling ... falling noiseless and unseen.... The cottage windows shine red, and moving lanterns of belated wayfarers define the void around them. Yet the night is far from dark. The forests and the mountain-bulk beyond the valley loom softly large and just distinguishable through a pearly haze. The path is purest trackless whiteness, almost dazzling though it has no light.'

Then the winter passes. Suddenly the yellow and white crocuses pierce the melting snow, while the torrents are thick with flood-water. Soon the fresh grass will begin to sprout in the meadows, and later, in June and May, the higher pastures will be star-scattered with a galaxy of flowers. 'In mid-summer,' Llewelyn Powys wrote in his sensitive descriptions of the Alpine scene, 'when the flowers are in blossom, to walk across these Alps is like being abroad on the wide paradise back of Olympus. The ground underfoot is as incense bearing as the enchanted soil of Cathay.'

39

The Lake of Lucerne (Vierwaldstättersee)

By now the woodman's axe resounds through the woods; and the cows are champing the grass in the lower fields. The well-manured lands will be protected from their keen appetite by a new fence. Everything wakes with the sweet smell of the spring. Soon the tinkle of the cow bell will be heard no longer in the valley, for the cattle have moved to the Alpine pastures. The scythe susurrates as the peasant and his family cut the lush grass. The hay is dried on the wooden tripods, and by moonlight these appear like an army of silent bears. When it is dry, the hay is carried to the chalets where it is stored for winter feeding.

The summer slips into autumn. The red berries gleam through the green leaves of the mountain ash. The trees become a brilliant motley of brown, orange, red and dark green. The peasants must cut the grass once more and manure the fields, while the cows come down from the mountains. The wind blows and the woods are carpeted with leaves. The trees stand bare, glistening silver in the wintry sun, among the dark pines, but the sky mists over and snow falls lightly on the pastures where the cowsheds stand dark and shuttered. For the people of the Alps the year follows a routine changed only superficially since the middle ages, and, except in the major resorts, immune from the impact of the tourist.

The peasants and the tourists are equally transient where the mountains wrestle and sleep. They will certainly outlive the Atomic Age and will perhaps outlast the life of man himself. 'The mountains from their heights reveal two truths,' so wrote Hilaire Belloc, 'They suddenly make us feel our insignificance and at the same time they free the immortal mind, and let it feel its greatness, and they release it from the earth.'

2

THE FOREST CANTONS

THE FOREST CANTONS which border the lake of Lucerne are the historic centre of Switzerland. The green slope of the Rütli, the chapel erected on the spot where William Tell is supposed to have jumped ashore and escaped from his Austrian captors, the statue of Tell in the market place at Altdorf, the avenue at Küssnacht where Tell killed the Austrian governor, Gessler, illustrate the extent to which the present is constantly reminded of the past. There are many more historic memories of Alpine history in the towns and villages of the forest cantons, battlefields where the apple trees blossom in spring, old houses, ancient shrines, and villages where pacts were signed and treaties broken. Apart from its historic setting, the lake of Lucerne, or Vierwaldstättersee as the Swiss call it, is a fitting gateway to the Swiss Alps. The lake is in the form of an ungainly St. Andrew's cross, the uppermost bar consisting of the grandiose Gulf of Uri, the crossbar extending from the little bay of Küssnacht to the village of Alpnachstad. The town of Lucerne itself is at the end of the lower bar.

Lucerne has been called an 'Edwardian watering place,' its bay bright with sailing craft, its front brisk with vast hotels, its streets crowded with tourists. In certain respects it is indeed the capital of Alpine tourism. When it rains, it may appear a grey, depressing place, but on a dull, damp day even the canals of Venice seem reminiscent of some of the more uninviting reaches of the Thames. I should not myself choose to stay at Lucerne for it is admittedly only on the periphery of the Alps. In fine weather, however, its situation is enchanting. Behind the town Mount Pilatus rises, appearing the more precipitous by reason of its very detachment, the green heights to the north forming pleasing foothills to its stony crags. On a clear day, the far horizon of the lake is shielded by distant snow mountains. The visitor emerging from its noble modern railway station—there is an admirable Transport Museum at Lucerne—becomes immediately aware that Lucerne has, what Interlaken and Montreux seem to lack, a rich historic past. For the swift-flowing river Reuss which divides the city is spanned by two medieval bridges, the interstices of their roofs decorated with colourful scenes. A part of the city walls and no less than eight round towers survive as a reminder of turbulent centuries long ago.

Indeed Lucerne's past illustrates the depth and complexity of Switzerland's history. The town and its neighbourhood was not one of the first cantons to form a pact to resist the Hapsburg overlords, but the burghers soon saw that it would be to their interest to join the Forest Cantons. They were more especially concerned with the control over the trade which went eventually over the St. Gotthard to Italy. But the burghers, who were under the suzerainty of the Emperor, were not eager to cut the links which bound them to their imperial overlord until it was clear that the mountain cantons were sufficiently strong to hold their own against him. On the battlefield of Morgarten, now a quiet spot close to the little lake, the Agerisee, the Hapsburg army was decisively defeated in 1315. Seventeen years later Lucerne entered into a perpetual treaty of friendship with the cantons of Schwyz, Uri and Unterwalden. The Swiss now controlled all the waters of the lake of Lucerne as well as the traffic passing over the St. Gotthard. The very next year they began to build the famous Kapellbrücke which catches the visitor's eye as soon as he leaves the railway station. This covered timber bridge was part of a defensive system, embracing the towers and walls, some of which survive, against a Hapsburg attack as well as a link between the two parts of the city. The bridge was decorated in the early seventeenth century with scenes from Swiss history by H. H. Wagmann and his son.

Lucerne's future was now decisively bound up with the youthful Swiss Confederation, though the citizens had to face centuries of political and religious unrest before they settled down to their placid existence. Naturally the Hapsburgs did not easily give up the idea of recovering one of their rich cities; but as the Austrian soldiers moved towards Lucerne they suffered a crushing defeat at Sempach in 1386 and three years later the city was able to assert its complete independence. In 1404 the other remaining wooden bridge, the Spreurbrücke, was built. It is decorated with scenes from the Dance of Death painted by Kaspar Meglinger and his contemporaries. The bridges over the fast-flowing green waters of the river, the old houses, many of them now replaced by modern blocks, and the swans still give a momentary impression of the rich medieval trading city.

In the sixteenth century Lucerne confronted a new crisis. The Protestant Reformation had come to Zürich under the lead of Ulrich Zwingli, and Zürich sought to evangelise and to control the lands near to her. The patrician merchants who governed Lucerne and kept the trade guilds tightly under their control were alarmed by the ambitions of their northern neighbour. They joined with the forest cantons, and Zug, as well as with their old enemy, the Emperor, to defend the Roman Catholic faith in a pact signed at the little lakeside town of Beckenried. In one of the wars which followed Zürich was defeated and its Protestant leader, Zwingli, was left for slain under a pear tree on the battlefield of Kappel.

For the future Lucerne was to sustain the Catholic cause in Switzerland. The sixteenth-century Pope, Paul IV, sent a special nuncio, Ottaviano Rovere, bishop of Terracina, to Lucerne, to forward the work of the Counter-Reformation. A native of Unterwalden, Melchior Lussy, arranged for Swiss troops to help the Pope, men who were the forerunners of the modern Swiss Guards at the Vatican and assisted in the negotiations for the establishment at Lucerne of a seminary which was opened in 1577. The town has still two splendid witnesses to the power of the contemporary church in seventeenth-century Lucerne, the Hofkirche on the edge of the old city, not far from the lakeside approached by steep steps, and the Jesuit church of St. Francis Xavier. The delicate twin steeples of the Hofkirche St. Leodegar were built between 1504 and 1515, all that now remains of the original building after it had been destroyed by a fire in 1635, caused, so it was said, by shooting crows on the roof. The remainder of the church was designed by Jakob Khurer of Ingolstadt between 1635 and 1644. It has a pleasing lofty interior, notable for its good early baroque side altars, its choir stalls carved by Nicholas Geissler, a splendid organ and a metal choir screen. The Jesuit church, built in 1666–75 by Christopher Vogler, a venture in discreet baroque, lovely, dainty and colourful, has a spacious, refined interior, the rose tints of the altar and pulpit contrasting with the white walls.

Lucerne's vigorous championship of the Roman Catholic cause made difficult its relations with the Protestant cantons. By the early nineteenth century there had been some alignment between the conservative and Catholic forces, and the radical and Protestant cantons. In 1841 the canton of Aargau decided to secularise the Catholic monasteries. There was an immediate storm of protest in Catholic Switzerland, more especially in Lucerne where the popular Joseph Leu von Ebersol had been at work in an attempt to reconcile the sovereignty of the people with that of the pope; he had won permission for the re-establishment of the Jesuits in the canton from the Great Council of Lucerne in 1844. On the other hand the Swiss radicals regarded this decision as a challenge, and forthwith began to raise companies of armed volunteers. In March 1845, an armed band of some 3,600 men under the command of a Bernese politician, Ulrich Ochsenbein, actually invaded the territory of Lucerne. In the face of this threat, the Catholic cantons came together under Lucerne to form the Sonderbund to protect their interests. But the Diet of the Swiss Confederation decided, though by a narrow majority, that the formation of the Sonderbund was an illegal act.

Tension grew as each side took up arms. The Sonderbund was itself divided. Its leading politician, Constantin Siegwart of Lucerne, an able diplomat but no soldier, hoped that the Austrians would intervene. Its military commander, Johann Ulrich von Salis-Soglio from the Grisons, was a brave if unskilled soldier and no politician. Skirmishes took place, with comparatively few losses,* in the bitter cold of winter at Gisikon and Meyers-kappel. The Catholic leaders saw the futility of further conflict and with their Jesuit advisers fled by night across the lake to Flüelen. The next day the victorious Confederates entered the defeated city. Violence precipitated a new constitution and a balance of forces within the federal state which, in spite of occasional tensions, welded the divergent elements into a compact and patriotically-minded nation. Such was the last war fought on Swiss soil.

If Lucerne's dramatic past hardly impinges on the tourist, it yet helps to show that the modern city is not simply a mushroom growth of the Victorian era. Yet for the tourist Lucerne is principally a gateway to an extensive and beautiful Alpine world.

To the south-west the town is dominated by the serrated crags of Mount Pilatus up which a rack-and-pinion railway has run from Alpnachstad since 1889. In this way a superstitious legend met its final doom. For long it was said that after his suicide Pilate's body had been thrown into the Tiber; but an immediate storm caused the superstitious to drag it out. It was taken to Vienne and thrown into the Rhone with similar results. The same thing happened at Lausanne when it was flung into the lake of Geneva. As a last resort it was thrust into the little lake on Mount Pilatus and here on Good Friday the sorry Roman official may still be glimpsed, sitting on his judge's throne in the centre of the lake dressed in scarlet. However, anyone sufficiently unfortunate to see him is doomed to die within the year. Not surprisingly the lake was initially subject to the storms which had already afflicted his previous resting places. It was, however, discovered that exorcism could reduce their incidence, though squalls appeared to follow the throwing of any large object in the lake. To prevent such disturbances the burgesses of Lucerne forbade anyone from visiting the mountain and they punished severely six priests who had the temerity to try to climb Pilatus in 1387. In the summer of 1518 the Burgomaster of St. Gall, Joachim von Watt, a future Protestant reformer, was granted permission to ascend the mountain. Some time later in the sixteenth century Johann Müller of Lucerne actually dared to throw stones into Pilate's lake without any obvious manifestation of his wrath. And now a rack-and-pinion railway, with a specially-designed rack with a double row of teeth set horizontally to cope with the steep ascent, takes the traveller up a slope with a gradient of 1 in 2 to the hotels at the summit. The line was electrified in 1937. Conquered in this way, Pilatus may seem to have lost something of its glamour; but its isolated position makes it a fine viewpoint, and in shape and substance it is every inch—or in every foot, all 6,790 feet, a mountain.

The south-western stretch of the lake, known as the Alpnachersee, is itself

---

* The Confederates had 78 dead and 260 wounded, the Sonderbund, 50 dead and 175 wounded.

an opening to a mountain world closely associated with the Swiss struggle for independence and liberty. A few miles away from the lake to the south-east there lies the charming little town of Stans, quiet, spruce and distinguished. It was mainly rebuilt after a fire in 1713 and boasts a very elegant public square. The Breitenhaus, built in 1791, was designed by Nicholas Purtschert who was also responsible for the classical churches at the nearby lakeside villages of Buochs and Beckenried. It is from here that the Stanserhorn, a little lower than Pilatus but with an even finer view, can be ascended by a funicular. The poet Wordsworth and his sister came this way in 1820 but their memories of Stans were marred by an argument with their driver who tried to overcharge them. What was more he refused to give up their coats and cloaks until Wordsworth handed over 27 francs he demanded. The indignant Englishman, who had earlier, at Herzogenbuchsee, spent the night in his char, enduring fleas and a heavy thunderstorm, rather than pay six francs for a bed, at once made for Stansstad, hired a boat to Lucerne and the next day at Sarnen laid a complaint before the magistrates who sentenced the driver to a month's imprisonment and secured the return of the Wordsworths' luggage.

After leaving Stans the road to Engelberg passes through orchards and meadows with mountains towering on either side, slips quickly through a number of villages, Wolfenschiessen the most interesting, and then mounts in noble curves to the winter and summer resort of Engelberg. The village itself is a cluster of rather uninteresting hotels, but the green valley is hedged about by great snow mountains, most dominant the sledge-hammer massif of the Titlis, one of the first snow-covered mountains to be climbed in Switzerland, in 1744. 'We breakfasted,' Dorothy Wordsworth wrote, 'in view of the flashing, silver-topped Mount Titlis, and its grey crags—a sight that roused W's youthful desires, and in spite of weak eyes and the weight of fifty winters, he could not repress a longing to ascend that mountain. He had much earnest conversation with the waiter, who had attended an English gentleman on that perilous adventure, and shewed us the snow pattens with which they were shod, described the scarification of their cheeks, and the blinding of their eyes by insufferable light (though they wore black veils), the excessive fatigue of the Englishman, and his resolution never to trust himself again to like perils. But my brother had his own visions of glory, and, had he been twenty years younger, sure I am that he would have trod the summit of the Titlis.' The cragged spurs of the Spannörter, a little further up the valley, are perhaps even more impressive.

The village and the valley are still dominated by the plain but imposing buildings of the great Benedictine Abbey founded eight hundred years ago. Indeed the word Engelberg is said to be a German derivate of Mons Angelorum, the name by which Pope Calixtus II called the abbey. Its undistinguished abbey church, rebuilt in the eighteenth century, hardly bears comparison with that of Einsiedeln, though the architect, Johann Rueff, had worked at that church, but its general lay-out, its spotless corridors, its trim flower gardens, its dairy and its school, all suggest continuing prosperity and carry a faint flavour, if no more, of that time when its abbot was virtually the independent ruler of the whole valley down which flows the Engelberg Aa.

The abbey has had a long history, full of vicissitudes. Its foundation in 1124 opened a splendid and exciting period, for it became a centre of scholastic learning and the illumination of manuscripts, more especially under the rule of abbots Frowin (d. 1178) and Berchtold (d. 1197), both of whom were the authors of learned theological and philosophical tracts. Among the 80 manuscripts from its medieval workshops which still survive, there is an interesting and particularly early piece of music for the organ written in the twelfth century. Another treasure is the beautiful silver processional cross decorated with precious stones. Its territorial possessions, however, brought the monastery into constant conflict with the peasants of the neighbouring cantons. It had too to endure other troubles. Fire destroyed its buildings in 1199 and 1309. The Black Death carried off seven monks, and decimated the adjacent convent of nuns, for some 116 died. This convent flourished until the middle ages, but was moved to Sarnen in 1615. The abbey was subject to the laxity which affected so many religious houses at the end of the fifteenth century; subsequently the regular observance of the rule was enforced by abbot Barnabas Bürky and, after another period of relaxation, by Benedict Sigrist who was abbot between 1603 and 1619. In the nineteenth century it established a house at Conception in the United States, which was raised to the status of an abbey in 1881; and another house was founded at Yaoundé in the Cameroons in 1932.

The indefatigable Archdeacon Coxe paid the monastery a visit in the eighteenth century. The abbot had been kind enough to send horses down to Stans. 'We rode,' Coxe wrote, 'through a fertile valley . . . began to ascend along a road winding by the side of a steep precipice, and through "unsunned forests" of beech intermingled with poplar, mountain ash, Spanish chestnuts and pines, the torrent Aa impetuously foaming in a stony channel, and forming a succession of cataracts. The wild horrors of the circumjacent rocks, the incessant roaring of the waters, and the solitary gloom of the forest, reminded me of Gray's beautiful Ode on the Grande Chartreuse.' At the abbey Coxe and his party were entertained 'with all the plenty of feudal times, and comforts of the present age.' He was especially impressed by the large collection of modern historical and miscellaneous works in the library 'which does honour to the taste of the abbot, and proves him to be a warm friend to polite literature.'

46

Engelberg is no longer as remote or as awe-inspiring. A thrilling *téléphérique*, the longest rope-span of its kind in the Swiss Alps, lifts the traveller to the Trübsee; but even modern conveniences such as this cannot altogether spoil Engelberg's character as an Alpine resort. The Trübsee itself is a sparkling little lake surrounded by high mountains. The walk here to the Joch Pass, 7,260 feet high, and thence to Meiringen was a favourite excursion with the Victorians; but the creation of a chair-lift from the Trübsee to the summit of the pass, and the building of the Susten road has somewhat curtailed its length. The view from the Joch Pass is limited, but the walk down to Engstlen Alp and Meiringen, stony and rugged till it reaches the pastures, is well worth the labour. The early traveller, Johann Stumpf, remarked on a miraculous spring of water at Engstlen Alp: 'This spring only flows twice a day, once in the morning and once in the evening. . . . When at the end of August the new snow has fallen and the cattle are driven on to the lower pastures, the spring ceases to flow, and does not start again until the following June, when the cattle are brought back.'

The Joch Pass conveys the traveller from the land of the forest cantons to the Bernese Oberland. The motorist and the traveller by rail will follow the broad valley which passes the little lakes of Sarnen and Lungern to the wooded Brünig Pass. The valley has many attractive features, for the orchards are bright with pink and white blossom in springtime and in the autumn the colouring of the trees is immensely rich. The landscape is friendly and unassuming, full of farmsteads with great wooden eaves. There are, too, some picturesque towns. Sarnen, where the men of the canton of Unter-walden meet in the well-designed public square on the last Sunday in April to elect the magistrates or executive council, has a number of elegant buildings. The most impressive is the noble Pfarrkirche, built to the design of Franz and Johann Anton Singer between 1739 and 1742. There is a fine view of the little lake and the distant mountains of the Oberland from the terrace in front of the church. This countryside of gentle alp and reedy lake, strongly Catholic, is above all associated with the saintly Swiss hermit, Nicholas von der Flüe. In the fifteenth century he retired from the world and married life (though his wife had borne ten children) to become a hermit in the nearby gorge of the Ranft where for twenty years, from 1467, he lived a life of great austerity. The fame of Bruder Klaus, as he came to be called, attracted so many pilgrims that his friends had to intervene to protect him from their pious importunities. He was born at the little village of Flüeli and lies buried in front of the high altar of the new church built at Sachseln in 1672. He was canonised in 1947 and his shrine still attracts pilgrims, fascinated perhaps less by his personal sanctity than by his love of peace which led to occasional intervention in the turbulent Swiss politics of his time. It was on his advice that the diet which met at Stans in 1481 came to agreement over the vexed questions of the admission of Fribourg and Solothurn to the Swiss Confederation and over the division of the spoils of war taken from the Burgundians.

The marble for the church in which Bruder Klaus lies buried was taken from the Melchtal, and it was near the valley's opening, south-east of Sarnen, that Bruder Klaus spent his declining years. There is, in fact, a church of considerable interest, with a detached medieval tower, high above the little village of Flüeli-Ranft where the roads twists round to enter the wooded gorge which leads to the Melchtal. This lovely valley remains remote from the tourist onslaught. Its green slopes dotted with chalets, its streams rushing through woods, its gritty roads, give it an air of perfect tranquillity all too unusual in the near vicinity of Lucerne. At the valley's head, reached either by a narrow curving road or by a cable railway from Stöckalp, there is the delectable resort of Melchseefrutt, set amidst treeless green pastures besides a small lake some 6,000 feet above sea level. It owes its scenic attraction, as Sir Arnold Lunn has observed, partly to the contrast between the long recession of the snow-covered Titlis range and the gaunt austerity of the great cliffs of the Glockhaus and Hohenstollen precipices. There are many fine walks, to the Engstlen lake, to the Tannen Alp and along its green ridge to the Erzegg or even further on to the Balmeregghorn which provides fine views of the mountains by the Rhone glacier and of the ravine of the Gental below. Melchseefrutt is not merely a resort where good skiing lasts until the late spring. In the Second World War it was one of the redoubts to which the Swiss would have retreated if Hitler's armies had invaded their country. Yet nowhere can be more peaceful than the Melchtal; and in more harried times I think longingly of the picnic by the stream when the warm sun melted the butter and the chocolate off the biscuits.

After leaving the lake of Sarnen the road rises steeply. There is a track part of the way round its western shore but latterly this becomes a country lane and is unusable after heavy rain as it involves crossing an unbridged torrent. The little lake of Lungern is set within a frame of high mountains, the snow-covered peaks of the Oberland appearing to the south. It is least attractive in the spring since its waters have been drained during the winter to supply electric power, leaving an ugly tidal mark around the lake. In summer its green-blue surface reflects the surrounding alps. After leaving Lungern the road climbs easily through finely wooded slopes to the summit of the Brünig Pass, the frontier of Unterwalden and the Bernese Oberland. Although the pass is a comparatively low one, 3,300 feet, the change of scene is dramatic. Far below the green valley of the Hasli is hedged by the steep cliffs and grandiose peaks of the Bernese Alps. It is here too that Protestant and Roman Catholic Switzerland part company. The

Wordsworths came over the Brünig from the canton of Berne in 1820. Subsequently Dorothy Wordsworth noted in her *Journal* that the peasants of the Catholic canton into which they had come 'would neither give nor sell anything to us Protestants except in the regular way of trade,' but when she reached Sarnen she also commented that 'in our rambles on foot, how thankful have we been to the Roman Catholics for the open doors of their churches.'

The forest cantons must be seen in their historic setting and nowhere else in all Switzerland recalls so vividly the making of the Swiss Confederation as the lake of Lucerne. The lake is bordered on the southerly side by Unterwalden and to the north by Schwyz; the eastern section of the lake known as the Gulf of Uri and certainly its most beautiful part is mainly in the canton of Uri. In the early middle ages much if not most of the lands of these cantons was worked by serfs, under feudal lordship, but even then there were some communities of free peasants. The free peasants naturally resented any attempt at domination. The great aristocratic families, the Zahringers and Hapsburgs, held a general lordship over these mountain valleys; but their jurisdiction was only exercised occasionally. Such remoteness from the seat of lordship must have favoured the comparative freedom enjoyed by these Swiss.

The situation was, however, changing. The German Emperors of the twelfth century had ambitions in northern Italy and were therefore concerned with securing control over the St. Gotthard Pass, only recently made practicable for horses and mules. In 1231 the Emperor Frederick II declared that Uri was to be immediately subject to Imperial lordship. Actually the remoteness of the control thus claimed was a stimulus to a movement for independence. Similar events occurred in nearby Schwyz, which, with Nidwalden,* had come under the governance of Rudolf III of Hapsburg-Laufenburg, who was an opponent of Frederick II. As a result the Emperor Frederick declared that Schwyz was freed from Hapsburg control.

The scene became rather more confused towards the close of the thirteenth century when a member of the Hapsburg house, Rudolf IV, who had bought the claims over Schwyz and Unterwalden from other members of his family, became Emperor. For he now added to his hereditary dynastic claims the right to direct Imperial control over Uri, Schwyz and Unterwalden. He was as well a shrewd statesman who perceived that he could increase his revenues by making tighter his hold over the increasing traffic which made use of the St. Gotthard route. The peasants foresaw that they were in danger of losing their cherished freedom. Their leaders forgathered, as I have mentioned earlier, on the green meadow above the lake of Lucerne at the

---

* Unterwalden consists of two separate cantons, Nidwalden, the lower valley of the Engelberg Aa, and Obwalden, the valley of the Sarner Aa.

Rütli, more or less opposite the modern resort of Brunnen, in August 1291, to join together against their enemies and to preserve peace and justice among their peoples. It is very possible that the treaty, the actual manuscript of which was not rediscovered until 1760 in the archives of Schwyz, was simply a repetition of an earlier understanding; but for the Swiss the year 1291 marks the definite beginning of Switzerland.

Naturally enough the Hapsburgs did not lightly surrender their claims to lordship and a long struggle with the Austrians ensued. The three original cantons were soon joined by others who wished to get rid of Hapsburg authority, Lucerne (1332), Zürich (1351), Berne (1353), Glarus (finally in 1388) and Zug in 1365. The hardy mountain peasants, assisted by the wealthy burghers of the cities, developed a military skill which brought disaster to the Austrian cavalry in a series of battles, at Morgarten in 1315, Sempach in 1386, Näfels in 1388. Towards the end of the fifteenth century the Hapsburg Emperor Maximilian made one further attempt to reimpose his authority over the Swiss, only to meet with defeats which made him realise that it was no easy task to bring the 'bull of Uri' under the yoke. The treaty of Basle, signed in 1499, virtually recognised the independence of this amorphous confederation henceforth known by the name of the canton of Schwyz, a word used by the Austrians as an expression of opprobrious contempt.

The struggle for Swiss independence is inevitably linked with the shadowy figure of William Tell. The countryside around the lake of Lucerne was the supposed scene of his activities. There is a fine statue in the pleasing little town of Altdorf where, for refusing to salute the Austrian power, he was ordered to shoot the apple from his son's head. At Küssnacht (near where a modern chapel commemorates the death in a road accident of Queen Astrid of Belgium) the Hohle Gasse marks the supposed site of the assassination of the Austrian governor, Gessler. On the Axenstrasse, just beyond Sisikon, a modern chapel, adorned with colourful rather than artistic frescoes portraying the events in his life, commemorates the occasion when Tell escaped from his Austrian captors by leaping ashore from a boat in which he was being carried to prison. In the Gulf of Uri, a large rock, the Mythenstein, has a tablet commemorating Schiller's play. William Tell has been lately a familiar figure to the viewer on the English Independent Television service. Perhaps indeed the young idealised Hollywood hero portrayed there, with his democratic sentiments, courage and nobility, his skill at outwitting the hated foe was not so far short of what the ordinary Swiss may well believe Tell to have been like.

It is therefore with reluctance that it must be stated that Tell may well be a myth. He was first mentioned in the White Book of Sarnen, written about 1470, a century and a half after the incidents which it records. The narrative has great dramatic power, but it is full of proven error and sheer impossibility. The myth of William Tell, so the professional historians say, was derived from Scandinavian mythology through the twelfth-century chronicler, Saxo Grammaticus. Yet popular sentiment, and who shall gainsay it, will no more freely hand over William Tell to his critics than it will Robin Hood. The remains of castles destroyed in the rising linked with his name have been unearthed by archaeologists. An Austrian Vogt may well have ordered the Swiss to salute his hat as the symbol of his jurisdiction, and a peasant leader such as Tell may have later slain him. At least Tell personified the courageous resistance of the Swiss to Austrian rule and the spirit of independence which brought Switzerland into being.

The lake of Lucerne or Vierwaldstättersee may thus claim to be the heart of Switzerland and its mountains the authentic home of Swiss freedom. It is a lake of varied enchantment and temperament. Its surface may be as calm and clear as a sheet of glass but there are occasions when it is grey and angry, white waves lashing its shores. The valley of the Reuss, like other Alpine valleys, those of the Rhine, the Linth and the Hasli in particular, is visited by the warm wind of the south known as the föhn. Before its advent, or during its early stages, the atmosphere becomes pellucid because the dry wind has greatly reduced its humidity. Colouring is brilliant and intensified. Distance is diminished. Great vistas are opened. After a few days of this almost unnaturally fine weather, the wind drops and the rains come. This wind from the south can be very destructive. A spark may set a village alight. Meiringen, Grindelwald, Glarus and Bonaduz have all been destroyed by fires during the period of the föhn. I have observed at Brunnen and many other places notices warning people not to smoke in the open when the föhn blows. In the spring it melts the snow and helps the new crops growing, and even in the autumn it may postpone the advent of winter. Yet it is also said to affect men and beasts unpleasantly, to heighten nervous tension, and to give feelings of tiredness and sickness. I have never felt such effects myself, but the roaring of the wind, the breaking of the waves against the bank, the total absence of dew and moisture, seem in some sense uncanny because unusual.

In the summer the lake is smooth and a pleasant highway for the traveller on the old, white, comfortable steamers. The road around the northern section of the lake, more especially that part known as the Axenstrasse, is often unduly crowded. The steamer moving from side to side provides an infinite variety of view, little clean Swiss towns with their clusters of hotels, Weggis, Vitznau, Gersau, Brunnen, Beckenried, and each with something to say for itself. I was staying at Weggis when the pound was devalued in 1931 and the English ceased for ever to receive 25 francs in exchange. 'Oh,' gasped the proprietress of the hotel at Weggis with becoming feeling, 'to think that England is now on the brink of revolution.' At Vitznau the mountain railway up the Rigi starts. This, the first mountain railway in Switzerland, was built at the initiative of a Swiss engineer, Nicholas Riggenbach, in 1871. It went up to Staffelhöhe, one and a quarter miles below the summit of the Rigi for the simple if political reason that this was the frontier of the cantons of Lucerne and Schwyz. The people of the latter canton, hoping to build their own railway from Arth at the south end of the lake of Zug, had refused the concession to the Rigi Railway. The summit of the Rigi was at last attained in 1873 and two years later the railway from Arth-Goldau to the Rigi was also completed. It was electrified in 1937. As a mountain the Rigi is unimpressive but the unobstructed views of the Alps which it provides on a clear day are singularly splendid. The track up the Rigi must be one of the most travelled of all mountain roads. Even before the railway was finished, the view drew crowds of travellers. Miss Havergal distributed religious tracts to the navvies engaged in the construction. César Ritz was once head-waiter at the Rigi-Kulm hotel. He used to recall the story of the English guest who had come to see the sunrise and appeared clad in a blanket. A sudden gust of wind disclosed his underwear to all the world. 'With a cry of horror he flung himself face downward in the snow and he would not budge until someone had caught the errant blanket and wrapped him in it!' The modern traveller has insufficient time and money to spend in staying at mountain hotels, many of which are now no more than restaurants. I confess to being somewhat unenthusiastic about many of the famous points of view. The fare is high, the company indifferent and too numerous, and the view, if splendid, is much the same as that provided by the neighbouring summit. It is just possible to have a surfeit of views. 'And now if you please, Sir,' Samuel Butler's Alfred told his master after he had taken him up the Rigi, 'I should like to lie down on the grass here and have a read of *Tit-Bits*.'

The boat steams from Vitznau to Gersau, a little town which had the distinction of being a semi-autonomous state until 1817. Archdeacon Coxe was particularly impressed by its picturesque and prosperous situation. 'The smallest spot of earth,' he wrote somewhat pompously but proudly, 'on which civil freedom is cultivated and flourishes, cannot fail of interesting those who know the true value of liberty and independence; and are convinced, that political happiness does not consist in great opulence and extensive empire.' Like the other lakeside towns, Gersau possesses tranquillity and charm.

Its nearby neighbour is Brunnen, known in Swiss history for the treaty concluded here in 1315 between Uri, Schwyz and Unterwalden but remembered by me as the site of early Swiss holidays. I shall not forget slipping on the steps going down to the lake, and emerging with my plus fours streaming with water; nor the walk to Stoos which we made one fine autumn day. From Brunnen a little funicular railway mounts to Axenfels and Axenstein, a resort beloved of Queen Victoria, and provides a starting-point to Stoos. I do not suppose anyone walks there now, since steel-grey cars now take visitors to Stoos by funicular from Schattli, a few miles from Schwyz. But Stoos was still comparatively undeveloped in 1931. It was on our way there up a track that wound through the forest that I first heard a genuine Swiss yodeller. He was driving a horse and cart, all the time emitting the warbling, throaty noises so dear to the Swiss. Yodelling is the vocal equivalent of the instrument known as the Alphorn which is thought by some to have originated among shepherds on the Asiatic steppes who used it to 'blow' prayers. It is a forbidding if deeply melodious sound. In the eighth century it was evidently associated by the monks of St. Gall with the contemporary equivalent of 'hot music,' for a regulation at the singing school there forbade the students from making sounds which imitated 'ribald jesters, yodeller Alp inhabitants, shrieking scolds or cries of animals.' Yet the solitary yodeller coming ever nearer down the forest road contributed to create the right Alpine background to the walk. There had been an early fall of snow and Stoos seemed completely deserted. But the sun blazed and I have an abiding schoolboy memory of making a snow-man and eating peaches and ham in the ecstatic frame of mind so rarely experienced in adult life.

Brunnen is also a centre for excursions into the countryside which lies behind the lake of Lucerne, to Zug, Schwyz and the Muotathal as well as to the majestic beauty of the abbey of Einsiedeln, so enthusiastically and admirably described by John Russell in his book on *Switzerland*. The old town of Zug, situated by its quiet lake, has some streets of extremely picturesque houses which retain the atmosphere of past sixteenth- and seventeenth-century Europe. It has too a fine example of late Gothic architecture in its parish church, constructed in 1478–83 by Hans Felder of Oettinger in Bavaria (though the tower dates from 1557), and dedicated to the English saint, St. Oswald of Northumbria. The interior has some good choir stalls, well-carved wooden statues and a picture of St. Oswald in prayer before the battle with Penda of Mercia in which he was killed.

It is worth while making a detour from Zug to visit the little-known and little-visited lake of the Ägerisee. It is small and peaceful, but its quiet setting, the gentle green meadows and its reedy banks provide a lovelier setting than some of the better-known lakes. Near its eastern basin the Swiss engaged in deadly if triumphant battle with the Austrians at Morgarten in 1315. The men of Schwyz, the canton which joins that of Zug, had taken umbrage at the way in which the powerful abbey of Einsiedeln had encroached on their Alpine grazing rights. In revenge they attacked the abbey early in 1314 and carried off some of the monks. The Hapsburgs, as protectors of Einsiedeln,

were presented by the Swiss with the excuse they wanted to bring the cantons to heel. The Austrian duke, Leopold, planned a triple advance, one army marching over the Brünig Pass from the Entlebuch to keep the men of Unterwalden in check, another, a naval force, was to move from Lucerne against the lakeside flank of Schwyz while Duke Leopold himself moved north from Zug along the right bank of the Ägerisee to meet catastrophe at Morgarten on November 14th, 1315. A service to commemorate the battle is still held annually in the old chapel of St. James, a mile to the south near Schornen.

Schwyz, which has given its name to the nation, is nobly situated at the foot of the symmetrical Mythen mountain. It is a small town with some good buildings, among them the exceptionally fine parish church of St. Martin built between 1769 and 1774 to the design of Jakob and Johann Anton Singer, the sixteenth-century Rathaus decorated with historic frescoes and the Arsenal where many Swiss victories, including that of Morgarten, are commemorated by captured standards. A road from Schwyz leads up the unspoiled Muotathal where I once had a memorable picnic, interrupted by the importunate attentions of a friendly flock of goats. It was here too that the Russian general Suvorov, advancing to help his allies against the French general, Masséna, during the Napoleonic Wars, was held at bay after an epic crossing of the Alps. When he reached Altdorf he discovered that the road marked on his Austrian map did not in fact exist. He was obliged therefore to make his way over the side ranges to the Muotathal. The march was made in single file in difficult conditions as a cold mist enfolded the mountains, but the general kept up the spirits of his men by constantly moving among them. When he reached the Muotathal, he learned of the French victory at Zürich. His situation was extremely precarious, for ammunition and food were running short while the French armies practically encircled him. None the less, 'relying on God and the wonderful devotion of the men,' he fought his way over the high mountain passes in the chill of October towards the safety of the Grisons. The Muotathal has no spectacular scenic features, but its verdant slopes and rocky heights afford a peaceful contrast with the roads thronged with the summer traffic round the lake of Lucerne.

The contours of the Alps restrict the traffic to comparatively few routes, and in the high summer, especially at week-ends, these become uncomfortably crowded. The road which goes from Schwyz to Brunnen and thence through Flüelen to the end of the lake is the principal route to Italy via the St. Gotthard Pass, with branching roads which lead by way of the Klausen Pass to Glarus and the north, of the Susten Pass to the Bernese Oberland and of the Furka to Brig and the Rhone Valley. The Klausen Pass which leaves the Gotthard road shortly after Altdorf has much to commend it. Its surface

The Kapell-Brücke over the river Reuss, Lucerne
Zug: the Kolin fountain

is still (in 1961) gravelled and the scenery it provides is fine rather than dramatic, but it is truly Alpine in character. Mounting through the Schächental, it goes to the little resort of Unterschächen, and traverses a rock gallery before achieving the summit of the pass, 6,404 feet high. The outlook is desolate and rough-hewn, with the irregularly-shaped Märcherstöckli prominent to the north and the Kammli, a spur of the Claridenstock, to the south. It leads eventually to Linthal, one of the chief towns in Glarus, but the road is still in the canton of Uri as it winds down past Vorfrutt, by way of the gorge of the Klus, to the rich pasturage of the Urnerboden. The men of Uri have had grazing rights here since they occupied it by force in the middle ages. The green pastures, brilliant with colour in early summer, resound to the constant tinkling of multitudinous cow bells.

The valley of the Reuss carries the St. Gotthard traffic, both road and rail. The scenery in its upper reaches is fine, for it blends the stony wilderness of the mountain peaks with the fertility of green meadows. At Amsteg the road to the Maderanertal branches off to the east. This lovely valley, watered by the rushing Kärstelenbach, is a remote and sparsely populated district, providing access to many high mountain passes and peaks. At Wassen the road to the Susten Pass leaves the St. Gotthard route. Beyond Göschenen where the St. Gotthard railway tunnel starts the character of the scenery changes dramatically. For the Schöllenen Gorge down which the turbulent Reuss foams in a creamy grey torrent is one of the bleakest spots in the whole of the Swiss Alps. The road has only recently been reconstructed and can take the heavy traffic more conveniently; but it has had the effect, I think, of diminishing the awesome fascination of the place. Shortly before reaching the little town of Andermatt the appropriately-named Devil's Bridge crosses the raging Reuss.

The scene here, even with the modern road bridge by the side of the old bridge, has still a touch of the infernal. Sir Edward Upton who subsequently has his journey described by his servant, Richard Smith, crossed over the 'ponte inferno' in 1563. The river, which he mistakenly thought to be the Rhine, 'hath such a fale among the huge stones that is merveylous.' The English traveller, William Brockendon, writing of his journey over the St. Gotthard in 1825, was more explicit and more impressed. The bridge, he said, had a span of 70 feet and was 100 feet above the cataract. 'It is not possible to conceive a more appalling scene ... the height of the rocks, the narrowness of the defile, and the roar and rush of the torrent beneath.' In fact Brockendon's bridge was not the one which Sir Edward Upton had passed, for a new bridge was built in the early eighteenth century by the Ticinese engineer, Pietro Moretini, to replace that swept away by the torrent in 1706.

The gorge has re-echoed to the sound of cannon as well as to the exhaust of coaches. A Greek cross hewn in the rock bears a Russian inscription commemorating Suvorov's campaign in 1799. The Russians, who were marching to join their allies, the Imperialists, had made their way over the St. Gotthard. On August 15th, 1799, the French in an effort to prevent the junction of their enemies forced the advance posts of the Imperialists back to their entrenchments at the Devil's Bridge. The French then charged the bridge, but it collapsed, thrusting the soldiers into the vortex of water far below. During the night, however, the Austrians retreated by the Oberalp Pass to avoid being cut off by General Gudin who had made a forced march over the Grimsel and Furka Passes with incredible difficulty. All this had taken place before Suvorov and the Russians came down the St. Gotthard. When they eventually reached the Devil's Bridge, they were able to push the French back and to repair the bridge by throwing beams across it and lashing them together with officers' scarves. Ultimately this astounding march proved fruitless and as we have seen Suvorov was obliged to sound the retreat in the Muotathal.

For long the narrow defile across the torrent was not the only obstacle to travellers. After they had crossed the bridge the way to Andermatt was obstructed by a sheer cliff. They could only circumvent this by passing over a frame or scaffolding affixed to the rock, a dangerous and difficult operation. In 1707 Pietro Moretini, who had had considerable engineering experience as a builder of some of Louis XIV's fortifications, and who had furthermore broken his leg a year previously in making the journey, decided to bore a tunnel. The tunnel or Urnerloch as it was called was only nine feet in breadth, ten in height and 120 in length, but it greatly eased the journey of travellers and pack-horses. A road was made through the Urnerloch in 1820.*

'There is a character of repose and tranquillity in the little plain of Andermatt, which is strongly contrasted with the scene upon which the traveller enters when he leaves the Val Urseren to follow the course of the Reuss.' So William Brockendon wrote in 1825. I would find it difficult to subscribe to such a verdict to-day. The Val Urseren, surrounded by the bare mountains, is certainly a pleasing green and fertile valley. In winter Andermatt has a deserved reputation as a skiing resort. In the summer, however, lying at the junction of many passes, its street is noisy with heavy traffic, private cars, coaches and leather-garbed motor cyclists, coming from every part of western Europe. It is, moreover, an important military centre and shares in the drabness characteristic of all garrison towns. My own short stay at Andermatt, interrupted at a very early hour by the passing of military lorries and the insistent clangour of church bells, is also remembered for a singular

* In 1825 Brockendon put the length of the road as 220 feet and the height and breadth at 12 feet.

discovery which I made while hunting for something to read in a bookcase in the lounge of my hotel; innocently titled and demurely bound was as pornographic a novel as ever fluttered the dovecotes of the Customs authorities at Dover or Folkestone. Little blame lay with the management, for the book was in English, and I wonder whether some salacious-minded Englishman or American still regrets the inadvertent loss of what might have been an important addition to his collection of *curiosa* or whether he had decided somewhat cynically to abandon an embarrassing piece of contraband before facing the examination of his baggage on the English side of the Channel.

I hope I have not been too unjust to Andermatt, and so many of our judgements on places are ultimately personal and subjective, for it is at the very centre of the Swiss Alps, and of the chain of communications which knits its communities together. The road up the Oberalp Pass to the Grisons curls steeply north of the town. The St. Gotthard route traverses the Val Urseren (Andermatt was formerly called Olsera), goes through the villages of Hospenthal, its name probably derived from the hospice once maintained here by the Capuchin friars, and Realp, and mounts towards the summit of the pass by the splendid road which has been reconstructed recently.

Swiss mountain passes, for that matter all mountain passes, have a certain superficial similarity, a tarn of dark water, the inevitable hotel which has replaced the original hospice, the gaunt mountains. The St. Gotthard has all these characteristics and, surrounded as it is by granite peaks of no particular eminence, Monte Prosa, Sasso di San Gottardo, Blauberg, it lacks the spectacular and scenic qualities afforded by some other Swiss passes. Archdeacon Coxe thought that the scenery was 'exceedingly dreary,' and I am not sure that he may not have been correct.

The St. Gotthard is none the less in all probability the most significant and the most historic of the Swiss Alpine passes. Once the Devil's Bridge had been built, the road carried a constant stream of travellers, for it provided the quickest, if not the easiest, route from the Rhine and South Germany to the riches of Italy and the south. Merchants travelling in caravan, papal emissaries, diplomats, pilgrims, mercenary soldiers, plodded the weary, dangerous and difficult track long before the tourist era. The Spaniard, Pero Tafur, crossed the pass in August 1438, sitting on a kind of trailer made of trees and drawn by oxen. From time to time his servants let off firearms to bring down avalanches, a seemingly unnecessary precaution in high summer; but perhaps the summer was worse in 1438 than it has even been in more recent years. In 1504 the papal legate, Raymond von Petrandi, made his descent to the Val Leventina on a litter carried by two shifts of eight peasants who had been specially conscripted for the job. An Englishman, Mr. Greville, was the first man to drive up the pass in a phaeton much to the

astonishment of the natives. The exploit, which occurred on July 25th, 1775, cost him 18 louis as he had to employ a gang of men to help the carriage over the steeper parts. There had been a regular service over the pass since 1693. Although Greville had shown the way, the road was still impracticable for carriages when William Brockendon travelled over the St. Gotthard in 1825; but he met engineers who were surveying the road with a view to improving it to that end. The road was complete by 1834. In 1842 a diligence conveyed passengers and luggage over the pass in summer. The *Mons Tremulus* of the medieval chronicler was rapidly becoming a tourist route. Even so, the inhospitable mountains could still show their dislike of human intrusion. In the winter of 1874 avalanches killed a driver of the mail coach in the Val Tremola and five Italians near Hospenthal.

Travellers over the pass for long could find shelter at a hospice maintained by Capuchin friars. The Swiss scientist Bourrit regretted that they did little more for travellers than say Mass; but Coxe's experience was more fortunate. As one of the friars was away, he was given his room and was entertained royally. 'Our host has just supplied us with a dinner, consisting of delicious trout . . . eggs and milk, together with excellent butter and cheese.' The hospice was destroyed by an avalanche in 1775 and rebuilt on a larger scale in 1777. When Coxe revisited it in August 1785, he found a friar engaged in saying Mass before a congregation of twenty people; but later he made him very welcome. The French pillaged it in 1799; and it was eventually replaced by a hotel.

The significance of the St. Gotthard made it, as I have already observed, a focal point of Swiss history. The Hohenstaufen Emperors were quick to realise the importance of controlling the road, as were the Hapsburg princes who tried unavailingly to stem the autonomous powers of the local aristocracy and of the rich peasants of Schwyz and Unterwalden and Uri who exploited its economic and political possibilities. Indeed, towards the beginning of the fifteenth century, the Alpine cantons sought to extend their influence to the south. A petty baron enjoying the entertaining title of Freiherr von Sax zu Misox sold his rights over the district around Bellinzona to Uri and Obwalden. Three years later the powerful Visconti rulers of Milan challenged this action and in 1422 put to flight the irregular levies from Lucerne and its allies on the battlefield of Arbedo.

The importance of the St. Gotthard route was such that it was bound to be considered by the railway builders. The construction of the railway up the Reuss valley was itself a triumph of skilful engineering. Between Erstfeld and Göschenen, where the tunnel starts, the line is raised some 2,080 feet in 18 miles. As later with the Lötschberg line between Frutigen and Kandersteg, the difficulty of enabling the railway to climb from the various levels of an increasingly narrow valley without too steep a gradient was met by a series of

The Alps on the Klausen Pass, Uri

spirals. The Pfaffensprung tunnel at Gurtnellen is completely circular and the passengers emerge 120 feet higher up the mountainside and facing the other direction. At Wassen there is a double loop which raises the train some 400 feet. At Göschenen, some 3,638 feet, whence the metre gauge Schöllenen railway runs to Andermatt, the 9¼ miles of tunnel begins. The boring of the tunnel started in June 1872, but it was 10 years before it was opened for passenger traffic. The engineers had profited by their experience in piercing the Mont Cenis (which had been opened some nine months earlier), more especially by the use made of an improved version of the compressed air rock drill invented by Sommeiller. The two bores met on February 28th, 1880, but unfortunately the engineer responsible for the tunnel, Louis Favre, died after a fatal seizure in the tunnel in July 1879, and lies buried in the churchyard at Göschenen.

The St. Gotthard tunnel is some 3,145 feet below the road. For a time it seemed as if it might well put the road out of business, but the invention of the motor car brought the pass back into prominence.

It is a truism to speak of the St. Gotthard as the king of passes, and the newly constructed road with its series of wide curves is without doubt one of the finest in Europe. Its supremacy is, however, less a scenic than a geological phenomenon. A very quick glance at the map will show that the Swiss Alps are divided by a cleft which starts at Martigny and pushes up the Rhone valley to Brig. It then turns towards the north, leading via Gletsch and the Furka Pass to Andermatt; thence it goes up the Oberalp to Disentis and Chur. At a remote period of prehistory the highest mountains of Europe may well have been here, and during the glacial period a thousand feet of ice lay over the pass. The mountain ranges which rise to the west still contain the high peaks of the Bernese Oberland; to the east the marine granite heights are pierced by the Schöllenen Gorge and the St. Gotthard Pass. Here in the prehistoric past a stream of ice opened the way for future travellers by a way of a ravine and a col, and so brought southern and northern Europe into closer cultural, economic and political contact.

The canton of Uri, the most easterly of the forest cantons, has its frontier on the Furka Pass, 7,992 feet, the summit of the road which, opened in 1867, leaves the St. Gotthard on the left-hand side. After leaving the St. Gotthard Archdeacon Coxe walked down to Hospenthal and made his way over the Furka. 'It was,' he wrote later, 'a single path, up a steep mountain, where a horse with some dexterity, could just put one leg before the other: and this path sometimes lay upon the edge of a precipice, very craggy and stony; where, if my steed had happened to stumble, we must both inevitably have perished.' They had to cross swollen torrents and in one place the track was blocked by a fall of rock. 'With much difficulty, and after having crossed several large drifts of ice and snow, the torrents at the same time rumbling under our feet, we reached by a very steep ascent, the summit of the Furka.' Goethe passed the same way about the same time, making his journey, however, in mid-November 1779, when the snow was so deep that it came half-way up his waist. Nearly a hundred years later, the young Joseph Conrad and his tutor were making their way, and the tutor was trying to persuade Conrad against his decision to go to sea. The sight of an Englishman travelling over the pass in some curious way clinched Conrad's determination to become a seafarer.

Conrad travelled over the pass after the road had been completed. It mounts through landscape bleak but grand. The crags of the Dammastock and Galenstock, with their attendant glaciers, break the comparative monotony. It was here that strangely enough I was involved in a bitter argument with an English spinster which, I confess on looking back at the incident, may not have been wholly to my credit. We had joined the Swiss postal bus at Andermatt. This was its starting point; but it was also the terminus of the bus route from Altdorf. The spinster had been in the previous bus, and, knowing that it was to take her further, had reserved the front seat by leaving there her coat and umbrella. Now the Swiss postal bus service gives intending travellers the right to occupy the seats they wish according to the priority of their reservations. We had been the first to reserve our seats and knew nothing of the lady with the umbrella. I removed the offending instrument and did not hear or ignored the irate tirade that this action produced. I was soon, however, to realise the iniquity of what I had done. From Andermatt to the summit of the Furka Pass the offended lady maintained an incessant stream of vituperation, in English for our benefit and in German for our discomfiture. It would, perhaps, have been easier, and possibly more graceful, to have surrendered the seat, but I thought at the time that I was more offended against than offending. At the Furka Pass hotel the bus stopped to allow the travellers to take refreshment. I put down my sweater on the seat. 'See,' said the enraged lady, 'he thinks that I am going to take *his* seat.' Restraint no longer ruled, and battle was joined.

Such trivia should not be allowed to weigh against the 'inexpressibly beautiful' view of the Alps as the road turns towards the Rhone valley. Beyond the Furka hospice the Finsteraarhorn appears in all its magnificence. 'A moment before, all was dullness,' Mark Twain wrote in *A Tramp Abroad*, 'but a step further on placed us on the summit of the Furka; and exactly in front of us, at a distance of only 15 miles, this magnificent mountain lifts its snow-wreathed precipices into the deep blue sky.' Further on the road passes by the majestic Rhone glacier, its ice pinnacles gleaming in the sun. The glacier is nearly eight miles long, but the ice-fall which used to dip right into the valley has shrunk considerably since I first saw it some 30 years ago. It is at its best in late spring or early summer when the Alpine flowers blossom on its slopes; and at its worst on an August Sunday when the crowd of visitors to its ice grotto and the heavy traffic make one yearn for the remote Alpine valleys. The view from the Furka embraces the snow peaks of the Bernese and Valaisan Alps, and looks towards the little hamlet of Gletsch whence the Grimsel road winds its way into the Bernese Oberland.

3

THE BERNESE ALPS

Interlaken and its neighbourhood

THE BERNESE ALPS can be seen on a clear day from the wooded Juras, sixty or seventy miles away. The plain and the lake of Neuchâtel may be veiled in a thin mist but in the distance the sun glints on the snowy peaks of the great mountains, as individual as humanity and yet cruelly impersonal. If they glisten now in the sunlight, to-morrow they may be storm-clad and wrapped in impenetrable fog. They can be seen too on a fine day from the famous Känzli terrace at Berne. When Joseph Addison visited Berne in 1701 he described the view, albeit he mistook the district for the Grisons, as the 'noblest summer-prospect in the world . . . for you have a full view of a huge range of mountains that lie in the county of the Grisons, and are buried in snow.'

Neither the Jura mountains nor the capital city are quite the gateway to the Bernese Oberland. If there is an approach which admits the casual visitor more quickly than any other to the intimacies of the high mountains, it lies through Thun and the lake which bears its name. The countryside between Berne and Thun is a patchwork of meadows and fruit-trees, of small villages and undulating woods, of timbered farmhouses. As one approaches the town of Thun, the mountains begin to appear on the horizon, the massive Stockhorn, the pyramidal Niesen and, if the day be clear, the majestic snow-covered peaks of the Eiger, the Mönch and the Jungfrau. The country ceases to be merely pastoral and becomes alpine.

Yet it is worth exploring the hinterland north-west and north-east of Thun, for there are unrealised delights here. It is a country so remote from the tourist, so different and yet still distinctively alpine that it possesses on an August day when the main roads throb with coach and car a rare, refreshing quality. The road which ascends through Steffisburg, a little suburb of Thun, traverses a country of orchards, running streams and beautiful farmhouses with great eaves and intricate wood carving. The mountains are only the foothills of the Alps but they have a shape and character all their own; rocky precipices and slopes dark with pine form a fitting background for the green meadows. From the little village of Oberei a gravelled road climbs in twists and turns over the Schallenberg. There is a breath-taking view from the verdant summit, not indeed of the great mountains, but of wide grassy valleys, the Emmental in particular, of rounded hills and bare mountains, Wachthubel, Honegg, Hohgant, Schwandfluh, before the dusty descent to the covered wooden bridge over the river Emme brings the traveller to Schangau, Marbach and at Wiggen to the road to Lucerne. This countryside, so little known, so uncommercialised, affords an unrivalled picture of sub-alpine life.

The town of Thun itself, though possessing a Kursaal and excellent tea-shops, is an ancient city in its own right. It has arcaded streets and old houses with overhanging roofs, clustering under the shadow of a castle tower, said incidentally to have been modelled on that of the Temple at Paris. It belonged to the counts of Kyburg before they sold it to the burghers of Berne in 1384. Thun, it will be remembered, was the scene of Matthew Arnold's romance, *Marguerite*:

> *The clouds are on the Oberland,*
> *The Jungfrau snows look faint and far:*
> *But bright over those green fields at hand,*
> *And through those fields comes down the Aar.*

> *And from the blue twin-lakes it comes,*
> *Flows by the town, the churchyard fair;*
> *And 'neath the garden-walk it hums,*
> *The house!—and is my Marguerite there?*

The hills rise gently around the Thunersee, though the rocky cape known as the Nase which projects into the far northern shore of the lake had to be pierced with tunnels to enable the road to complete its journey. The northern shore of the lake is bright with small watering-places, Oberhofen with a fine medieval castle, Gunten, Merligen. Shortly after Merligen a track, and a funicular, leads to Beatenberg on the slopes of the Güggisgrat, a summer and winter-sports resort with fine views of the Oberland peaks. The village takes its name from a Celtic saint, Beatus, who supposedly inhabited a cave in the cliffs below. The saint had somewhat ungenerously displaced the dragon who lived there by making the sign of the Cross. He was helped in his work of evangelising the villages around the lake of Thun by his ability to float on a capacious cloak, a means of journeying not unfortunately available when I visited the cave at Beatushöhlen in 1947. This was to be regretted as we had missed both the last bus and the last boat and had to make the tiring walk back to Interlaken. I am bound to confess that I find caves singularly unre-warding places to visit and speleologists engage my imperfect sympathies.

The road around the southern shore is the more widely used, and passes above the little town of Spiez, which has an ancient castle and an anchorage for sailing yachts. Behind the lake rises the cone-shaped Niesen. Spiez is a junction for rail and road, whence the Lötschberg line climbs to Kandersteg and the Rhone valley while the Montreux–Oberland–Bernois railway saunters along the Simmental to Zweisimmen and the lake of Geneva. Above the lakeside resorts which dot the shore between Spiez and Interlaken, Faulensee, Leissigen, Därligen, a charming road with marvellous views over mountain and lake leads to the quiet villages of Krattigen and Aeschi. The lake of Thun is 11¼ miles long and 2 miles wide. Its blue-tinted waters, upon which little white steamers ply, afford glimpses of the great mountains, but its particular beauty arises from the gradation of the hills which surround it, the lower slopes emerald green with grass merge into dark tree-covered hills, topped finally by bare rock and towering snowy pinnacles.

Interlaken, situated on a marshy plain, the Bödeli, interposed between the lakes of Brienz and Thun, is the tourist capital of the Bernese Alps. It is so rooted in the tourist industry, so much the product of Victorian enthusiasm, that out of the season it seems like some seaside resort devoid of life. Yet the suburb of Unterseen on the northern bank of the river Aar which flows from one lake to the other here has many quaint corners and old houses which point to its earlier history. The original lord of Interlaken, as of much of the surrounding region, was its Augustinian monastery, founded by Baron Seliger von Oberhofen and taken under direct papal protection in 1133. In 1279 Count Berchtold von Eschenbach-Oberhofen with Imperial approval founded a town at Unterseen on land belonging to the monastery. The monastery was determined to uphold its rights over this land, and to restrict the activities of the burgesses of Unterseen, even to the extent of damming the river to ensure control over the fish (the dam was not actually removed until 1855). The hatred with which the people of Unterseen regarded their lords made them sympathise with the Bernese government's acceptance of the reformed religion in 1528. Nor did the prior and his monks put up a stout fight. In the belief that discretion was the better part of valour and present compensation better than future hardship, the monks surrendered their house with its very extensive property. Their former subjects soon discovered that they had exchanged one harsh master for another. There were risings against the Bernese in the Haslital, at Grindelwald, Lauterbrunnen, and at Frutigen; but the citizens of Unterseen for the most part remained loyal and in return received the Sefinen Alp, near Mürren, as a reward. The revolt, helped, albeit weakly, by men from Uri and Unterwalden who had come over the Brünig, was quickly suppressed, and its leaders, Christian Kolb of Lauterbrunnen among them, were put to death by being torn apart by horses.

Modern Interlaken is the product of Victorian and Edwardian tourism. In another setting it could be a prosperous English spa, dignified by its strangely designed Kursaal with a magnificently kept garden, its tea-time music and its evening concerts, its clean streets, its well-stocked shops and grandiose hotels. There are few shops or tea-rooms where English is not clearly and correctly spoken, which is more than can be said of some of its modern British visitors. 'There's no paper like the *News of the World*,' a stout Englishwoman observed with relish as she bought a copy at the kiosk in the Hoheweg, where the English papers are usually available the day of their publication, often before lunch. The more sophisticated and intellectual Englishman will avoid Interlaken, and many other resorts in the Bernese Ober-land, as he would avoid Margate or Blackpool, preferring the picturesque remoteness of some Apennine village. Yet it is fair to say that Interlaken, suffering the economic changes contingent on two world wars and enter-taining a different class of tourist, has met the challenge offered to it. It cannot be other than a tourist resort but judged simply as a tourist resort it has many merits. It might have become dowdy, as in some respects Montreux has become, but it is spruce and prosperous. Its hotels, or at least most of them, are comfortable and good; the refreshments offered at Schuh's or Ecken-berger's restaurants are of the high Swiss standard. It has without doubt the most splendid, as well as the most photographed, view in all the Alps, that of the Jungfrau. When clouds muffle its peaks or its slopes glow rose in the sunset, its beauty is of a theatrical quality. Finally, Interlaken is still an incomparably fine centre for the exploration of the Alps.

Yet when all that can be said in Interlaken's favour has been said, its greatest advantage is the opportunity of getting away to more exciting places in its vicinity. Within a range of 50 miles the mountains open their mysteries, some ravished by chair lift, funicular and mountain railway. When one is young in years the arrival of the tourists by these modern contraptions at the summit of the Niesen or the Schynige Platte, or at the beautiful Oeschinensee may seem a desecration of nature, a vulgarism invented by the capitalist and exploited for gain. I have often felt as did the Alpine traveller, Walter Larden, who when he was climbing in 1904 glimpsed the building of the Eiger Glacier Station below and wrote: 'Not only mountaineers, but all travellers of just taste, must surely feel that this railway is a desecration of nature; something like a merry-go-round in Westminster Abbey.' Nor shall I forget the rush of English schoolboys from the funicular urged on by their schoolmaster to see 'which house' could first achieve the summit of the Niesen. 'He says,' one boy observed somewhat bitterly, 'we've got to beat the record.' Yet, when all is said and as middle age deprives the limbs of youthful vigour, the funicular and mountain railway provide many with the opportunity to see the mountains at close quarters. The Bernese Oberland, honeycombed as it is with roads and rail-ways, surfeited with hotels and souvenir shops, can yet within a short

distance of all these things bestow tranquillity and grandeur, remoteness and beauty.

The eastern range of the Bernese Alps forms an irregular block of mountains, Wellhorn, Wetterhorn, Schreckhorn, Eiger, Mönch, Jungfrau and many another stretching as far as the Fafleralp and the Lötschen valley. The north-west slopes are almost uniformly precipitous. The southern side of the Alps provides a wonderful glacial highway, stretching from the Lötschenlücke at the head of the Lötschen valley to the Concordiaplatz, a veritable glacial crossroads whence climbers can make their way down the great Aletsch glacier to Belalp and Riederalp and so to Blatten and Brig in the Valais, or climb straight on to the Grünhornlücke, up the south-east ridge of the razor-edged Finsteraarhorn, and so through the gap known as the Gemslücke to the Oberaar glacier. It is not far from here to the Grimsel hospice. This vast, irregularly-shaped range of mountains with its snow-fields and glacial valleys has long been a mountaineering paradise, even for the comparatively sophisticated climber.

Times have certainly changed, at least in the valleys, since Leslie Stephen wrote his classic work *The Playground of Europe*, first published in 1894, but his enthusiasm for the Bernese Alps still stands and deserves quotation. 'No earthly object,' he wrote in his account of the first ascent of the Schreckhorn, 'that I have seen approaches in grandeur to the stupendous mountain wall whose battlements overhang in mid-air the villages of Lauterbrunnen and Grindelwald; the lower hills that rise beneath it, like the long Atlantic rollers beaten back from the granite cliffs on our western coast, are a most effective contrast to its stern magnificence; in the whole Alps there is no ice-stream to be compared to the noble Aletsch Glacier, sweeping in one majestic curve from the crest of the ridge down to the forests of the Rhone valley; no mountains, not even the aiguilles of Mont Blanc, or the Matterhorn itself, can show a more graceful outline than the Eiger—that monster, as we may fancy, in the act of bounding from the earth; and the Wetterhorn, with its huge basement of cliffs contrasted with the snowy cone that soars so lightly into the air above, seems to me to be a very masterpiece in a singularly difficult style; but indeed the very names stand alone in the Alps for poetical significance—the Maiden, the Monk, the Ogre, the Storm Pike, the Terror Pike, and the Dark Aar Pike—would each repay the most careful study of the youthful designer. Four of these, the Jungfrau, Mönch, Eiger, and Wetterhorn stand like watchhouses on the edges of the cliffs.'

The Lütschine torrent which flows into the lake of Brienz near Bönigen and which, it is said, was first canalised by the nuns of Interlaken has its source at the foot of these cliffs, the Black Lütschine streaming down from Grindelwald, the White from Lauterbrunnen. They meet and join at Zweilütschinen. The valleys down which they flow, leading to the very

The Alpine Garden, Schynige Platte, near Interlaken,
rnese Oberland

heart of the great mountain chain, are amongst the loveliest, if most frequented, in the Alps. Here there is a marriage of rushing torrent and stately
pine, with the mountains rising on every side to peaks never free from ice
and snow.

The valley of the Black Lütschine ends at the village of Grindelwald,
situated in an amphitheatre of green meadows surrounded by mountains,
the Wetterhorn, with the Upper Glacier sloping towards the valley, the
stern rocks of the Mettenberg concealing the sharp-toothed Schreckhorn, the
Fiescherhörner appearing in the middle distance above the Lower Glacier,
and dominating the scene the giant bulk of the Eiger. To the east the valley
is closed by the gentler height of the Grosse Scheidegg over which a splendid
track takes the walker to Rosenlaui and Schwarzenalp, to Meiringen in the
Haslital. The path mounts through grassy pastures towards the saddle of the
Grosse Scheidegg with the great cliffs of the Wetterhorn on the right. At
the top there is a fine view of the Hasliberg ridge and the mountains
beyond but, more particularly, looking backwards, of the green bowl in
which Grindelwald is situated. It was at this spot that Roundell Palmer,
Lord Selborne, met the Prince of Wales, the future Edward VII. 'I remember
well that we met him . . . with his tutor Mr. Gibbs,' the future Lord Chan-
cellor commented gravely 'just after we had been decorating our hats with
the beautiful *Gentiana asclepiadea*.' The track to Schwarzenalp and Rosenlaui
is very beautiful, descending through pine woods, to the green velvet
plateau of G'schwandenmadt, near the Rosenlaui hotel, cradled in wild
mountains and ice-clad peaks, the spiky crags of the Dossenhorn, the rocky
pile of the Wellhorn and the sheer falls of the steep sides of the Wetterhorn.

From the Grosse Scheidegg a path to the right, passing the cow huts of
Oberlager, leads along the green terraces of the Schwarzhorn and the
Faulhorn, giving a marvellous view of the amphitheatre of peaks above the
village. The Faulhorn and the Schwarzhorn are also magnificent points of
view. A chair lift can now raise the traveller some 3,265 feet of the way, in
two and three quarter miles, from Grindelwald to First, 7,122 feet high.
There are intermediate stations at Oberhaus, Bort and Egg, giving access
to fine walks and, in winter, to good skiing slopes. This is in fact one of the
most ambitious chair lifts in the Swiss Alps, with a greater passenger-
carrying capacity than any other. Alternatively, the walk down from the
Faulhorn past the mirrored surface of the little Bachalpsee and through the
silent pines is a rewarding experience.

To the west the Kleine Scheidegg, towards which the railway climbs with
thousands of passengers desirous of seeing the Jungfraujoch, gives an even
more intimate view of the great peaks. The path from Grindelwald ascends
through meadows and woods under the shadow of the towering Mittellegi
ridge of the Eiger to the little hamlet of Alpiglen. I remember meeting one of

74

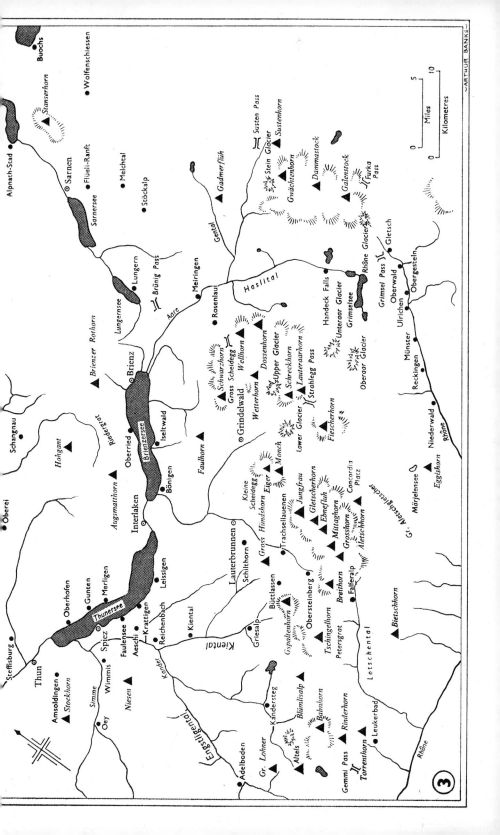

the maids from the hotel where we had been staying who had left Grindelwald for Alpiglen because the former had become too noisy. The Kleine Scheidegg itself is both a mountain saddle and a railway junction, giving ingress through the Jungfrau railway to the very heart of the Alps; but there are also lovely walks along the gentle green slopes of the Männlichen which separates Grindelwald from the Lauterbrunnen valley. The Wordsworths came over the Kleine Scheidegg to Grindelwald in 1820. 'Soon the vale lay before us with its two glaciers,' Dorothy wrote, 'and, as it might seem, its thousand cabins sown upon the steeps. The descent became so precipitous that all were obliged to walk; deep we go into the broad cradle valley; every cottage we passed had its small garden, and cherry trees sprinkled with leaves bearing half-grown, half-ripe fruit. . . . When near the bottom of the declivity we were almost stunned by the roaring of the stream . . . and from the centre of the wooden bridge we beheld it issuing from its icy cavern beneath the snow-like roof of the larger glacier. . . . The sunshine had long deserted the valley, and was quitting the summits of the mountain behind the village; but red hues, dark as the red of rubies, settled in the clouds, and lingered there after the mountains had lost all but their cold whiteness and the black hue of the crags. The gloomy grandeur of the spectacle harmonised with the melancholy of the vale; yet it was a heavenly glory that hung over those cold mountains.'

The village of Grindelwald itself is surrounded by green pastures on which the little brown chalets are dotted in a haphazard yet picturesque fashion. Possibly the site of a Celtic settlement, it first appeared in history when it was granted to the monks of Interlaken in 1146. Nearly half a century later the remnants of a baronial force which had rebelled against Duke Berchtold V of Zähringen, retreated towards Grindelwald where it was crushed on Good Friday, 1191. Although Grindelwald's glaciers were visited comparatively early in Swiss history, it was not until the nineteenth century that it became a fashionable centre. I fear that the village has not wholly improved with the passing of the years. The charming little Adler hotel has been expanded into a big modern building as a result of the destruction by fire of the Bear Hotel. This was the second occasion upon which the Bear met with disaster. The first was in 1892 when the whole village was burned through a fire fanned by the relentless föhn. 'I can still shut my eyes and see the Eiger snows blood-red in the glare reflected from the flames,' Sir Arnold Lunn recalled. 'Houses, hotels, railway station, wagons, haysheds, fences, cornfields, telegraph-poles, all were ablaze!' the climber Julius Kugy commented. 'Kaufmann saw his house threatened, but still standing. His money was inside. We raced down, but by the time we were below, his house was a smouldering ruin. He took his place calmly at the fire-hose, while Bonetti and I laboured the whole afternoon, and throughout the night till next dawn,

14 *Looking from the Kleine Scheidegg; the cloud formation shows the approach of the Föhn*

in the water-chain.' Grindelwald has, however, become too popular. There are too many souvenir shops and too many, though necessary, car parks. I do not think that I shall again find an old woman from a chalet offering me mountain raspberries piled with fresh whipped cream for the equivalent of 10d. Yet tourism here, as elsewhere, significant as it must be in the summer and winter economy of Grindelwald, may serve to conceal the real life of the place.

For Grindelwald, rich as it is in green pastures and variegated trees, walnut, alder, birch and pine, is basically the great mountains which surround it. They are the lords of the place. Even the most modest walker can get a thrill by climbing up the great ladder-way which leads to the ice grotto in the Upper Glacier and seeing face to face the immensity of the great ice-field beyond brilliantly tinted in sapphire and turquoise. Better still he can walk past the Chalet Milchbach and up the wooden stairway, the Leiterweg, built in the chimney of the rock, to a fine view point. Thence a short crossing of the glacier leads to the Gleckstein hut, 7,600 feet, on a shoulder of the west ridge of the Wetterhorn. The climb to the Bäregg Inn, above the dust-strewn Lower Glacier, conveys another taste of the mountains. From the Bäregg the path goes high above the glacier with a fine prospect of the vertical cliffs of the Schreckhorn to the Strahlegg hut, where begins the rock and glacial track to the Grimsel Pass.

Grindelwald's mountain scenery has long attracted visitors, even if they were few before the nineteenth century. The English diplomat Thomas Coxe, not to be confused with the peripatetic Archdeacon from whose works I have quoted, visited the glaciers in 1690, bringing such a crowd of attendants with him that it cost the governor of Interlaken 120 crowns to entertain him. Twenty-one years previously Johannes von Muralt described the glaciers in the *Philosophical Transactions of the Royal Society*. The early observers were already interested in the problem of the growth and recession of glaciers. There was a little medieval chapel dedicated to St. Petronella near one of the glaciers which with the houses near it had been overwhelmed by the ice. The bell, dated 1440 (though one record read 1044), survived but disappeared in the great fire which burned down so much of Grindelwald in 1892. The warm summers between 1539 and 1563 were accompanied by a shrinking of the ice, but the chapel, though shown in Schöpf's map of 1578, had completely disappeared.

The glaciers of Grindelwald, like the Rhone glacier, are less impressive than they were at the beginning of this century. Ninety per cent of the Swiss glaciers are now in the course of retrogression, the Morteratsch by as much as 50 feet a year. There are, it has been reckoned, over a thousand glaciers in the Swiss Alps, covering as much as 772 square miles. They move at a rate of 130 to 650 feet a year, the ice in the centre of the glacier flowing faster than

79

The Wetterhorn and the Mettenberg seen from the Kleine Scheidegg,
ese Oberland

at the side. The drag exerted by the outer ice on the central mass causes the appearance of marginal crevasses. The steepness of the incline accounts for the transverse crevasses. Crevasses, those 'dark blue caverns of fathomless depth, with long pendants of lustrous ice fringing the sides, and hanging in fantastic groups from the translucent roof,' cross each other, forming the beautiful glinting ice towers known as séracs. The colouring is often wonderful, ranging from bright sea-green to deepest azure, its brilliance depending not on the sky but the depth of the ice. A stream emerges at the foot of every glacier, grey-coloured because of suspended particles of rock ground off by the mass of moving ice. Glaciers are often edged and strewn with dust-coloured debris, the rubble forming the various kinds of moraines. When they are covered by dirt, they are unpleasing to look at; Leslie Stephen compared the terminal of the Lower Grindelwald Glacier to a dead whale. When, however, they are seen in all their splendour, glittering in the sunlight, a fairy city full of towers and castles, with unfathomable dungeons of deep azure, they are amongst the loveliest of Alpine creations.

Early travellers noted particularly the apparent 'health and contentment' of the people of Grindelwald. Marc Bourrit who visited the Alps many times between 1769 and 1819 was impressed by their 'cleanliness, simplicity and bliss.' He also described one of the first crossings of the Kleine Scheidegg, where he found some 300 young men and women who had walked from Grindelwald to watch a wrestling match there. Sir Gavin de Beer has pointed out in his *Escape to Switzerland* that the first Englishman to cross the Scheidegg was a country clergyman, the Rev. Norton Nicholls, rector of Lound and Bradwell in Suffolk and a friend of the poet Thomas Gray. He walked to Grindelwald from Lauterbrunnen in company with Karl Viktor von Bonstetten and Jakob Wyttenbach in 1771, staying with the local pastor at Grindelwald. Archdeacon Coxe naturally came to Grindelwald, travelling from Meiringen over the Grosse Scheidegg and was thrilled with the view from the top of the pass 'which so far exceeded them in wildness and horror, that we unanimously exclaimed "There is the Schreckhorn, or the Peak of Terror,"' but he was disappointed by the glaciers.

The sage of modern Grindelwald was an Oxford don, the Rev. W. A. B. Coolidge.* An American by birth, he was educated at St. Paul's School. Concord. In 1864 he accompanied his mother, his aunt and his sister to Europe, which they were never to leave again, when he was fourteen years old. The next year, 1865, he made his first visit to Switzerland with his aunt Meta Brevoort, and walked over the glacier pass, the Strahlegg, which leads eventually to the Grimsel. 'We had,' he told his mother, 'to be tied together for some time and to cut steps in the ice. Peter Bernet came first, then I, then the shepherd, Rudolf Boss, aunty, and Jossi. We reached the summit at

* Ronald W. Clark, *An Eccentric in the Alps* (1959).

12 a.m. and then went down the ice wall which was entirely bare, both snow and ice having melted away. We came down from the top, having already crossed the Upper and Lower Eismeer of Grindelwald, and crossed the Finsteraar Glacier and then the Unteraar Glacier, enjoying beautiful views of the Finsteraarhorn and Schreckhorn.... We reached the Grimsel at a quarter to nine p.m., having been gone 18 hours from the chalet on the Eismeer.' Mr. Baedeker, the guide-book writer, who had started two hours after them, he added, arrived half an hour before them. This was the first of some 1,200 or more ascents which Coolidge was to make in the next thirty years. The Bernese Oberland was not indeed to be his only sphere of action. As his biographer has observed, 'The map of their wanderings is a cross-hatch of routes, thickest in the Dauphiné and the Oberland, but covering all except the most easterly Alps.' But Grindelwald, which he made his home from 1896 to his death in 1926, was the start and finishing-point of his alpine life.

In his early Alpine climbs Coolidge was accompanied by his indefatigable aunt, Meta Brevoort (until she died in 1876), and by his dog, Tschingel. In her short canine life, Tschingel climbed no less than 66 *grandes courses*, made 11 first ascents and went on some 100 minor Alpine expeditions. She had been given to Coolidge originally by his guide, the Grindelwald-born Christian Almer, in compensation for Coolidge's disappointment at failing to climb the Eiger. Almer himself had bought Tschingel at Kippel in the Lötschental and her Alpine career had been initiated by going up the Torrenthorn. Henceforth Tschingel, later made an honorary member of the Alpine Club, was always to the fore in Coolidge's climbs until old age imposed retirement. Her first ascent with Coolidge and his aunt was the (second) ascent of the Blümlisalp, followed by climbs up the Balmhorn and the Aletschhorn. With her master she conquered the Eiger in 1871. As the ascent was difficult, they had intended to leave her to guard the knapsacks. 'We were about half-way up the bad rocks when the last man spied her coming after us. We were divided between displeasure at her neglect of duty in abandoning the knapsack and great amusement at her feverish zeal for mountain climbs.' For the final ascent she was roped, but elsewhere she climbed freely. 'Although bleeding profusely in each of her paws, she led the way over rocks and ice, finding her way wonderfully, avoiding every wide crevasse, in short, a born guide, and with an excellent appetite withal.' To prevent the paws from bleeding, Coolidge had small boots made specially for her but she did not take to these. Her master held that the dog actually grew to appreciate mountain scenery, and it certainly seems that by being able to sniff the cool air coming from crevasses she contributed to the safety of crossing a glacier. When she was ten, Tschingel climbed the Klein Schreckhorn, and made an ascent of Mont Blanc. As a result, she was much fêted by the people of Chamonix. A cannon was fired in her honour, and

81

she presided at a reception in the lounge of the hotel for guides and others who wished to make or renew her accquaintance.

Coolidge was not himself a great or adventurous climber; but he was tough and pertinacious. He was in part responsible for making use of high bivouacs, and for popularising winter climbing. He made the first winter ascents of the Wetterhorn and the Jungfrau. Above all he was unrivalled in his knowledge of Alpine lore and history.

He had become, and remained to his death, a fellow of Magdalen College, Oxford, and in spite of continuous absence after 1896, he retained his love for his college, in earlier days always seeking to commemorate the founder's day by making a notable ascent on July 22nd. At the age of thirty, he was rather surprisingly ordained (and for a time he acted as curate of South Hinksey), but outwardly religion made little impact on his life. Yet, when no chaplain was available at Grindelwald after the outbreak of the First World War, he readily took the services at the little Anglican Church there (of Low persuasion and, rather characteristically, locked when I last tried to enter it). He was a scholar of the crabbed type, enormously meticulous and erudite, brutally and unnecessarily critical of others, loving a quarrel, yet ponderous and uninspired. But the sage of Grindelwald had one love; he worshipped the mountains. It was, perhaps, a weakness that conferred ultimately, as such a love must, loneliness and misanthropy; but since his first visit to Grindelwald in 1865 it proved the guiding light of his life.

Coolidge was not indeed wholly untypical of his generation of Alpinists. While he did not lack powers of aesthetic appreciation, as some of his critics said, it was an even deeper if inarticulate satisfaction that he enjoyed as a result of climbing and living in the Alps. Other Victorian mountaineers were as opinionated, as temperamental, and as tough. It was in his fanatical concern with historical accuracy and topographical exactitude that he was also their unrivalled peer. Indeed he made many of his later climbs simply to confirm facts. Like his contemporaries, he placed great reliance on his guides. His guide, and one of his few friends, Christian Almer, then aged 70, with his wife, Margherita, also aged 70, who had never before climbed a snow peak, celebrated the golden jubilee of their wedding by an ascent of the Wetterhorn. Coolidge is buried in the churchyard at Grindelwald, under the shadow of the mountains he had grown to know so well.

Two mountains dominate Grindelwald, the Wetterhorn and the Eiger, while a third, the Schreckhorn, invisible from the village itself, towers above the bare cliffs of the Mettenberg. The Wetterhorn consists of three peaks of much the same height, the lower one of which, the Hasli-Jungfrau, overlooking the fields of Grindelwald, was climbed by two Swiss guides in 1844. The famous ascent of the mountain was made in 1854 by a barrister, Alfred Wills, who was some forty years later to preside at the trial of Oscar

Wilde. 'In front rose a steep curtain of glacier,' Wills wrote in his *Wanderings among the High Alps*, 'surmounted, about five or six hundred feet above us, by an overhanging cornice of ice and frozen snow, edged with a fantastic fringe of pendants and enormous icicles. This formidable obstacle bounded our view, and stretched from end to end of the ridge. . . . We foresaw great difficulty in forcing this imposing barrier; but after a short consultation, the plan of attack was agreed upon, and immediately carried into execution.' They hacked steps in the ice and made slow progress. 'Hence, the blocks of ice, as they were hewn out, rolled down upon us, and shooting past, fell over the brink of the arête by which we had been ascending and were precipitated into a fathomless abyss beneath.' Then the way seemed obstructed. 'The cornice curled over towards us, like the crest of a wave, breaking at irregular intervals along the line into pendants and inverted pinnacles of ice. . . . They seemed the battlements of an enchanted fortress, framed to defy the curiosity of man, and to laugh to scorn his audacious efforts.' Yet they broke through and achieved the summit. 'The instant before, I had been face to face with a blank wall of ice. One step, and the eye took in a boundless expanse of crag and glacier, peak and precipice, mountain and valley, lake and plain. The whole world seemed to lie at my feet. The next moment, I was almost appalled by the awfulness of our position. The side we had come up was steep; but it was a gentle slope, compared with that which now fell away from where I stood. A few yards of glittering ice at our feet, and then, nothing beneath us and the green slopes of Grindelwald, nine thousand feet beneath. I am not ashamed to own that I experienced . . . a profound and almost irrepressible emotion. . . . We felt as in the more immediate presence of Him who had reared this tremendous pinnacle, and beneath the "majestical roof" of whose deep blue Heaven we stood, poised, as it seemed, half way between the earth and sky.' The Wetterhorn has claimed its victims, among them a young Englishman, William Penhall and his guide, killed by an avalanche, in August 1882, but it is by its normal route a comparatively easy mountain to climb.

The Schreckhorn has a forbidding name, the peak of terror, and its conspicuous pinnacles stand out handsomely. It can be seen from the little village of Schwendi, though not from Grindelwald itself. Leslie Stephen, who made the first ascent accompanied by the guides, Peter and Christian Michel and Christian Kaufmann, has described the climb in his *The Playground of Europe*. 'The two summits of the Schreckhorn (the other, southernmost peak, is now called the Lauteraarhorn) form, as it were, the horns of a vast crescent of precipice which runs round a secondary glacier, on the eastern bank of the Grindelwald Glacier. This glacier is skirted on the south by the ordinary Strahlegg route. The cliffs above it are for the most part bare of snow and scored by deep trenches or gullies, the path of avalanches, and of the still more terrible showers of stones which, in the later part of the day, may be seen every five minutes discharged down the flank of the mountain.' Perturbed a little by his guides' appetites—'Every driblet of water seemed to be inseparably connected in their minds with a drop of brandy, and every flat stone suggested an open-air picnic.'—Stephen made the ascent without serious difficulty, though the rocks were steep and slippery and in places covered by a treacherous layer of thin ice, while driblets of snow and rock below the summit slid down with a sinister hiss. 'I can only say,' Stephen wrote of the panorama from the peak, 'that there is something almost unearthly in the sight of enormous spaces of hill and plain, apparently unsubstantial as a mountain mist, glimmering away to the indistinct horizon, and as it were spellbound by an absolute and eternal silence . . . on that perfect day on the top of the Schreckhorn, where not a wreath of vapour was to be seen under the whole vast canopy of the sky, a delicious lazy sense of calm repose was the appropriate frame of mind.' As they made their way down, 'A huge cloud, which looked at least as lofty as the Eiger, rested with one extremity of its base on the Eiger, and the other on the Mettenberg, shooting its white pinnacles high up into the sunshine above. Through the mighty arched gateway thus formed, we could see far over the successive ranges of inferior mountains, standing like flat shades one behind another. The lower slopes of the Mettenberg glowed with a deep blood-red and the more distant hills passed through every shade of blue, purple and rose-coloured hues, into the faint blue of the distant Jura, with one gleam of green sky behind. In the midst of the hills the lake of Thun lay, shining like gold. A few peals of thunder echoed along the glacier valley, telling us of the storm that was raging over Grindelwald.'

Some eighteen years later, in July 1869, the Schreckhorn claimed a victim in the young mountaineer, the Rev. Julius Elliott. Elliott had been at Zermatt, where his ascent of the Matterhorn, the first after the tragic accident which marred the first triumph, had evoked praise from Théophile Gautier. 'A tall young man,' so he described him, 'robust but elegant, in jacket and waistcoat and breeches of brown velour, gaitered to the knees, his felt hat pulled down to his eyebrows, manly and determined in his features, having the air of a perfect gentleman.' 'We muse,' he added prophetically, 'upon the unconquerable passion of some men for dangerous ascents . . . keen delights . . . once they have been tasted, he cannot do without them, but must return until he finds there his own destruction.' The young clergyman had, perhaps, a touch of hubris. He preferred to go unroped in spite of the admonitions of his guide, Franz Biener. He lost his footing and his body plunged at speed to the crevasses of the Lauteraar Glacier over a thousand feet below. He was buried at Grindelwald and F. W. H. Myers was inspired to write:

Here let us leave him; for his shroud the snow,
For funeral-lamps he has the planets seven,
For a great sign the icy stair shall go
Between the heights to heaven.

One moment stood he as the angels stand,
High in the stainless eminence of air;
The next, he was not, to his fatherland
Translated unaware.

Mountains exercise a profound fascination over men and sometimes the enchantment is fatal. There can be little doubt that this has been pre-eminently true of the mighty, well-named Eiger. In the short story *Riesenberg* by Ford Madox Ford one of the characters imagined the mountains as survivals of the old pagan gods, occasionally waking from their age-long sleep to demand a sacrifice. We know in our scientific age that all such imaginings are absurd, and yet mountains more than many natural objects seem to possess both individuality and character. A young Englishman, Charles Barrington, was the first to climb the Eiger, on August 11th, 1858. Accompanied by Christian Almer and Peter Bohren, he went up the north-west ridge. 'We got to the top—the two guides kindly gave me the place of first man up—at 12 o'clock, stayed about ten minutes, fearing the weather, and came down in four hours, avoiding the very steep place, as, looking down from above, we found out a *couloir*, down which we came, and just saved ourselves by a few seconds from an avalanche. I was met at the bottom by about thirty visitors, and we went up to the hotel. They doubted if we had been on the top until the telescope disclosed the flag there. The hotel proprietor had a large gun fired off, and I seemed for the evening to be a "lion." Thus ended my first and only visit to Switzerland.'

A year later, practically to the day, August 9th, 1859, Leslie Stephen, William and George Mathews, with their guides, made the first ascent of the mountain pass which leads from the Wengern Alp to the Rhone valley, the Eiger-Joch. At that time the first major obstacle was the fearsome ice-fall, 'unique among the glaciers of the Alps for its gigantic crevasses and its ice pinnacles of marvellous form and variety.' There was considerable rivalry between the two sets of guides accompanying Stephen's party. When they entered the glacial labyrinth, the Chamonix guides advised against speaking for fear that it would bring down an avalanche; but Stephen's guide, Ulrich Lauener, learning of this, shouted at the top of his voice. This 'failed . . . to dislodge any séracs, and Lauener, going to the front, called to us to follow him.' They first tried the southern Eiger-Joch and found it impassable. They then turned to the northern Eiger-Joch and cut their way up the ice-fall. 'Time slipped by, and I gradually became weary of a sound to which at first I always listen with pleasure—the chipping of the axe, and the hiss of the fragments as they skip down the long incline below us. Moreover, the sun was very hot, and reflected with oppressive power from the bright and polished surface of the ice. . . . The action of resting one's whole weight on one leg for about a minute, and then slowly transferring it to the other, becomes wearisome when protracted for hours. . . . At last, as I was counting the 580th step, we reached a little patch of rock.' Two hours later they emerged on the snow-covered saddle. 'Behind us the plain of Switzerland stretched away to the Jura. On our left a huge amphitheatre of glacier sank down, marked in long concentric curves by tier after tier of crevasses to the level of the Grindelwald Glacier. Beyond rose the sheer cliffs of the Wetterhorn, and further back from the plain the black cluster of rocks of the Schreckhorner.' It was now late and the descent to the Eggishorn entailed a night on the mountains. As the moon rose 'Lauener took this opportunity of remarking that he had been very unwell. He added presently that he could not see, and did not in the least know where he was going.' Stephen observed tartly that 'I do not implicitly believe either of these statements, which struck me as being rather ill-timed.' They spent the hours of darkness on some sharp stones under a big rock as a cold wind blew in gusts from the glacier. Stephen betrayed his toughness by saying that he really rather enjoyed the night. 'Partly the excitement and partly the beauty of the perfectly still and silent night prevented its seeming long. The huge snow-covered mountains that glimmered faintly through the darkness, the long glorious glacier, half seen as it swept away from our feet, and the perfect stillness of the scene, were very striking.'

Subsequently mountaineers conquered the south-west ridge of the Eiger in 1847, the south ridge two years later. In 1885 Grindelwald guides descended the difficult Mittelegi ridge but it was not climbed until 1921, by three guides, Fritz Amatter, Samuel Brawand, Fritz Steuri and a young Japanese, Yuko Mati. In 1932 Dr. Hans Lauper and Alfred Zürcher reached the summit of the Eiger by the north-east face. Every side of the great mountain had now been climbed successfully except the north wall. This was well known for its treacherous qualities, for the volleys of falling stones, its storms, its smooth rock-face 'bread-crumbed with snow, ice and rubble.' Its only unalterable features, according to Heinrich Harrer who has written recently its enthralling history in The White Spider, 'were its pitiless magnificence and its utter unapproachability.'

The first attempt on the north face of the Eiger was made in mid-August 1935, by Max Sedlmayer and Karl Mehringer from Munich. The two young men made progress at first up the steep cliffs but then the weather broke, and the north face was assailed, as was and is its custom, by hail, thunder and

a biting wind. The men survived—after five days spent on the face, but they were trapped by avalanches and falling rocks. Again the weather broke and as the curtain of mist descended on their last bivouac at the upper rim of the third ice-field their fate was sealed.

A second attempt was made in July 1936, by two young Austrians, Edi Rainer and Willy Angerer, and two Bavarians, Anderl Hinterstoisser and Toni Kurz. They managed the exceptionally severe crack below the Rote Fluh successfully and by the end of their first day were more than half-way up the face. Angerer had, however, been hurt, probably by a falling stone, and on the third day only two of the climbers, Kurz and Hinterstoisser, could be seen by those watching far below. They climbed down to the bivouac where they had spent the night, probably in an attempt to bring Angerer down. The weather became worse and as the temperature fell the water on the rocks hardened into ice. 'Hinterstoisser came off and fell the whole way down. The rope pulled Rainer up against a snap-link. He froze to death there. And Angerer's dead too, hanging below me, strangled by the rope when he fell.' So Kurz was able to inform his would-be rescuers but the weather was such that they could make no attempt that night. He lived until dawn but though they arrived at a point about 130 feet below where he was hanging on a rope, they could not reach him, and he died.

Various efforts to climb the north face were made in 1937 and 1938, involving loss of life; but in July 1938, the first successful ascent was made by Heinrich Harrer, Andreas Heckmair, Ludwig Vörg and Fritz Kasparek. Their starting-point was the little hamlet of Alpiglen below the Kleine Scheidegg. Harrer and Kasparek began independently but teamed up with Heckmair and Vörg. Harrer has described the climb in his fascinating book *The White Spider*: the bivouacs on the narrow ledges, the climb up the sheer walls over which stones fell constantly, the glazed rocks, the ever-changing weather and perhaps above all the relentless avalanches which poured forth from the steep patch of snow or ice on the almost vertical face known to climbers as *Die Spinne* or the Spider. 'The howling of the wind increased, gathering a very strange note,' Harrer wrote later, 'a banging and swishing, a whistling hiss. This wasn't the voice of the storm any more coming down out of the wild dance of ice-particles and snowflakes, but something quite different. It was an avalanche and as its harbingers, rocks and fragmented ice! I snatched my rucksack up over my head, holding it firmly with one hand, while the other gripped the rope which ran up to my companion. I jammed myself against the ice-cliff, just as the whole weight of the avalanche struck me. The rattle and hammering of stones on my pack was swallowed up by the clatter and roar of the avalanche. . . . The pressure decreased, but I got no time to draw new breath or to shout before the next avalanche arrived. Its fury exceeded that of the first. . . . The pressure of the avalanche . . . ceased.

The Jungfrau and the Silberhorn, Bernese Oberland
The Mönch, Bernese Oberland

The snow and the ice-granules were tinkling away into the gulf.' In spite of the poor weather, the bad visibility and the constantly whistling flakes of snow, they achieved the summit. 'The storm was raging so fiercely on the summit that we had to bend double. Thick crusts of ice had formed around our eyes, noses and mouths; we had to scratch them away before we could see each other, speak or even breathe. We probably looked like legendary monsters of the Arctic, but we felt in no mood for the humour of such a reflection. Indeed, this was no place in which to turn handsprings or shriek with joy and happiness. We just shook hands without a word.' One further quotation epitomises the experience of those who have dared to climb the north face. 'On that climb the mountaineer will find every experience mountains can offer man in the menacing terror as well as in the beauty of nature at her most savage, and the mountaineer who climbs it must combine in himself every attribute that marks a true man of the mountains.'

Since the first successful climb 13 further successful ascents have been made, two in 1947, two in 1950, six in 1952, one in 1953, and one in 1958; the first winter ascent was made in March 1961. On July 26th, 1950, Erich Waschak and Leo Forstenlechner climbed the face in a single day of eighteen hours and bivouaked on the summit itself. The mountain has, however, continued to claim numerous victims. The most tragic attempt, partly because the most publicised, was made in August 1957 by two Italians, Claudio Corti and Stefano Longhi, and two Germans, Günther Nothdurft and Franz Meier. The struggle for survival was watched by the world but in the end the mountain won. Corti alone survived, but his account of the climb and the subsequent tragedy, described at length by Heinrich Harrer, contains such manifest inaccuracies as to be thoroughly misleading.

The valley of the White Lütschine which leads to Lauterbrunnen and the hamlet of Stechelberg is shorter and narrower than the Grindelwald valley. It is fenced by precipitous cliffs over which water cascades, and the road ends at the very foot of the great Oberland range. Although the deep glen gets very little sun, the upper part of it remains my favourite Swiss valley and the walk from Stechelberg to the Obersteinberg, or to the little Oberhornsee, the loveliest of walks. I was pleased to note that it was also Claud Schuster's considered opinion that the Obersteinberg was a finer place to view the glories of the Oberland peaks than the Wengernalp, Leslie Stephen's choice.

Lauterbrunnen, which means 'clear springs,' a well-chosen name as the traveller seeing the water plunging down the steep sides of the valley in wet weather recognises, was first mentioned in 1240 when Walter von Wadiswil gave the mountain pasturage, the Sefinen Alp, above Mürren, to the monastery at Interlaken. The heiress of the Wadiswils, who were at this time lords of the district as well as of the upper Kandertal, at the beginning of the fourteenth century married a Valaisan nobleman, Jean de la Tour Châtillon of Niedergarten. Under his direction some of his Valaisan tenants crossed the Lötschental to settle in the Lauterbrunnen valley. Indeed, it seems likely that the bell in the parish church at Lauterbrunnen, the fifteenth-century Lötscherglocke, was transported across the Wetter-Lücke, a mountain pass some 10,368 feet high between the Breithorn and the Tschingelhorn, as a present from the people of the Lötschental to the colonists in the valley of Lauterbrunnen. The choice of this high and difficult passage was made because of a quarrel with the grasping monastery of Interlaken which had so far resisted a demand for the construction of a new church at Lauterbrunnen, because the church at the hamlet of Gstseig, six miles distant between Interlaken and Zweilütschinen, attended by the Lauterbrunners, was under its jurisdiction. The peasants were determined to prevent their precious bell falling into the hands of the monks.

In the late eighteenth and early nineteenth century the little village had many famous visitors, for its characteristic features made an inevitable appeal to contemporary romanticism. Goethe was there in 1779. Byron and his friend, John Cam Hobhouse, stayed with the parish priest and described the Staubbach falls behind the village in a letter to his half-sister, Augusta: 'The torrent is in shape curving over the rock, like the *tail* of a white horse streaming in the wind. . . . It is neither mist nor water, but a something between both; its immense height (nine hundred feet) gives it a wave or curve, a spreading here, or condensation there, wonderful and indescribable. . . .' It also received honourable mention in *Manfred*

> the sheeted silver's waving column
> O'er the crags headlong perpendicular.

Later he crossed the Kleine Scheidegg to Grindelwald and thence by way of the Grosse Scheidegg to Meiringen. Wordsworth had been at Lauterbrunnen in September 1790, and he told his sister 'We are now upon the point of quitting these most sublime and beautiful parts . . . the idea of parting from them oppresses me with a sadness similar to what I have always felt in quitting a beloved friend.'

The modern village is pleasant enough, and still dominated by the film-like spray of the Staubbach waterfall, glittering rainbow-like in the sunlight. Beyond Lauterbrunnen the Trümmelbach falls, fed by the snows of the Jungfrau, Mönch and Eiger, tumble through a cleft in the rock in five cascades. In spite of the commercialisation, the falls leave a sinister and even hostile impression as their harsh roar re-echoes in the dripping caves through which the stream rushes. After Trümmelbach the road narrows and ends at the little hamlet of Stechelberg where the pleasant hotel has been recently enlarged and re-equipped.

A mule track goes from Stechelberg to Trachsellauenen and the Obersteinberg. It is, I think, one of the finest walks in the Alps. Each twist and turn of the valley reveals spectacular mountain scenery; glacier and rock, snow and spruce, dwarfing the little timbered chalets and the cows on their alpine pastures. The green slopes in spring are yellow with marsh marigolds and other flowers, and in autumn the mauve crocus grows freely in the fields. The valley is walled in by a mountain range, 12 to 13,000 feet above sea level, from the Schwarz Mönch, where the chamois breed, which hides the Jungfrau from view, to the Gletscherhorn, the level summit of the Ebnefluh, Mittaghorn, Grosshorn, Breithorn, Tschingelhorn. After Trachsellauenen, there are two possible approaches to the Obersteinberg, passing near the Schmadribach falls and the Untersteinberg, and the other, mounting by the Ammerten Alp, to the Obersteinberg. The latter is the better way, giving splendid views of the mountains and of the Upper Schmadribach Fall, for the lower path is slippery and uneven. An hour's walk from the scattered and remote hamlet of the Obersteinberg brings the traveller to the little lake of the Oberhornsee, 6,800 feet high, below the Breithorn glacier. After that the path becomes a climber's pass, crossing the Tschingel glacier between the Tschingelhorn and the Gspaltenhorn. The Tschingel Pass itself, 9,265 feet high, is situated between the Blümlisalp and the Mutthorn. A steepish descent from the pass through the wild Gasterntal leads eventually to Kandersteg.

Another track goes from Stechelberg up the Sefinental. It affords a lovely view of the Sefinen falls as they tumble down to the valley while the walk up the valley itself, enclosed by woods and steep slopes, to the foot of the Büttlassen, is wild and rugged. In spring and early summer there is an abundance of gentian and mountain rose. I last walked there on a dull September day when a cold mist was encircling the mountain peaks. The only man I met was a chamois-hunter, a dead animal slung across his broad shoulders. The head of the valley has a lonely grandeur which makes the villages and towns of tourist Switzerland seem many miles away.

In fact, a track branching off to the right at the opening of the Sefinental leads, via the little hamlet of Gimmelwald, to Mürren. Accompanying Brahms on a walk from Mürren to Gimmelwald, Widmann commented that it was impossible to fix the magnificence of the mountain scenery at which they were looking in the human mind 'and to reproduce it in poetry or in art.' Brahms agreed, adding 'Everyone else who goes for a walk in the Alps with me usually says "that is just as in your third symphony."' Yet critics have recognised the impact of the Alpine scene upon Brahms' music, more especially in his double concerto for violin and cello in A Flat.

Mürren is poised superbly on a steep cliff. It has no motor road and is reached by funicular from Lauterbrunnen to Grütschalp and thence by a light railway which must have one of the finest views from its carriage windows in the world. The village itself is mainly a group of hotels. It is indeed essentially an English foundation, with an English church designed by Street, but its Anglicisation, most obvious in the winter season, cannot deprive it of its grandiose situation. Nowhere else affords such easy and intimate views of the high mountains. 'I would not,' John Addington Symonds wrote with characteristic exaggeration, 'take Rome, Florence or Naples in exchange for the chalets of Mürren.' Even in 1869 a traveller complained that it was 'crowded with English people.' Yet the ecstatic mood prevailed. Archbishop Benson vented his scorn on those who played tennis in the 'sight of the Jungfrau,' here an incomparable silky white. Mürren affords many opportunities for the moderately energetic walker, to Allmendhübel with its superb views over the surrounding mountains and so up the Schilthorn where the unfortunate Mrs. Arbuthnot was struck by lightning on her honeymoon in 1865, or further afield by the high passes to Kiental and Kandersteg. The path to these leads through Gimmelwald to the Sefinen-Furgge, the saddle 8,583 feet high, between the Büttlassen and the Schilthorn. The track descends sharply with the serrated crags of the Gspaltenhorn to the left towards the Kiental. The track on the other side of the stream winds steeply upwards to the Hohtürli and so down to the lovely Oeschinensee and Kandersteg.

Mürren is a refreshing place for a relaxing holiday, for there is no need to wander far from the village to improve the view. One can lie in the hot sun and look at the white snows of the Jungfrau through the sweet-smelling mountain grass or, if the weather is bad, watch the lightning strike the iron-coloured cliffs of the Schwarz Mönch. Delightful as it is, perhaps above all in early summer and autumn, Mürren is best known as a winter sports resort. Sir Henry Lunn first used it for this end in 1910. The Kandahar Ski Club was founded at the Palace Hotel, with which he was closely associated early in 1924. Yet I would be wiser to leave this side of the village's activities to those who have indulged in them there, and perhaps above all to Sir Henry's son, Sir Arnold Lunn, who has described them in his book on the *Bernese Oberland* and elsewhere.

From the shelf on which Mürren stands the sun can be seen glinting on its fellow winter sports resort, Wengen, on the other side of the valley. Its sunny slopes, ablaze with flowers in the early summer, provide delightful walks among pine woods and meadows, to the Leiterhorn, along the Steinwaldweg looking into the green chasm where Lauterbrunnen lives, or up to the Männlichen or the Kleine Scheidegg. At the Wengernalp, which Leslie Stephen held to be the loveliest viewpoint in the Alps, there is an unparalleled glimpse of the Jungfrau, so-called, it is said, because of its likeness to the habit of the nuns of Interlaken. It is the loveliest of mountains, noble in shape and size, reflecting every changing light; its subsidiary peak, the Silberhorn, deep in smooth snow, shimmers in the sunshine. 'Of the three peaks which overlook the Wengern Alp,' the mountaineer Frank Smythe wrote, 'the Jungfrau is the most beautiful. Her long flowing glaciers, with their network of crevasses, suggest the robes of a Grecian maiden, whilst her dark precipices, friezed with gleaming ice, are symbolical of an unapproachable virginity. The Mönch is more staid; he suggests his name and stands aloof from the affairs of life, his firm square summit in commune with the stars. And lastly, the "Ogre" springs from the pastures of Grindelwald and the Little Scheidegg in one tigerish sweep of rock and ice.'

The Kleine Scheidegg, as I mentioned previously, is primarily a junction for the highest mountain railway in Switzerland, indeed, in Europe, that which goes to the Jungfraujoch, a depression about two thousand feet lower than the Mönch and the Jungfrau itself, some 11,333 feet above sea-level. The Bernese Oberland Railway to Grindelwald and Lauterbrunnen was finished in 1890. A plan was mooted to carry the line to Stechelberg and thence work upwards towards the Jungfraujoch. Fortunately this plan, which would have completely spoiled the beautiful valley which begins at Stechelberg, never came to anything. In any case, it would have meant carrying the line nearly 9,000 feet. Then, in 1893, a Swiss engineer, Adolf Guyer-Zeller and his daughter, having climbed the Schilthorn above Mürren, saw the smoke of the railway engine as it chugged towards the Kleine Scheidegg. He was at once convinced that it was from here rather than from Stechelberg that the Jungfrau line must start. It might require a longer tunnel but it had to surmount very much less height. The work began in 1896 and it took sixteen years to complete the $5\frac{3}{4}$ miles of line. In his interesting book, *Switzerland's Amazing Railways*, Mr. Cecil J. Allen has described the immense difficulties which had to be overcome before the work was finished, the need to transport materials during the summer season, the constant falling avalanches, the rarefied air which affected the health of the workers, the shortage of water in spite of the masses of snow and ice, the hardness of the limestone rock and the even harder gneiss after the Eismeer station. An immense amount of tunnelling was necessary. Indeed, for the greater part of the journey the train is in a tunnel—$4\frac{1}{2}$ miles of tunnel in all—though at the intermediate stations, Eigerwand and Eismeer, great windows reveal an extensive prospect reaching over mountain and valley. The summit station consists of a modern hotel, the Berghaus, a tourist hotel, and an observatory. The panorama is stupendous and yet wonderful as it all is, it is difficult not to feel that this is an intrusion into the silence of the Alps. I would much rather watch the clouds floating over the Tschingelhorn at the Obersteinberg than visit the palace of ice or watch the husky dogs frisking over the snow at the Jungfraujoch.

It is inevitable that what I have written about the Bernese Oberland should give the impression that this is a mountain playground in which everything seems subsidiary to the needs of the tourist. The high season of tourism is, however, happily short. Even in the winter sports resorts the greater part of the year is free from the alien invaders. It is then that the Swiss Alps and the people in them follow the life that has been familiar to them for centuries. The souvenirs are packed away for another year; the bazaars close. The little hotels that are still open are left to their permanent clientele, the farmers and the labourers of the village. The snow falls silently, wrapping the trees, muffling every footstep. The spring flowers gradually pierce the melting snow which lies like patchwork on the dead grass; and the air is crisp and clean. The routine of farming proceeds uninterruptedly while the mountains watch and listen. Although the valleys would suffer in prosperity if there were no tourists, their real life is independent of those who come so far to view their beauty.

4

THE BERNESE ALPS

Passes and valleys

THE AREA which includes the Grindelwald and Lauterbrunnen valleys is certainly the principal region of the Bernese Alps; but the mountains to the east and south as well as the Haslital, the Susten and the Grimsel passes are also a part of the Oberland. Further, the districts south of Spiez, Kandersteg, Adelboden and the Simmental, are geographically and socially united with it. Finally the Lötschental, though a part of the Valais, seems sufficiently linked to the Bernese Alps to be included within their province.

The lake of Brienz, or the Brienzersee, is west of Interlaken. It is a little smaller, 9 miles long and 1½ miles wide, than the lake of Thun, with which it was once conjoined, but it is in my view more beautiful. The mountains, thickly wooded with beech and pine, slope steeply down to its blue-green waters. Its colouring is indeed exquisite, and ever changing as light and shade themselves differ. One day its surface will be a smooth aquamarine, mirroring the mountain peaks; the next, as the föhn blows from the Haslital its waters will be ruffled and grey, breaking against the rocky shores with untamed violence. The tints of the trees and the mountains are as varied. There is an immense diversity in the shades of green, yellow-green, blue-green, olive, emerald, apple, of the grasses and trees of the Alpine regions. Nor are the mountains ever the same colour; sometimes bare rock, sometimes white with snow; sometimes brown; sometimes green, ever reflecting the changing lights, rose, purple, grey. Every detail may stand out in rain-washed air or be veiled in the golden haze of a summer day. I think, perhaps, the most splendid colouring of all occurs in autumn after a fine sunset when the sky becomes a deep ice-blue, against which the mountains stand dark silvered, their serrated peaks silhouetted against the sky-line. In spring and autumn the shades of evening are soft and pastel. The colouring of the flowers in the Alps is brilliant, almost coruscating. Zinnias, dahlias, geraniums bedeck the weather-tanned chalets which stipple the meadows and slopes. Below the crests of the mountains the meadows in spring, early summer and autumn are carpeted with an infinite variety of blooms. It is possible to see the same view day after day and yet to enjoy a different experience every hour, as the prospect continually changes. This is especially true, I think, of the Brienzersee and its immediate neighbourhood, though no doubt those who treasure their own particular corner of the Alps can argue with equal vigour for their own chosen spot.

The lake of Brienz is a narrow sheet of water with the road and the railway situated close to each other on its northern shore. The southern shore, above which a road is to be completed in 1962, is still comparatively remote. A narrow highway meanders by the lake and then winds up and down through the woods to the little village of Iseltwald, situated on a promontory. This is a place of delight and tranquillity. The swans drift along the lake. A fishing boat moves placidly towards the little Schnecken-Insel with its small chapel. The ancient chalets are decorated by ornate carving. I thought that a pastoral symphony could well be composed here as I watched a peasant family wash their cows, who had just come down from the mountains, with water from the lake, singing and laughing as they did so. A very attractive soft, mossy path with fine views of the mountains on the opposite side of the lake, the Augstmatthorn, the Rieder Grat and the Brienzer Rothorn, passes through meadows and woods of larch and pine from Iseltwald to Giessbach. 'The path ascended gently to a point which suggested a pause,' Sir Arnold Lunn wrote in his description of this lovely walk. 'Above me on the right was a limestone cliff, fluted by the spray of two frolics of falling water, too immature to be described as waterfalls. Their soft murmur blended with the gentle breeze whispering through the trees. Below me I could see the lake through a pattern of beech trees, young and tender with no fear of autumn frosts. . . . There was a purity in the water as if the frost had cleansed it to match the fresh wonder of spring colours on the land. Facing me was a range of medium mountains, a range with a character all its own, and the slopes near the lake were stripped of snow and green; higher up the young grass had not yet worked its alchemy on the tired browns, and higher still there was dark earth and rocks.'

Giessbach was a popular resort with the Victorians who came to see the spectacular series of cascades that foam over a broad cleft in the wooded cliff, and rush down to the lake. A large hotel was built there and later a funicular was constructed to take visitors from the landing stage to the falls. In the summer evening all are illuminated. In spite of such commercialisation the seven cascades are an impressive sight, especially after heavy rain. Behind Giessbach a narrow road winds to the little village and resort of Axalp, on the green slopes of the Axalphorn and under the shadow of the Schwarzhorn.

Little white steamers serve the lake of Brienz. On a fine day when the boat is relatively empty, there can be no pleasanter way of travelling as the steamer crosses from side to side, from Ringgenberg to Bönigen, along the southern shore to Iseltwald and Giessbach, occasionally touching at Oberried and so making its way to Brienz. On the southern side appear the bare tops of the mountains that separate the lake from the Grindelwald valley, Faulhorn, and Schwarzhorn, while opposite to them the slightly lower range, the rocky Augstmatthorn, the flat ridge of the Rieder Grat, the Gummihorn and the Brienzer Rothhorn. In summer they are void of snow; in spring and autumn their white peaks are reflected in the smooth surface of the lake. The steamers started as early as 1839, but their early voyages were not without drawbacks. An English traveller, a Mrs. Bray, was told that sparks from the engine had burned the Lutheran minister's wife's umbrella, and to her chagrin found that her parasol and her husband's coat suffered a similar fate. Three years later another traveller noted that a group of English ladies came aboard at Giessbach. To accommodate them on deck the hatch leading to the saloon was covered and chairs placed on it. A tourist who wished to descend found himself seized by the crew, pushed over the railings and in through a port-hole to the deck that he wished to visit. There are still occasions when the boats here, and on other lakes, are unpleasantly crowded, and the wise will certainly not travel if the steamer carries a party of English, often grossly undisciplined, or Swiss schoolchildren, for the Swiss like to show their children the beauties of their own country, a splendid idea if the children's enthusiasm were on occasions a little more perfectly under control.

The northern shore of the lake can be too populous, especially at week-ends during the summer when the Swiss drive to the mountains as the English make for the sea. Yet few visitors take the trouble to leave the main road for the lake frontages of the little villages along the route. Here on fine Sundays the peasants and shopkeepers may be found strolling, the men in dark suits, their wives in white blouses, black coats and skirts, the younger members of the family somewhat more gaily adorned. Unless the Swiss wear the national costume of their canton, they dress in a sombre and conventional fashion. When Monday comes round, the women will gossip round the washtub, a boiler by the lake will supply them with hot water and the lake itself provides a splendid rinser.

It is better to stay in the villages, where there are generally relatively good, inexpensive hotels, than in the larger resorts; for the people who live outside the towns are far less dependent on the exigencies of the tourist trade. Yet their general shops are extremely well stocked, better than their English equivalents, even though it is rare to find a butcher away from the towns, possibly a reflection of the comparatively small part that meat plays in the normal dietary of the peasant. The lakeside is everywhere carefully cultivated, the ground being divided into narrow strips in which the villagers plant potatoes, lettuces and other vegetables. Fruit trees cluster round the lake, their pink and white blossoms floating on the breeze in the spring. The hay is carefully stored for winter feeding. There are plenty of good fish in the lake, perch, pike and trout; and in early summer the Swiss take full advantage of their Sunday rest to bring out their rods. Grebes dive into the waters, warmed sufficiently by the sun in midsummer to permit bathing but otherwise testifying to their glacial origins.

There are many swans on the Swiss lakes and rivers. The swans of Oberried used to pay daily visits to the chalet where I was living, sometimes determinedly waking me at seven in the morning with their calls in the hope of being fed. The family consisted of father, mother and three cygnets (there had originally been four, but the fourth disappeared). We watched the young birds grow from balls of fluff carried on their mother's back into handsome young swans. The father, who was a noble, arrogant-looking bird, ruled the part of the lake which he and his family patrolled. At the first sign of an interloper either from the neighbouring village of Ebligen or across the lake from Iseltwald, his feathers would rise, and the other unfortunate birds would be chased whence they had come. I shall never forget the swans of Oberried, gliding along the lake in single file, the father in front and the mother, a solicitous and far from greedy bird, behind, the children twittering in the expectation of food, nor the feeling of sorrow I felt on our departure at the thought of the cold, dark winter facing them.

The steep, sylvan sides of the mountains which engirdle the Brienzersee narrow the number of possible excursions in its immediate neighbourhood. An upward track rises through beech woods to Schiphern and thence through meadows, dappled in summer with gentians of many shades of blue, to the pastures of the Bütschigrind, whence a stony path leads to the Tiefe Gumm. Here there is a fine view of the uplands in the direction of Lucerne, and especially of the rocky escarpment of the Hohgant. The panorama of the high Alps to the east and south is breathtaking, stretching from the Titlis and the Spannört to the Oldenhorn, and embracing every major peak of the Oberland range from the Aletschhorn and Bietschhorn to the great snow-covered giants of the more immediate neighbourhood. Four to five thousand feet below the lake of Brienz glitters like a sapphire bordered by emerald enamel. A similar view may be more easily enjoyed by using the little rack-and-pinion railway that climbs from Brienz to the summit of the 7,000-foot Brienzer Rothorn. The railway was built in 1892 (the hotel at the summit is twenty years older), but for economic reasons the service was suspended between 1915 and 1930. Its little red carriages are pushed up the mountainside by the most charming and friendly of steam engines. They chug their way to the top with tremendous enthusiasm. I think that the Brienzer Rothorn railway is one of the most attractive in all Switzerland, and the journey one of the most pleasurable; but I prefer the panorama provided by the less frequently visited mountains.

Brienz itself is a large village with many attractive chalets, and a lakeside promenade. It is the centre of the wood-carving industry; but it is unfortunately true that the somewhat highly-priced bears and dogs lack any touch of creative originality and resemble each other as closely as T-model Fords. Indeed, the comment which Sabine Baring-Gould made as long ago as 1841 is still substantially correct. 'It is singular,' he said, 'the Swiss wood-carvers have not progressed in a century, but continue to cut the same uninteresting and inartistic salad-bowls and spoons, brackets, paper-cutters, chalets and little bears.' Conservatism of approach must in practice confine the products of the wood-carvers of Brienz and its neighbourhood to the souvenir hunter.

After leaving the lake the Hasli valley opens the way to the passes. The lowest of the three, the Brünig, ascends shortly after leaving Brienz and its summit marks the frontier between the Oberland and Unterwalden. It is gently circuitous, affords good views of the mountains and the Haslital below and descends through woods, a riot of colour in autumn, to the little village of Lungern. From the summit a road leads to a series of charming, seldom-visited villages, Hohfluh, Wasserwendi, Riedi, overlooking the snows of the Wetterhorn. They are situated on the high shelf above the Haslital and provide many a fine mountain walk.

The road up the Haslital goes through Meiringen, a pleasant village rebuilt after a disastrous fire in 1875 and devoid of architectural interest, leaves the narrow and sinister gorge of the river Aar on the left, and the Reichenbach fall on the right, and reaches the little village of Innertkirchen. 'It is, indeed, a fearful place,' wrote 'Dr. Watson.' 'The torrent, swollen by the melting snow, plunges into a tremendous abyss, from which the spray rolls up like the smoke from a burning house. The shaft into which the river hurls itself is an immense chasm, lined by glistening, coal-black rock, and narrowing into a creaming, boiling pit of incalculable depth, which brims over and shoots the stream onward over its jagged lip.' Here Sherlock Holmes met his foe, Dr. Moriarty. 'I found myself at the fall of the Reichenbach once more. There was Holmes's Alpine-stock still leaning against the rock by which I had left him. . . . Two lines of footmarks were clearly marked along the further end of the path, both leading away from me. There were none returning. A few yards from the end the soil was all ploughed up into a patch of mud, and the brambles and ferns which fringed the chasm were torn and bedraggled. . . . I shouted; but only that same half-human cry of the fall was borne back to my ears.' From Reichenbach a path leads to Rosenlaui and Grindelwald. At Innertkirchen the road forks, the right leading to the Susten Pass and the left to the Grimsel.

The Susten is the least historical of the Swiss passes but scenically one of the, if not the, most attractive. It eventually joins the St. Gotthard road in the valley of the Reuss at Wassen. It seems that when some Bernese soldiers captured in the first Villmergen war in 1656 were sent back to their homeland,

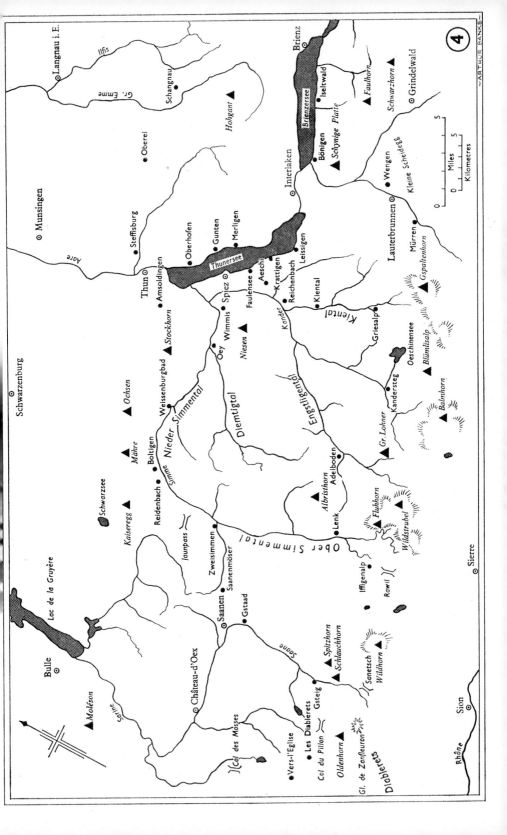

they were escorted by way of the Susten Pass (and the same thing occurred again in the second Villmergen War in 1712). The pass was first mentioned on a map in 1697 and in the literature of Alpine travel in 1760 by S. S. Grüner who described it as 'so cruelly steep that persons affected with giddiness cannot use it.' The comparative lateness of the Susten's appearance in history may well be the result of the former extent of the Stein glacier. The old track can still be seen on both sides of the summit, well beneath the splendid new road, moving in zigzags up the mountainside.

The new Susten road was constructed between 1939 and 1947 and cost 32,000,000 francs. Although the scene at the summit of the pass has a comparatively limited range, it is unquestionably one of the most beautiful of the high Alpine routes, mainly because of the way in which it blends in such perfect harmony green fields and pine-girt slopes with bare rock, glacier and snowfield. From Innertkirchen the road climbs through cornfields and meadows by the steep cliffs of the Gadmerflüh and the Titlis range to the hamlet of Gadmen, some 3,800 feet high. Shortly the valley contracts and the road mounts quickly in a series of finely-engineered curves to the Steingletscher Hotel. A path from here leads rapidly to the foot of the glacier itself. The road has still a thousand feet to rise. On its way to the summit, it brings the traveller into the intimacy of the high mountains, with extensive views of the majestic Stein Glacier and the murky little lake at its base and of the mountains which surround it, the Sustenhorn, the Gwächtenhorn, the Spitzhorn and peeping over the top the snow-white needle of the Tieralplistock. The view from the pass is less embracing than other summits, but the Oberland peaks appear in the far distance. The road descends the wild Meiental and the jagged peaks are splendidly austere.

The Grimsel Pass, which also starts at Innertkirchen, is the wildest of the great Apline passes. It is narrower and more tortuous than the Susten road, becoming steadily more forbidding as it mounts. The last village in the Haslital is Guttannen where the traveller Horace de Saussure noted an inscription in Italian (Italians frequented the pass in the eighteenth century) which read 'The past depresses me; the present displeases me; the future appals me.' De Saussure thought that the inscription was singularly untrue of the Swiss but would suit an Englishman 'devoured by the spleen.' After the Handeck Falls, where the Aar tumbles with, as William Brockendon put it rather unpoetically, 'a horrible fracas into a deep gulf,' the scenery becomes, to borrow his adjectives again, 'stupendous, savage and dreary.' The Alpine pastures round the summit of the pass, 7,159 feet, were bought in the middle ages from the wealthy patrician family, the Bubenbergs of Berne, by the commune of Hasli who held them until 1902 when they, together with the hospice which the commune had maintained, were purchased by the Oberhasli Power Company.

The Grimsel has had a long history since it was the connecting link between Italy, via the Gries Pass, and central Switzerland. In 1532 the humanist, Thomas Platter, having crossed the Brünig Pass, went up the Grimsel with his wife. 'The lady seemed none the worse for it although her clothes froze upon her.' Twelve years later Johann Stumpf described the hospice as a 'wretched building. . . . The people of Hasli keep this hospice and instal a host or hospice-master, who gives travellers food and drink for their money, and to those who cannot afford to pay he gives bread and food for the sake of God. It is a bad inn, but one can usually find good wine, brought over the mountains on mule-back from Valais and the Val d'Ossola.' De Saussure who came up from Guttannen in the eighteenth century could not sleep in the inn because of the overpowering smell of cheese and wine. He moved to a barn where the hay gave him a headache, and spent the rest of the night watching a distant but spectacular thunderstorm. Another eighteenth-century traveller, Archdeacon Coxe, went over the Grimsel twice during his Swiss tours but was not displeased at his reception. The hospice was no more than a 'hovel' but 'in this desert spot' they found all they required except beds, supping off cheese, butter, milk, good wine, and, unexpectedly, a portion of kid and a boiled marmot. The landlord usually arrived in March and remained to the beginning of December. When he left, he put provisions where travellers could find them. When Coxe returned ten years later, in August 1786, his guide and a local peasant 'suddenly started up at the sound of their favourite air, the *Renz des Vaches*, played upon a rebec by a shepherd, and danced several *allemandes*, perfectly in time, and not without grace; a picturesque group of spectators looking on and applauding.' Incidentally Jean-Jacques Rousseau avowed that Swiss mercenary soldiers were often so touched by this ancient chant of the Alpine shepherds, that they wept, deserted and sometimes died, until the officers forbade the singing of the song.

Since the Grimsel Pass has become part of the domain of the Oberhasli Power Company, the combination of natural austerity with engineering skill has contributed to create a scene of magnificence and grandeur, with at times sinister undertones as the mist drifts across the great slabs of bare rock. The former hospice was drowned in more than 90 feet of water when the Grimsel lake was dammed. The work was begun in 1925 and finished seven years later. The acres of grey glacial water hold more than 100 million cubic metres. The most massive of a number of barrages is the Spitallauenen on the Grimsel lake which is 374 feet high and 180 feet thick at its base. The dominant colour, of the road, of the rocky defile, of the lake, looking to the serrated pyramidal form of the Finsteraarhorn, is blue-grey. The Grimsel is a passionate, not a suburban pass. The little lake at its summit, now above the Grimsel Pass Hotel, the Totensee, is said to have been so-called because the corpses of the dead in a skirmish between the Austrians and the French were thrown into it, but as Grüner called it by this appellation as early as 1760, it seems likely to have taken its name from its stagnant or frozen surface. 'What a chaos of mountains are here heaped upon one another! A dreary, desolate, but sublime appearance, it looks like the ruins and wreck of a world.' There is certainly something primordial about the Grimsel Pass which the twentieth century engineers have sought to control and harness but which still gives the impression of a world's beginning.

The Finsteraarhorn is the last major mountain of the eastern range of the Bernese Alps before the great primeval cleft down which the infant Rhone begins its long journey to the sea. But the Bernese Alps are not confined to the range which stretches thus far. The westernmost portion of the Alps which slope towards the Rhone Valley itself provides scenery as fine and climbs as difficult as those of the other parts. The western Alps consist of a series of great peaks, descending sharply towards steep valleys on the southern side, with gentler sub-alpine valleys to the north.

The western range is crossed by high walking or climbing passes, for there is no road until the Col de Pillon. Medieval travellers used the 8,000-foot Lötschen Pass which goes from Kandersteg to Ferden in the Lötschental. The Gemmi, which also starts at Kandersteg and takes advantage of the gap between the massive ramparts of the Balmhorn and the Wildstrubel, is better known. It mounts in zig-zag fashion through the forest above the Gasterntal, and leaves the canton of Berne at the stony pasturage of the Spitalmatte where the Altels glacier once broke apart and killed the herdsmen and their cattle. There are many mountains to be climbed from the Schwarenbach Hotel, the Balmhorn, the Altels and the Rinderhorn. A path to Adelboden by the Engstligen-Grat begins here. Then the track skirts the Dauben-See from which a subterranean stream runs to the Rhone Valley near Sierre before the final ascent to the summit, 7,620 feet, between the Daubenhorn and the Plattenhörner. The white peaks of the Pennine mountains, from the Mischabelhörner and Monte Rosa to the Weisshorn, and Dent Blanche appear in all their dazzling beauty. Below the summit and the Hotel Wildstrubel, the path curvets down 2,000 feet of precipice to Leukerbad in the Valais. Sebastian Münster crossed the Gemmi in 1546 and compared its meanderings to a 'snail-shell or screw, with continuous turns and bends to right and left; it is a narrow path and dangerous, especially to drunkards and persons subject to giddiness, for whichever way the eye looks, there are only precipices and deep sheer drops to be seen, so that even those whose heads are steady cannot regard them without horror.' In the eighteenth century the track was improved. A mule path was carved out of the solid rock between 1736 and 1741 at the joint expense of the two cantons concerned, Berne and the Valais. There are two other walking passes from the Oberland to the Valais, the Rawyl from Lenk to Sion and the Sanetsch from Gsteig to Sion.

19   *The Steingletscher as seen from the Susten Pass r*

Further to the west the mountain masses, perhaps less majestic, are separated by good roads. The route over the Col de Pillon begins at the resort of Gstaad, made fashionable in recent years by film stars, industrial magnates and minor royalties (and perhaps epitomised by the name of its major restaurant, Charley's Bar); after leaving the charming village of Gsteig, beneath the sheer sides of the Schlauchhorn and the jagged Spitzhorn, it works its way through rock and pine above the foaming Reusch to the Col de Pillon, between the Palette d'Isenau and the Oldenhorn. In late spring and early summer the meadows are gay with white crocuses and buttercups. From the Col the road descends by way of the Les Diablerets to the Rhone Valley and the lake of Geneva. Near to the quaintly-named village of Vers L'Église, there is a magnificent view of the cragged peaks of the Les Diablerets and the Glacier du Dard.

Before the road has dropped very far a branch to the right takes the traveller over the undulating Col des Mosses. This gentle pass is the gateway to a different world of grassy slopes, clear, crystal streams embedded in moss, running through beech and larch, underneath aquiline mountains reminiscent of the Dolomites. The road leads eventually to Bulle and Fribourg but a right-hand turn leads to the village of Château d'Oex, where the countryside, lacking the mass and grandeur of the Alps, is yet strikingly beautiful. The village which is a winter sports resort is pleasant but undistinguished, save, perhaps by the young ladies whose education receives its final polish here. They may be seen riding through the main street or, less elegantly, playing the juke-box in the local café.

The road to the Col de Pillon left the heart of the Bernese Oberland at Spiez by the lake of Thun by means of the picturesque Simmental. There is, however, another cleft in the mountains between the valleys of the Lütschine and Simme which opens enchanting vistas. This valley too starts at Spiez, and follows the rushing Kander river, past the conical Niesen and its funicular to Reichenbach (not to be confused with the falls) and Frutigen. The Kander runs into the lake of Thun, but originally it flowed into the river Aar near Thun, in flood time, especially when it carried the melted snow from the mountains, causing considerable damage to farming land. In the eighteenth century a plan was put forward to divert the river into the lake. The engineer, Samuel Jenner, decided to make a tunnel, piercing the original lateral moraine of the Aar valley which had deflected the river to the west since the Ice Age. Some two hundred men were employed on the project, marching to and from their work to the sound of drum and fife. The work was finished in 1714. As the tunnel was nearly twelve times shorter and steeper than the old course, the river was easily diverted to its new bed. Then the roof of the passage fell in and the channel became the gorge which it still remains.

The new Grimsel Hospice, dam and artificial lake;
steraarhorn in the background

The Kiental valley opens to the south-east near Reichenbach. This is still a mountain fastness, peacefully remote from the tourist, disturbed only by the tinkle of cow bells and the rush of water. Yet it was here that a congress of the extreme left of the Socialist International, composed of Lenin's immediate supporters, met in 1916. Lenin had arrived at Berne in September 1914, and at once pledged himself to work for the overthrow of the Czardom and the defeat of the Russian armies to ensure the liberty of the 'toiling masses of all the peoples of Russia.' Not all the members of the International agreed with Lenin, and subsequent conferences at Berne and Zimmerwald revealed the possibility of a potentially dangerous split among the revolutionary socialists. Lenin, who moved from Berne to Zürich in 1916 to finish his *Imperialism as the Highest Stage of Capitalism*, worked enthusiastically for the acceptance of his views. His left-wing group was joined by representatives of the newly-created Spartacus group. Meeting at Kiental they reaffirmed that the 'new International which must rise again after the collapse of the old one on August 4th, 1914, can be born only of the revolutionary class struggle of the proletarian masses in the most important capitalist countries.' Less than eighteen months later, Lenin left his innocent refuge for the throes of revolutionary Russia, travelling in a sealed coach with 20 other Bolsheviks through Germany to Sweden, reaching Petrograd on April 3rd, 1917. Thus this lovely unspoiled Swiss valley served as one of the nurseries of Bolshevism. The narrow road which passes through Kiental leads eventually to the hamlet of Griesalp, a centre for fine mountain walks and climbs, beneath the towering buttresses of the Gspaltenhorn and the Blümlisalp. One pass goes over the Sefinen-Furgge, an opening in the toothy crags linking the Gross-Hundshorn and the Büttlassen, to Mürren. Another, the Hohtürli, takes the walker to Kandersteg.

The Kander valley turns south-east at Frutigen, leaving the road to Adelboden to the right. There is a tourist attraction on the route in the Blausee, the little blue lake the translucent waters of which reveal the macabre shapes of dead trees with their branches strangely interwined. Nearby there is a fascinating trout-farm. Kandersteg itself is 3,864 feet high and reached by the main Lötschberg-railway which has to climb 1,642 feet in 13½ miles from Spiez. The train in fact covers 19½ miles, accomplishing the ascent by a series of ingenious loops on a gradient of 1 in 37. The old baronial castle of Felsenberg appears first above, then level and finally below the traveller. The Berner-Lötschberg-Simplon line provides an all-important connection between Berne and Italy. The idea of making such a link was first mooted as early as 1857. Among the many plans considered was one for building the railway up the Lauterbrunnen valley and tunnelling under the Breithorn but happily this never materialised. In fact everything ultimately depended upon making a tunnel under the Simplon, connecting the Rhone

Valley with Italy. The building of the Simplon tunnel started in 1898, and increasing interest began then to be displayed in the proposed construction of the Lötschberg line.

The cantonal authorities gave the scheme their backing and financial support, but it was not until 1913 that all the various difficulties were overcome. The Kander valley, like so many other Alpine valleys, was formed by glacial action. The river itself rushes down through three glacial basins, up which the railway had to climb after leaving Frutigen. These difficulties were overcome, as I have said, by a series of well-devised loops which thus enabled the train to pass into the flat and fertile pastures around Kandersteg. But the engineers were now faced with the problem of piercing the Alpine barrier which forms the southern flank of the Bernese Alps. The original plan was to tunnel straight through the mountain mass, east of the opening of the Klus, down which the river Kander tumbles from the high glacial basin of the Gasterntal, enclosed by the great precipices of the Petersgrat on the south and the Doldenhorn on the north. The boring of the Lötschberg tunnel started in March 1906, before the connecting links from Frutigen on the north and Brig in the south-east had been built. This in itself greatly accentuated the difficulty of bringing up the equipment. The tunnel's construction was indeed marred by tragedy. The workers' camp on the southern side of the tunnel at Goppenstein was destroyed by an avalanche in February 1908, causing 12 deaths. The following July, after the tunnelling had already proceeded some 3,000 yards, the explosion of a charge penetrated a thin barrier of rock, releasing a torrent of glacial water and debris which killed 25 workmen and destroyed all the boring equipment. This was a major setback which could only be overcome by diverting the tunnel to the east. The Lötschberg tunnel, nine miles long, was opened on July 15th, 1913.

Kandersteg itself is beautifully situated but I do not think I should wish to stay there long, for it is too hemmed in by the high mountains; nor can precarious memories as a reluctant boy scout make me the more ready to prolong a visit to Kandersteg, because it was here that a great international boy scout rally was held. Apart, however, from a number of fine mountain walks and climbs, there is an easy uphill walk from the village to one of the loveliest spots in the district, now, unfortunately, even more easily reached by chair-lift. This is the little mountain lake of the Oeschinensee, whose waters reflect the snows of the Blümlisalp. The best time to visit it is the early summer before either of the refreshment houses are open or the summer crowds have had time to deposit their litter on its shores. The remnants of snow still carpet its rocky verge and float like miniature icebergs in the lake itself; but the trees are bursting with new green and the meadows are starred with crocuses and the piercing blue of the gentiana vernia. The stillness is broken only by the thud of a distant avalanche. It is then that nature creates perfection.

The Lötschental, on the other side of the massive mountains by Kandersteg, is reached from Goppenstein, the station at the other side of the Lötschberg tunnel. A narrow road also winds up the grim Lonza valley from the main Rhone Valley. It is situated politically in the Valais but it is geographically connected with the Bernese Alps. It is still one of the most beautiful and least visited of the Alpine valleys; its dark timbered chalets, their window boxes in summer ablaze with geraniums, are singularly attractive. In the seventeenth century it was the centre of a school of wood carving and the choir of Sion Cathedral and of the church of Ernen in the Gomstal were made here. Wedged between the Oberland and the Rhone Valley, it seems to possess some of the features of a miniature Alpine republic. Its hotels are less pretentious than those in other parts of Switzerland, and the peasants' life is comparatively unaffected by the tourist season. There is, however, an infinite variety of walks and climbs. The head of the valley is dominated by the white snowfield of the Fafleralp. The bright green of its pastures, the broad reaches of the rock-strewn torrent, the wayside shrines, most especially the picturesque chapel of Kühmatt, the rich, sombre wood of the chalets create a picture of unsurpassed beauty. It is a Roman Catholic valley and the festival of Corpus Christi is celebrated at Kippel, the chief place in the district, with picturesque ardour.

The Lötschental is also a good climbing centre. The visitors' book in the hotel at Ried goes back to the middle of the nineteenth century and contains the names of nearly all the great mountaineers. Some of them described their climbs, and others questioned the accuracy, indeed, the truth, of claims made by rivals. An entry for August 14th, 1877, records an ascent of the Bietschhorn with Alex. Burgener as guide. We 'left the hotel at 1.30 a.m. Bad weather set in on the rocks and we completed the ascent in mist and snowstorm with strong wind,' an account which provoked Messrs. J. W. Hartley and F. C. Hartley who arrived at the hotel the next day acidly to comment 'These gentlemen did not ascend the Bietschhorn at all but stopped at a point some way from the top, as was discovered by the Messrs Hartley who saw their track on the mountain'.

The Bietschhorn, the mountain in closest proximity to the Lötschental, was first climbed by Leslie Stephen in August 1859 in company with W. and G. Mathews and described by him in amusing fashion in his *Playground of Europe*. They started off with the local priest of Kippel, Father Lener, who had some pretensions to be a climber, and local guides, dressed in tailed coats and top hats. One of the latter proved good. 'Of the others, the less said the better.' The priest was soon left behind, and the summit was reached soon after midday. 'I have been,' Stephen recorded, 'on wild enough mountain tops before and since, but I doubt whether I ever saw one so savage in appearance as that of the Bietschhorn. It consists of a ridge some hundred yards or so in length, with three great knobs, one at each end, and one at the middle—the articulations from which the great ribs of the mountain radiate. It was hard to say which of the three knobs was highest, and at first sight it also seemed hard to pass from one to the other. The sharp-backed rocky ridge was splintered and torn into the wildest confusion. It looked like the mockery of a parapet, in which the disfigured ruins of grotesque images were represented by the distorted pinnacles and needles of rock. The cliffs on each side sank steeply down into the broken masses of cloud which concealed from us all distant views. . . .' On his return to Kippel, Stephen was regaled, if that is the right word, by the old priest, on the ground that it was a fast day, with a dinner consisting entirely of soup and cabbage stalks.

At Frutigen a road to the south-west leads up the Engstligental to Adelboden. The village is attractive, though it is more a winter than a summer resort, being the first centre to be used by the Public Schools Alpine Club. It was here too that Vivian Caulfield, the author of the text book *How to Ski* (1910), challenged the current custom of 'stick-riding,' that is putting the two sticks together to reduce speed or help out a turn. The historian, G. G. Coulton, who went on one of the first of Sir Henry Lunn's winter sports excursions to Adelboden, has described the expedition in his autobiography *Fourscore Years*. Among his fellow travellers there were a bishop and his daughter, an A.R.A., a professor of Greek, two public school headmasters, his former pupil from Sherborne, Murray, and Miss Ilbert, the niece of Sir Courtenay Ilbert, Clerk of the House of Commons, whom he eventually married. On one of their excursions, they made use of a deserted chalet not far from the village, even to the extent of lighting a fire on its hearth to dry their wet clothes. But, in spite of damping down the fire with slabs of frozen snow, they were horrified to see later in the evening that the chalet was ablaze. Indeed, it was burned to the ground, with some resultant cost to the company.

Adelboden is also the starting-point for many good climbs, including the Wildstrubel, 10,667 feet, the table-top summit of which stands out so characteristically against a blue sky, and the rocky Tschingellochtighorn. My own memory of Adelboden is associated with the presence of a frisky black dog who joined our picnic near the Engstligen Falls, snatched an unguarded sandwich, ate it at a safe distance and then hungrily returned for more, and left us very reluctantly. Among the walking passes from Adelboden one of the more interesting, especially in springtime when the meadows are carpeted with wild flowers, is over the Hahnenmoos to Lenk.

Lenk is the highest village in the Simmental, 3,514 feet, and another centre for winter sports. It is grandly situated under the towering Wildstrubel.

The village itself is not particularly interesting but the narrow road which goes through the hamlet of Oberried towards the Simme Fall is the starting point for a fine walk, skirting the rushing waters of the Simme, to the little brown chalets of Stalden and Razliberg and to the Siebenbrunnen where the Simme emerges in seven springs in the steep cliffs of the Flühhorn. Further on the path becomes steeper, leading up the Flühwande to the little clear tarn of the Flühseeli and the summit of the Flühhorn. There are many other lakes, the Iffigensee for instance; and numerous climbs, the Wildhorn, the Niesenhorn, and the Wildstrubel itself, have their starting point at Lenk. The Rawyl Pass, as I mentioned earlier, begins here, goes past the Iffigen Alp, zigzags up the stony slope to the summit, 7,923 feet, a desolate waste surrounded by snow-clad mountains. It descends to Ayent in the Valais whence a road goes to Sion. The valley in which Lenk is the chief town contains a number of villages, St. Stephan, Blankenberg where there is an eighteenth-century castle, and is as quiet as it is full of charm. I lunched there in the woods on a late October day after early snow. The woods were still white and the logs were deeply crusted with frost, but the sun burned brilliantly and the only sound, except for the jangling bells of a passing herd of cows, was the steady drip of the melting snow.

The Simmental begins shortly after Spiez, actually after leaving the village of Wimmis which has a finely situated castle. The valley has much to commend it, though the scenery is comparatively gentle. There are engaging villages where the gardens of the chalets are bright with flowers, good inns, meadowland and pasture. The Simme is a rushing stream, grey in the spring but in summer blue-green in colour, with woods on either side. Indeed where river and road are close together, the scenery is not unlike that of the Exe Valley between Wheddon Cross and Dulverton. At Oey-Diemtigen, six miles from Spiez, a narrow road goes to the little mountain resort of Grimmialp. A short way from Weissenburg, where there is a delightful inn, is the miniature spa of Weissenburg Bad, situated in the wooded gorge of the Bunschibach. Its waters were said to be good for bronchial complaints. After Boltigen and Reidenbach the road to the right goes in wide sweeps up the Jaun Pass, memorable for its view and, for me, the unpleasing and noisy manœuvres of the Swiss army which spoiled the sight. The chief village in the upper Simmental is Zweisimmen, which has an old church and some decorated wooden chalets; here the road forks, one branch going to Lenk and the other over the easy Saanenmoser Pass to Saarnen and Gstaad.

The Bernese Alps provide within a comparatively narrow area an immense range and variety of scenery and Alpine experience. There are so many places that only infrequently see a visitor in a region often surfeited with tourists. The Stocktal, for instance, under the shadow of the crags of the

Stockhorn is as quiet in summer as it is in the other seasons of the year, while the little village of Amsoldingen, only four or so miles from Thun, with a noble medieval church beside a little reedy lake reflects a Switzerland all too often forgotten in the search for more theatrical beauty and more grandiose scenes.

5

THE VALAIS
The Rhone Valley

THE VALAIS presents a startling contrast with the Bernese Oberland. Indeed, in certain respects, it seems a curiously un-Swiss canton. Many have commented that its scenery is reminiscent of Spain. The vegetation is stunted, the rocks are stark and the vineyards which drape the slopes are prolific and dusty. The light is exceptionally strong and translucent, save when a summer haze shrouds the Rhone Valley. 'We enter the burnt-up white landscape of little African hills,' Cyril Connolly wrote in *Ideas and Places*, 'like the homes of Spanish troglodytes, the rainless apricot country between Sion and Sierre. Here the cicada is found, and up each long lateral valley is some curiosity of wildness, women of Saracen descent, smugglers' headquarters, rare Arolla pines, or the archaic village-kingdom with strange costumes and marriage laws, of Evolène. Above Sierre, pitiless in the sun, we struggle up through the vineyards and peach or walnut orchards, past the ragged tawny romanesque villages with their untidy and sunny poverty which is so soul-refreshing after the northern neatness to our last literary pilgrimage, Rilke's tiny castle at Muzot.' But Connolly recognised correctly that it is unjust simply to compare the Valais with Spain. 'It is,' he went on to say, 'an incomparable country. . . . Shrines, crucifixes at every cross-roads, uplands ribbed with vineyards and in late season all curly with their foliage; fruit trees, each with its tender shade and (oh, so sightly!) single fully grown poplars dotted about.'

The distinctive characteristics of the Valais arise not merely from its climate and vegetation, but from its past history. Climatically it is the driest part of Switzerland. While some 157 inches of rain fall on the great mountains which rise on each side of the Rhone valley, the average rainfall at Grächen, a little village between Zermatt and Visp, is only 21 inches a year. Sion has annually 350 more hours of sunshine than Zürich. Indeed in the exceptionally warm year of 1921 Sierre had only ten inches of rain, less than the Sahara desert. I cannot, however, forbear from remarking that the traveller who visits the Rhone valley in the belief that the sun always shines there may be sorely disappointed; I have known days where rain falls no less heavily than in other parts of the Swiss Alps. The vegetation may appear similar to that of Spain or of the Ticino, but it is not typically Mediterranean in character.

The steep sides of the mountain valleys are clothed with larches and pines. Vines droop grey-green against the dusty soil and white rock of the broad valley of the Rhone. They have been there since Roman times and the annual output in a good year will be as much as fifteen million litres. The best known wines, incidentally, are Fendant du Valais, Mont d'Or and Johannisberg, the latter descended from German Riesling vines introduced from the Rheingau. Slim poplars, their leaves soughing in the wind, line the roads. There are orchards of apple, apricot and plum, their blossoms brightening the valley in springtime. But the predominant colours are shades of grey and green, poised against a skyline of grey mountains peaked with snow.

It is indeed so arid a land that the dryness of the countryside constitutes a continual problem to the Valaisan peasant. He has tried to solve it by constructing irrigation canals to bring water from the glacial streams of the high Alps to his parched fields and vineyards. These watercourses, known as *bisses*, and originally no more than hollowed-out tree trunks, sometimes flow for miles, often along the sides of precipices where they are supported by wooden or iron pegs driven into the rock face. The Bisse de Saxon is 17½ miles long. Many of them date back to the middle ages. That which brings water from the Brozet and Zanfleuron glaciers to the vine-growers of Savièse was certainly flowing in the thirteenth century. Naturally the question of water-rights has afforded constant occasion for friction and litigation. A dispute between the commune of Stalden, not far from Zermatt, and its high-lying neighbour of Embd lasted a quarter of a century. Contrariwise, as with the control of the cattle on the Alpine pastures, economic needs have furthered communal co-operation. At Savièse the use of the water is divided between 830 shareholders. Each shareholder must be a member of the commune and he is entitled to have water turned on to a certain area of his land for three hours a day, and he may, if he so wishes, sublet his quota.

But it is neither the climate nor the geography, distinctive as these are, which account wholly for the character of the Valais. This is something deeply rooted in its past history. It is difficult to say what accumulation of races are represented by the modern Valaisan, but the original Celtic population were at a comparatively early date subdued by the Romans. There are still Roman remains at Martigny and at Sion where a Roman inscription is immured in the vestibule to the seventeenth-century Hotel de Ville. Later there were inroads of Saracens, who may possibly have colonised some of the southerly Alpine valleys. The Valais, however, had long accepted the Christian faith. St. Maurice boasts the oldest abbey in Switzerland, founded in 515. The seat of the bishopric was moved from Martigny to Sion at the end of the sixth century for fear of the Lombard invaders who made their way over the St. Bernard Pass. During the middle ages the Bishop of Sion was the virtual ruler over a rich province (and he still knows no superior save the Pope); but the peasants were ever-ready to protect their privileges and to extend their rights. The communes were organised in 'dizains' or 'zehnten' and in the early fifteenth century were in contact with the democratic communities north of the Alps. The other Swiss cantons were interested in the Valais because they feared that the powerful Duke of Savoy might seek to absorb the region into his domains. Thus, by 1400, the Valais was knit by a loose alliance to the Swiss Confederation, though it did not achieve full cantonal status until 1814.

Matthias Schinner, the sixteenth-century Bishop of Sion, was a figure of European renown. An arch-intriguer, a militant prelate, the friend and emissary of Pope Julius II, Schinner never forgot the land of his birth. He believed the French to be the chief threat to the Valais as to the Papacy, and made good use of the murder of two Swiss envoys at Lugano to persuade his fellow countrymen to take up arms against them. But the death of Pope Julius in 1513, disunion among the allies and the fine fighting force of King Francis I of France brought disaster to the Swiss ranks at Marignano in 1515. Travellers to the Valais in the seventeenth and eighteenth centuries found the Valaisans less accommodating, dirtier and prouder than the other Swiss. They showed, said Archdeacon Coxe, 'uncleanliness . . . disgusting beyond expression,' and his good Protestant instincts made him suspect that their strong attachment to the Roman Catholic faith was ultimately responsible. He and other travellers commented on the prevalence of goitres and cretinism in the region. At the end of the eighteenth century the French revolutionary armies entered the Valais and were at first greeted warmly by the French-speaking peoples of the district who sympathised with their boasted love of freedom and planted a tree of liberty in the public square at St. Maurice. They soon found that their new masters would not readily acquiesce in their ancient privileges. There were risings, at Ascensiontide near Sierre in 1798 and again the next year when the patriots were heavily defeated by the French soldiers in the forest of Finges. The region was strategically important for Napoleon because of its passes, the Great St. Bernard and the newly-constructed Simplon. He declared that the Valaisans, to whom he had granted independence, were incompetent to govern themselves and by dictatorial degree in 1810 the Valais was joined to France as the Simplon department. Even after 1814 the determination of its people to preserve their way of life and to stress cantonal autonomy give them an independence of character. There is an element of self-containment and of autarchy, that accord with the geological barrier imposed by the great mountain ranges which separate the Rhone valley and the valleys which flow north and south from it from their fellow Swiss and from the Italians.

The Rhone valley itself, stretching from St. Maurice to Brig, is comparatively broad and flat. The river flows hurriedly through meadows and orchards, vineyards and dusty copses towards the lake of Geneva. The towns and villages along its course proclaim the long history of the Canton. St. Maurice, the first town after the frontier of the canton of Vaud, is picturesquely situated between the river and the cliff. Known to the Romans as Agaunum, it takes its name from Mauritius, the *primicerius* of the Theban legion which refused to abandon the Christian faith and was subsequently massacred by order of the Emperor Maximilian. A basilica to commemorate his memory was built as early as the fourth century under the first bishop of the Valais, Théodule. Its parish church contains the tomb of the sixth-century king of Burgundy, Sigismond, in whose presence the monastery was founded in 515. Since 1128 it has belonged to the Augustinian order and from 1840 the abbot has been bishop of Bethlehem *in partibus*. The present church, which incorporates remains of the medieval building, was erected between 1611 and 1627. The glory of St. Maurice is its treasury which houses works of art of outstanding interest. The earliest in date is a sardonyx vase of reddish brown, veined in milky blue, ornamented with a frieze. Tradition asserted that it came from heaven to rest in the hands of St. Martin during a pilgrimage. The setting dates from the sixth or seventh century but the vase and its ornaments, thought to represent the funeral of Achilles, is possibly Greek in origin and second century in date. There is a golden ewer of singular beauty, decorated with rich enamel and filigree work, of earlier date than the ewer itself, and oriental in character. The jug is said to have been given to the abbey by the Emperor Charlemagne and it has been suggested that the decorative inset may have been part of the loot, even possibly a part of the royal treasure, of the Avars conquered by Charlemagne. There are a number of fascinating reliquaries, one, Merovingian in character, called the coffer of Theuderic, another of silver set with precious stones in the shape of a hand in benison containing relics of St. Bernard of Menthon, as well as lovely ciboriums and a silver head of St. Candidus of twelfth-century workmanship. Among the later treasures there is a relic of the holy thorn given by St. Louis IX of France.

The road from St. Maurice to Martigny passes a picturesque waterfall, the Pissevache, a cascade of the river Salanfe with a fall of some 200 feet. Some years ago our then Minister to Switzerland told me that it had been his pleasant duty, a few weeks earlier, to act as host to an English Princess. He arranged a motor drive for her entertainment and the cars stopped opposite the waterfall. Later in the day a young attaché described to the Minister his acute embarrassment when the Princess had the innocence or the temerity to enquire the precise meaning of the waterfall's strange name. I am afraid I have forgotten the free but just adequate translation which the attaché managed to produce without too noticeable a pause.

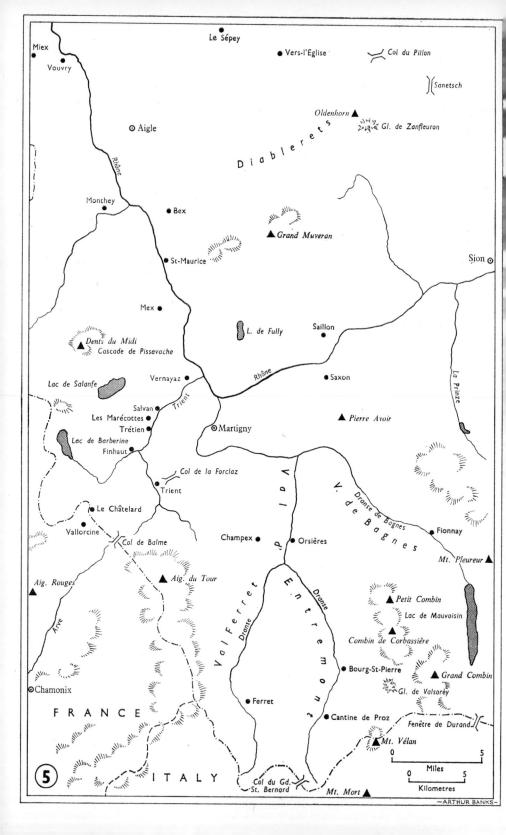

Martigny has long been enriched by the traffic passing up the Rhone valley or down the St. Bernard Pass. It was originally a settlement of a Celtic tribe, the Veragri, attacked by Julius Caesar who, as he said, was eager to 'open up the Alpine route [that is the St. Bernard Pass] through which traders could only travel at great risk and on payment of exorbitant tolls.' The Veragri put up a stout resistance but Servius Galba and his third legion eventually brought Octodurum, as Martigny was then called, to Roman rule. The round, embattled tower of La Batiaz, conspicuous to all who travel through the town, was captured and rebuilt by Peter II of Savoy in the mid-thirteenth century. An exceptionally fine timber-covered bridge crosses the torrential river Drance at Martigny. It is a pleasant little town, though not one where people stay for long. Yet they may be assured of a warmer welcome than the one which greeted Goethe and Duke Charles Augustus of Saxe-Weimar when they arrived there from Chamonix. Their guide had advised them to bathe their tired feet in a mixture of red wine and clay. The servant girl at the local inn was so haughty that her guests obliged her to dry their feet herself.

The road, and the railway, pass rapidly through apple orchards from village to small town. Saillon, which lies a little off the main route, had a ruined castle of Peter II of Savoy and provides an interesting example of a medieval walled town. Saxon was the scene of an abortive attempt to establish a Swiss casino until the Swiss government decided to ban roulette. In 1953, its apricot growers, incensed by the government's refusal to protect their fruit against Italian growers (whose apricots ripened earlier than those of the Valais), burned several railway trucks of Italian fruit by way of protest, another testimony to the Valaisan love of independence.

The cantonal town, Sion, is one of the oldest and most fascinating cities in Switzerland. It is strikingly situated, dominated by two steep hills, the one crowned by a church and the other by a ruined castle. Valeria (or Valère) houses a handsome medieval church of St. Mary de Valère which contains Romanesque capitals, a fine medieval choir and some excellent seventeenth-century carved stalls. On the other hill, Tourbillon, there stands the ruined castle of the bishops of Sion, built in the thirteenth century, burned in war in 1416 and finally destroyed by fire in 1788. The town itself has a number of interesting buildings, including the small but finely proportioned fifteenth-century cathedral. The seventeenth-century Hôtel de Ville, as I mentioned earlier, has a Roman inscription with a Christian monogram, originally in the church on Valeria, dated 377. The Rue de Conthay preserves the house of the humanist, George Supersaxo, friend and later enemy of the town's most famous bishop, Matthias Schinner.

Sion has more of interest than its neighbour, Sierre, though the seventeenth-century château of the de Courtens, a well-known hotel since 1885, is worth a visit. A melancholy reminder of former national pride and an apt illustration of the habits of British travellers before the First World War is the little English church near by. 'To Sierre,' Bishop Wilkinson wrote in the summer of 1903, 'where I dedicated a very beautiful little chapel in the hotel grounds. Everything—marble, oak-work, stained glass by Clayton and Bell—good.' But to-day the chapel, built by the then proprietor of the hotel, M. Michael Zufferey, is used as a storeroom.

Sierre's prominence arises in part from its chance association with the German poet, Rilke, who spent his last years at the near-by Château de Muzot. When he first came to Switzerland at the end of the First World War, his sensitive, artistic spirit was deeply wounded, nor did he expect that it would be soothed by Switzerland's bourgeois charm. 'It is a pity,' he wrote, 'that nature is so exaggerated in Switzerland, or so it seems to me. How pretentious these lakes and mountains are; there is always a bit too much of them. . . . The admiration of our grandparents and great-grandparents appears to have collaborated in producing these regions. There they came, travelling from their countries, where was "nothing" so to speak, and here they found "everything" in an *édition de luxe*. . . . A mountain? Good gracious no—a dozen whichever way you look, one behind the other. A lake? Certainly, but a superfine lake of the best quality with reflections of the purest water, a whole gallery of reflections, and God to act as a guide, explaining each in turn; unless of course he happens to be busy at the moment, in his capacity of stage-manager, directing the spot-light of the sunset glow on to the mountains. . . . I can't help it, the only way I can reach this assorted nature is through irony; and indeed I remember those happy days when, travelling through Switzerland, I used to draw the curtains in my compartment, whereat the other travellers in the corridor greedily devoured my share of the view.'

But, as his biographer has urged, 'the showy sanity of Switzerland was perhaps the only effective remedy for his deeply injured mind.' From Nyon he went to Soglio and thence to a gloomy pension at Locarno. He turned to Venice, found it astronomically expensive and came again to Switzerland, this time to the kind hospitality of the Castle Berg. On his return he had caught a glimpse of the Castle Höllinger near Berne. 'The large old chestnut avenue of the approach; at the end, behind the iron-barred gate, the steep little castle and sidewards beneath the row of trees, the long view over the horizontally-lit country—the tears came to my eyes again. An avenue like this, and a house like this, for the space of a year, and I would be saved.' So he wrote to Nanny Wünderly-Volkart. She obtained an invitation from Colonel Ziegler and his wife to Castle Berg on the Irchel. But the Château de Muzot, discovered by chance from a photograph in a hairdresser's window at Sierre, was to be his final resting-place. His kind friend, Werner Reinhart of Winterthur, first rented it for him and finally bought it. Remote and austere in appearance, not easy to domesticate—he himself said that it was was more like donning a suit of armour than moving into a house—the little stone tower enabled him to finish the *Duino Elegies* and here he died on December 29th, 1926.

The Valais had ultimately won his heart. 'How beautiful the Valais is. . . . Among the valleys of Switzerland I have seen none as spacious: the Valais is a plain, wide between the mountains, and these are nothing but the background, not intruding with their mass, but of a softness of contour that at times produces the imaginary impression of mountains as seen in a reflection.'

Two other towns deserve attention before the high mountains rim the Rhone Valley from which escape is only possible by way of the Furka and Simplon passes. Visp, enriched in the middle ages by merchandise passing over the Monte Moro and the Antrona passes, now known mainly as the junction for the Alpine resort and climbing centre of Zermatt, is a town of considerable charm, with a fine modern church which possesses some striking stained glass. Brig too was made wealthy by the trade passing through the town from Italy and central Switzerland. The castellated pile of the Stockalper Palace with an arcaded courtyard erected by the wealthy Catholic burgher, Kaspar Stockalper, between 1658 and 1678 epitomises the town's past importance. The parish church, some way outside the town itself at Glis, a village on the Simplon road, has been described by Sir Arnold Lunn in his book on the Valais as 'a felicitous blend of Renaissance and Gothic.' It was mainly the work of Schinner's architect, Ruffiner.

Such a catalogue of towns cannot do justice to the character and atmosphere of the Rhone valley and its people. Their combination of pride and independence, of passion and loyalty, is equally characteristic of the many lovely Alpine valleys, to the north and south of the valley of the Rhone. The Bernese Alps slope steeply on the northernmost side, penetrated only by high walking and climbing passes. There is, for the most part, an absence of lateral valleys of any significance. The two little resorts of Crans and Montana, the one known for its golf and the other for its sanatoria, stand on a shelf above Sierre. There is an astounding panoramic view of the great Pennine chain of mountains, but I can never visit Montana without thinking of James Elroy Flecker, the author of *Hassan*, and his hard comments on Montana's 'eternal whitewash.' The silent beauty of the eternal snows can only be cold comfort to the dying man; the challenge they evoke can only be resisted by the healthy in mind and body.

Beyond Sierre a narrow road goes up to Lonza valley to the Lötschental which has more in common with the Bernese than the Pennine Alps. Another short northern valley, seven miles in length, leads to Leukerbad, the terminus, as I have said earlier, of the Gemmi Pass from Kandersteg in the Oberland. Leukerbad, like other spas, is now in many respects a survival of a past which ranked hot saline springs to be of greater medicinal value than does the modern specialist. The health-giving properties of its waters were known for centuries and no less a person than the arrogant Valaisan prelate, Cardinal Schinner, had the bathhouses rebuilt in 1501. Even so, the standards they represented did not appear high nearly three centuries later to Archdeacon Coxe who commented acidly to a native Swiss on the inadequacy of accommodation. The man replied shrewdly that a 'concourse of strangers would only serve to introduce luxury among the inhabitants and insensibly destroy that simplicity of manners, for which the Valaisans are so remarkbly distinguished.' Coxe, probably with justice, felt that 'simplicity of manners' was a poor euphemism. The temperature of the springs is said to be about 120° F, and the early sixteenth-century traveller, Stumpf, declared that eggs and fowls could be boiled in the water. There is a comparatively easy walk from Leukerbad to the top of the Torrenthorn which provides a wonderful view of the Lötschental and of the Pennine Alps.

The great southern wall of the Pennine Alps, a massif of peaks even higher than those of the Oberland, which forms a frontier with Italy, are penetrated by a series of steep valleys of exceptional beauty. There are many climbing passes but only two roads, the Great St. Bernard and the Simplon, take the traveller from Switzerland to Italy. It should, perhaps, be added that the Col de Forclaz provides the opportunity for entry to France and the Mont Blanc range of mountains. Both the Great St. Bernard and the Col de Forclaz roads leave the main Rhone valley at Martigny, and it is below Martigny, between St. Maurice and Martigny, that the first of the lovely lateral valleys of the Valais has its starting point.

This is the valley of the Trient which emerges through a narrow gorge near Vernayaz into the Rhone valley itself. It has many of the geographical features typical of the other Valaisan valleys; a deep gorge making access difficult, opening out to a high plateau. Yet, like the other valleys, it has an entirely individual character. A rack-and-pinion railway starting at Martigny mounts steeply from Vernayaz to Salvan, the first of a group of small but attractive resorts, Les Granges where I remember eating the plumpest of sweet strawberries looking over a magnificent panorama of the Rhone valley far below, Les Marécottes, Le Trétien above the rugged Gorges du Triège and finally Finhaut, pleasantly situated on a high shelf above the river far below. The village looks towards the snow-covered Aiguille du Tour and Aiguilles Rouges. It possesses a noble modern church built by F. Dumas between 1928 and 1931, albeit in traditional Valaisan style. Finhaut is a magnificent centre for fine walks along the high shelf on which it is situated. A walk which slowly mounts through the flowery meadow and woodland eventually emerges at the artificial Lac de Barberine. The view of the French

21 *The Oeschinensee and the Blümlisalp, near Kanderste*
Bernese Oberla

Alps with their characteristic needle points dominated by the ice-bound bulk of Mont Blanc is one of the most majestic in Switzerland, comparable to that of the walk from Grütschalp to Mürren. The lake itself, its bare stony slopes studded in late spring by the alpenrose, really a rhododendron, surrounded by snow-capped mountains, shows little trace of its origin. A funicular descends from Barberine Château d'Eau to Le Chatelard Giétroz where the imprisoned water of the lake are converted into power by the Hydro-Electric Works of the Swiss Federal Railways, built in 1923–6. A mile further on Le Châtelard Trient marks the Swiss customs house. It is near here that the road from Martigny joins the main valley after climbing over the 5,000-foot Col de la Forclaz. The former road was noted for its extremely difficult and narrow hairpin bends but the new road is a splendid highway until it debouches for some inexplicable reason into a narrow, gravel track before the Swiss customs house is reached. It must have been over something like this that William Wordsworth travelled on his way from Martigny to Chamonix in 1790, a journey he later described in *The Prelude*.

There are walks through woods to the high pastures, Fenestral, and Emanay, and to the neighbouring cols and peaks. One of these, some four hours' walk from Finhaut, goes to the Col de Balme. When the Cambridge historian, G. G. Coulton, was staying at Martigny, he decided to walk to the Col, but the snow was deep, the way was long and the winter day was short. As dusk fell, he made for the hotel at Trient. 'The big summer hotel there was in its natural winter state; no guests but the family and servants hibernating in a kitchen and a little parlour with its iron stove. With them were the travelling cobbler and the travelling tailor, welcomed during the dead months to repair the ravages of winter wear. I was ready to do full justice to all the eatables and drinkables they produced, and listened complacently to their expositions of my folly. . . . Presently they started the subject of the Diamond Jubilee due in that year, 1897. It was pleasant to find how genuinely they were interested, and anxious to hear all I could tell them about my own country.'

Martigny is a major junction, for here the road divides, the principal route going, with the railway, straight up the Rhone valley, other roads leading via the Col de la Forclaz to Chamonix and via the Great St. Bernard to Aosta in Italy. The St. Bernard road forks at Sembrancher, each road following a branch of the river Drance. The right-hand valley, the Val d'Entremont, descends gently to Orsières where there is a further division, the main road ascending towards the St. Bernard and the others going up the Val Ferret or mounting to Champex. This high village, situated amidst the pines beside a miniature lake, has much that is idyllic. The snowfields of the Grand Combin are reflected in its calm waters. There are some fine walks, more especially up the Val d'Arpettaz with snow mountains at its head, and some interesting ascents but ultimately Champex is disappointing. It is, I think, too

Vineyards near Sion, Valais

artificial, too manufactured, being rooted in the holiday traffic rather than in native tradition. Its life seems attached, unlike most of the Alpine villages, to its summer visitors rather than to its pastures and meadows. It is, however, fair to say that my own experience of Champex was soured by a wakeful night occasioned by a drunken summer reunion of skiers (who infested every hotel in the locality), and the intrusion into my bedroom with the early morning tea of a still intoxicated diner who, in spite of all my protests, curled himself up on the couch and went to sleep. Not even a dramatic Alpine thunderstorm which the next evening put out every light in the place could quite reconcile me to the beauties of Champex.

I expect that I have been less than just, but memory plays strange tricks. From Orsières a little bus goes up the Val Ferret, remote from tourists, with wild walks and savage beauty; but more than its alps and chalets I remember the heat of the bus the windows of which, unusually inefficient for a Swiss bus, refused to open and the small boy who for some obscure reason brought his kitten with him in a knapsack, which was only saved from suffocation by the determined interference of a fellow traveller. Yet I shall also remember the grass and the flowers waving in the breeze beside the little chapel at Ferret itself outlined against the mountain and the sky.

The main road from Orsières passes through Bourg St. Pierre, where the Hotel Napoleon commemorates the meal the French general ate there on his crossing of the St. Bernard, and the Cantine de Proz en route for the summit of the famous pass. In its later stages the road is singularly barren and forbidding; nor in general is the scenery as attractive as that of many other Swiss passes. There is less breadth of view, and greater austerity, while the works associated with the building of the Great St. Bernard tunnel detract greatly from the approach, or at least did so when I was last there, imposing on the barren and desolate mountainside a film of industrialism.

The idea of building a tunnel in this region was raised first in 1936, but it was not specifically associated with the St. Bernard route until the ending of the Second World War. The tunnel itself, which is said to have cost some 56 million Swiss francs, is some 5·875 kilometres long and at a height of 5,700 feet. Since one of the objects in building the tunnel is to ensure that motor traffic can cross from Switzerland to Italy all the year round, the approaches above 4,500 feet, some four-and-a-half miles on the Italian side and three miles on the Swiss side, are to be covered by a concrete roof. The tunnel has been excavated by a mixed labour force, including many Southern Italians on the Italian side who have been made miserable by the severe climatic conditions, and, on the Swiss side, by some groups of former German SS men. In one place they had to pierce the face of a coalmine, buttressing and lining each section as soon as a foot of the mine had been scooped out to prevent a disastrous fall. At least three men died during the

23 *Mount Collon, near Arolla, Va*

building. As well as the road the Agip petrol company is sponsoring a pipe-line which will run from the port of Genoa to a projected refinery at Aigle in the Rhone valley. The heavy cost of the tunnel has been met largely by the Fiat company in Italy and the cantons of Vaud and Valais and the city of Lausanne in the belief that it is bound to promote the economic well-being of the nations involved. Certainly it will immensely shorten the land routes from the industrial north to the Italian plain while it will give the Swiss access all the year round to their free port of Savona.

The march of progress must, however, leave the old St. Bernard simply as a scenic museum piece, high above the rushing world of traffic 2,000 to 3,000 feet below. It will be less used, except by the summer tourists, than at any time in its long history. The world has indeed entered into the mountains with a vengeance; but the prior of the hospice of St. Bernard, Marcel Giroud, has signified that his order, the Augustinian canons, has as yet no intention of closing the House.

The pass, some 8,000 feet high, was used by the Roman legions and was long known as Mons Jovis from a temple erected near the summit to Jupiter Poeninus. Near Bourg St. Pierre there is a military column dating from the fourth century. The pass was a popular route for pilgrims to Rome during the early middle ages and there was certainly a hospice to cater for their needs there by the middle of the ninth century. In 972 the abbot of Cluny was actually held to ransom by the Saracens after descending the pass to Orsières. When exactly St. Bernard de Menthon founded the hospice is not known. King Henry II of England gave it land at Hornchurch in Essex which it held until William of Wykeham bestowed it on his foundation of New College, Oxford. Among many distinguished travellers the Emperor Frederick Barbarossa crossed it in 1162. Twenty-six years later the Canterbury monk, John de Bremble, experienced both fright and pleasure as he toiled wearily along the desolate paths, 'on the one hand looking up to the heavens of the mountains, on the other shuddering at the hell of the valleys' as he prayed 'Lord, restore me to brethren, that I may tell them, that they come not to this place of torment.' The traffic over the pass was so considerable that the eighteenth-century traveller, Marc Bourrit, who was precentor of the cathedral at Geneva, reckoned that over 8,000 people crossed it annually, and he said that one of the nights that he stayed at the hospice there had been 561 other travellers who consumed four oxen, twenty sheep and three sacks of wheat. Accompanied by one of the monks he ascended the Pain de Sucre and visited the glacier de Valsorey. An early nineteenth-century traveller. William Brockendon, was much gratified by the hospitality of the monks. 'One chamber is devoted to visitors, which may be considered the *drawing-room* of the establishment; it has its elegancies—a piano-forte,* books,

* Edward VII, when Prince of Wales, later presented a piano to the monastery.

24 *The Pyramids of Euseigne, Val d'Hérens, Valais*
25 *La Sage, Val d'Hérens, Valais*

prints and pictures, which have been presented by travellers.' He recalled an incident which had occurred shortly before his visit. In the winter of 1825 three of the hospice servants, with two dogs, returning with a traveller from the Italian side were overwhelmed by an avalanche; all but one dog perished nor were their bodies recovered until the following June. Brockendon was impressed by the morgue in which the victims were placed, preserved by the ice, to make possible later recognition by their relatives; on one body the clothes had remained for eighteen years. Longfellow's *Excelsior*, published in 1842, told the story of a high-minded youth struck by an avalanche on the St. Bernard road. The morgue remains but is no longer used.

The most famous crossing of the St. Bernard took place between May 14th and May 20th, 1800, when Napoleon Bonaparte led 40,000 troops to the Italian plains to defeat the Austrians at Marengo. Each regiment spent three days in the crossing where the snow was still on the ground. Many of the men lacked proper equipment and clothing, and were sadly suited to cope with the heavy wet snow of late spring. The guns were dismantled, placed in the trunks of hollowed-out trees and dragged up the pass by sheer man-power. Napoleon was himself conducted by a young Valaisan guide, Nicolas Dorsaz, whom he later rewarded generously. The monks who had given freely of their hospitality had, however, to wait two years before the bill for the army's provisions was met.

The historic rather than the scenic aspect of the pass holds the attention of the traveller; but its gloomy grandeur as the mist floats across the jagged rocks of the bare mountains is impressive.

Charles Dickens took the Dorrit family over the St. Bernard in late autumn in *Little Dorrit*. 'A craggy track, up which the mules in single file scrambled and turned from block to block. . . . No trees were to be seen, nor any vegetable, save a poor brown scrubby moss, freezing in the chinks of rock. . . . Up here in the clouds, everything was seen through cloud, and seemed dissolving into cloud . . . snow flakes drifting in among them.'

'"We have had, of course," said the young lady, who was rather reserved and haughty, "to leave the carriages and fourgon at Martigny. And the impossibility of bringing anything that one wants to this inaccessible place, and the necessity of leaving every comfort behind, is not convenient."

"A savage place, indeed," said the insinuating traveller.'

John Ruskin described a visit he made to the pass in 1835 in some detail. 'This convent,' he wrote, 'is, I believe, the highest dwelling constantly inhabited, in the known world, and a mournful habitation it is. . . . There are three buildings: the first is a sort of storehouse; then the principal building, and close to the hospice for the living is a narrow and small hut built against the crags of Mont Mort, the dwelling place of the dead. . . . Above this melancholy habitation rise the crags of Mont Mort, loaded with masses of thick snow. The grey steep rocks which remain uncovered are thinly greened with moss and lichen to a certain height, the limit of all vegetation except that of the lichens. . . . Above this line all is monotony, grey rocks, bare on the precipice side, lifting up coronets of snow upon their foreheads, climbing up on one another's backs into the deep, blue, silent heaven, gathering themselves around you on every side, gleaming in a pure, liquid crystal, frosty sunlight or with their white summits shining out, themselves like suns, from oceans of invidious cloud, white misty wreaths billowing beneath you, and whirling past you, and eddying above you, like the wings of mountain spirits.

'Beneath the sloping flanks of Mont Mort . . . rests a small, deep, calm, transparent lake. . . . It had not the bluish, verdigris green of the lac de Chêde, but a rich olive sort of green, like the green of phosphate of copper. . . . Beyond this lake the valley appears to be terminated by peaks of gneiss of a great elevation.'

A statue of St. Bernard de Menthon stands on the site of a former pagan temple looking over the little lake to the mountains of Italy and the Val d'Aosta. The Italian barracks, burned out by French partisans from the Savoyard Alps during the Second World War, have been rebuilt. The hospice itself, reconstructed after a fire in the sixteenth century, now only ministers to the pilgrims and the genuinely needy. The tourist is catered for at the neighbouring Hotel de St. Louis. During the summer some twelve to sixteen monks live at the monastery together with the maronniers or lay-brothers; but in the severe winters the number may be reduced to five. The famous St. Bernard dogs no longer play a significant part in the life of the monastery, but form an attractive show piece. There was a time when their capacity to follow the right road was an inestimable help in heavy snow; though the belief that they carried a small cask of brandy appears legendary. 'Every day in winter,' Ruskin noted in 1835, 'a courier, accompanied by a dog, goes down half way to St. Pierre on the Swiss side, and as far on the Italian, shouts loudly, and waits for ten minutes or a quarter of an hour before he returns.' The kennels of the dogs, said to be a cross between the Pyrenean sheep-dog and the Newfoundland, are certainly worth visiting, if the visitor is ready to tolerate a strongish doggy smell.

The St. Bernard road is in the course of becoming a first-class motor thoroughfare of great economic and strategic significance. At least it is better that, if the road had to be constructed, it should not have marred the precariously-defended beauty of others of the southerly lateral valleys. The St. Bernard road ascended the right-hand valley of the Drance as it left the village of Sembrancher. The left-hand valley, the Val de Bagnes, opens a very different prospect, leading to the quietly beautiful village of Fionnay, surrounded by immense cliffs and a good climbing centre for the neighbouring peaks. After Fionnay the scenery is of a magnificent order, the valley stark, austere and narrow, the heights superb and exciting.

An hour and a half beyond Fionnay the chalets of Mauvoisin are situated between the precipices of Mont Pleureur and the Pierre Avoir. It is a splendid starting point for many climbs and high-level walks, up the Grand Tavé, 10,348 feet, from the summit of which the Corbassière glacier and the Combin range can be seen glowing under the summer sun in icy splendour, or up the somewhat toilsome Mount Pleurer, 12,159 feet, or the Combin de Corbassière, 12,212 feet and, joined by a short ridge, the Petit Combin, 12,044 feet, with staggering views of the precipitous sides of its big brother, the Grand Combin, 14,164 feet 'with,' as Mr. Walker has described it, 'huge rock cliffs falling towards Italy on the south, and on the north, terrace after terrace of glaciers and snow rising to the very summit.'

The Chanrion hut, some three and a half hours further on from Mauvoisin is another fine starting point for high mountain walks and climbs, more especially for the ascent of Mont Vélan, 12,353 feet, the final point of the spur which includes the Grand Combin. Chanrion is on the route to the Col de Fenêtre de Balme, the long-used frontier pass which leads to Ollomont and the Italian Valpelline. The oft-repeated legend that John Calvin escaped over this Col after an unsuccessful attempt to protestantise the Aostans seems without historical foundation. The climber can make his way towards the Italian side of the range by ascending the lovely Otemma glacier, its six miles of startling whiteness relieved by the dark rocks of the cirque of peaks around it, notably the Pointe d'Otemma and the Pigne d'Arolla. A gap to the left of La Sziassa, forming the Col d'Otemma, provides a means of descent to Prarayé, a village situated amidst splendid scenery at the head of the Valpelline.

There are many high-level passes which can bring the climber or mountain walker back from the Valpelline to the Swiss valleys. The Col de Valpelline, 11,687 feet, leading towards Zermatt, gives a splendid view of the Tsa de Tsan glacier, flowing from the Tête Blanche, a mountain with an incomparable view. 'In front was the mighty obelisk of the Matterhorn,' F. W. Jacomb wrote, 'with, nearer still, the Dent d'Erins (Hérens), little less in height; whilst beyond the eye ranged over the many other well-known mountains and glaciers of the Monte Rosa district. Was not this a sight worth hours of toil to attain? Let those say who know what it is to stand upon a high mountain top in golden sunlight, and see the neighbouring peaks crowding to welcome them.' The view embraces all the major peaks of the Pennine chain and stretches as far as the Mont Blanc range and the Graian Alps. The Col des Bouquetins, 11,214 feet, situated between the Dents des Bouquetins and the Tête Blanche connects the snowfields of the Tsa de Tsan glacier at the head of the Valpelline with Arolla or Ferpècle at the extremities of the

Val d'Hérens. There is one other climbing pass, the Col de Collon, which goes from Prarayé by way of the savage Combe d'Oren over the Arolla glacier and around the foot of Mount Collon to Arolla itself.

The Val d'Hérens may be reached from the Val de Bagnes without entering Italy or going down to the Rhone valley. After crossing the bleak Val d'Hérémence, a track leads over the Col de la Meina, 8,878 feet, to Evolène in the Val d'Hérens. The climber can make use of the Col de Sevreu, 10,335 feet, which, passing the Glacier des Ecoulaies, goes down to the Alp de la Barma above Pralong where the Val d'Hérémence and the Val des Dix are conjoined. The path up the Col de la Meina, from which incidentally there is an easy ascent to the Pic d'Arzinol, mounts steeply from Pralong.

Enough, perhaps more than enough, has been said to indicate the opportunities afforded for high-level walking in the valleys which penetrate the Pennine Alps south of the river Rhone. They are honeycombed with tracks used immemorially by the peasants to drive their cattle to the high pastures or to bring down their hay. The postman can sometimes be seen jogging along on his mule to deliver letters or parcels at a remotely-situated hamlet or chalet. As the jingle of the mule's bells and the steady clip-clopping of the hooves diminishes in volume, and the silence of the woods and mountains descends again, I am reminded once again of the extent to which tourists and visitors are a transitory phenomenon in two thousand years of Alpine history.

6

THE VALAIS

The Pennine Alps

THESE SWISS VALLEYS, the physical features of which at first sight have so much in common, are very far from being similar. For centuries the people who live in them had comparatively little contact either with those of the neighbouring valley, or with the central authority in the Rhone valley below. They were virtually independent republics, islands in the mountains where life had a rhythm and routine all its own. Yet their life was not static. Many of the village people had, and have, a nomadic existence. The winter would be spent in the bigger villages in the main valley, and then with the coming of spring and the melting of the snow, the villagers would sometimes move en masse with their animals, their goods and even their priest to hamlets higher up the Alps. I have seen a jeep, a vehicle of the greatest use in these parts, crowded to its doors with household goods, with chickens squawking in cages, and grandma sitting in an arm-chair hoisted into the back, her heavy black boots hanging over the edge. This is, however, not the only form of nomadism found in the Valais. The inhabitants of the high village of Chandolin, perched on an eyrie some 6,350 feet above the Rhone valley in the Val d'Anniviers, own vineyards at Muraz near Sierre, nearly 5,000 feet below them, as well as Alpine pastures for their beasts nearly 4,000 feet above them. In February when Chandolin lies under a deep mantle of snow, they descend with their cattle and their goods to Muraz to work in the vineyards until the middle of April when they begin the move towards the higher pastures, a move not eventually completed until the end of June. In summer the family is inevitably divided as some of its members look after the vines, others cut the hay and tend the cattle. After the cows have come down from the high alps, the people gather once again at Muraz to take part in the grape harvest. When this is over, in November, the village moves back to Chandolin where the snow is falling and the deep silence of winter vests the wooden chalets. 'Life in the summer was one of fatigue high up on the sunlit pastures, in sight of the glaciers and the sky, in the winter one of repose in the darkness of the stable,' Guido Rey wrote of his memories of an Alpine village in the last century. 'During the latter season, when the little chalets are buried in the snow, when long, silver festoons hang down from the eaves, when the torrent is silent in the grip of the frost and the steps of the rare wayfarers are no longer heard on the soft layer of snow that covers the path, when the sun is only seen for a few hours above the horizon, the mountain people take their rest. Only at times, on fine days when the sun shines bright but cold on the vast white canopy and makes the trees with their icy beards glisten, do they leave their houses and go forth up the valley to look for the heaps of wood that they have made ready in the summer, and the hay they have stored in the highest chalets that they may bring it down on the useful highway of the snow; and the loaded sledges slide silently down the deep chute between the two white walls.'

This life, so remote from the outside world, is indeed challenged less by the tourist intrusion, which has affected Zermatt and Saas-Fee most adversely, than by the march of progress represented by the building of roads and dams. The great Mauvoisin dam is 780 feet high and, when completed in 1965, the Grand Dixence will be 940 feet, the highest in the world. These great engineering projects are indeed essential to Switzerland's economic livelihood. Upon them the electric railways, the heavy industries, the country's daily bread depend. The finished project will be a masterpiece of engineering skill and it may even add to the scenic values of the situation, as the Ober-Hasli power scheme has enhanced the forbidding character of the Grimsel Pass. Yet something is lost, something of the wild, unsophisticated nature of the mountains, something of the freedom and remoteness of Alpine life.

The Val d'Hérens, whether reached from the austere Val d'Hérémence or by road from Sion, is an enchanting valley, full of handsome villages, fascinating walks and good climbs. The people are proud of their ancient traditions and determined to preserve them. The women still wear even in their workday occupations their local dress, a long black skirt billowing around black boots, a white blouse, a black bodice and a red kerchief, and a black velvet hat. This dress must be as uncomfortable as it is picturesque in the hot days of summer; and the younger women are noticeably less eager to don it or to wear their hair long and neatly braided as do their mothers. Yet this colourful costume stresses the individuality of this peasant republic, giving it the appearance of a Ruritania come to life. Outwardly the peasants seem taciturn, aloof and even unfriendly, suspicious of the underclothed strangers who penetrate their valley during the holiday season and jealous of their independence. A friend of mine, anxious to secure a photograph of a haymaker and her goat, disappeared quickly from the scene after the good lady had brandished her scythe in a menacing fashion. At the beginning of the nineteenth century William Brockendon said of the people of the Val d'Hérens and the Val d'Anniviers that they were 'singularly primitive in their manners' and 'rather uncivil to their visitors.'

Although Christopher von Holder in 1803 spoke of 'friendly Evolena, surrounded by meadows and well-tilled fields,' adding sententiously 'How rich you are in dispensing with many things which have become indispensable to millions of mortals,' the somewhat hostile attitude towards visitors for long seemed to prevail. Over 35 years later Christian Engelhardt found the priest's housekeeper extremely unwilling to provide hospitality for the night until a tip was forthcoming. She 'would scarcely consent to give lodging at all, and when we spoke of wanting two beds, behaved out of malice and laziness like sourness personified.' It seemed that the curé, who here as elsewhere in Alpine valleys acted as hotelier until inns were established, provided the simplest accommodation for his guests; and the substitution for the housekeeper of the priest's sister made things worse, for she was a woman of 'ungovernable temper and rude manners, who seemed to find pleasure in the arrival of strangers only as fresh subjects whereon to vent her spleen.' But this was many years ago and Evolène at least has many good hotels during the short summer season.

Evolène is the chief village of the valley, some 16 miles from Sion. The road narrows after the village of Vex, riding high above the torrential Borgne which rushes through a dark canyon towards the distant valley below, and passes through the extraordinary rock cones known as the Pyramides d'Euseigne before it mounts towards Evolène itself. The scenery is most attractive. Looking down the valley over the forests and meadows, the peaks of the Bernese Oberland, and the Glacier de Zanfleuron in particular, appear through the summer haze. The valley itself is dominated by the stupendous bulk of the Dent Blanche, 14,318 feet, 'a vast pyramid perfectly symmetrical and ending in a point as sharp as though it had been finished off by a human hand,' as A. W. Moore described it, which was first climbed by two Englishmen, T. S. Kennedy and William Wigram in 1862. It was down its icy slopes that the Englishman, William Gabbett, a graduate of Lincoln College, Oxford, his guide, Josef-Marie Lochmatter and porter, Alexander, fell to their death some 2,600 feet below twenty years later, in August 1882. Each of the four ridges of the mountain has a marked character of its own. The east ridge was named the Viereselgrat by Ulrich Almer of Grindelwald after a long climb to the summit. *Wir sind vier Esel*, 'we are four asses,' he said of himself and his three companions, his fellow guide, Aloys Pollinger and two English climbers, G. P. Baker and J. Stafford Anderson.

The west ridge is especially associated with Owen Glynne Jones. In August 1899, Glynne Jones persuaded his school colleague, P. W. Hill, to attempt the ascent of the Dent Blanche by the Ferpècle ridge, a difficult route. They were accompanied by three guides, Furrer, Zurbriggen and Vuignier, and spent the first night at the chalets of Bricolla. They started the next day before dawn, slowly ascending the dangerous ice-glazed rocks until

136

they reached the foot of an overhanging spur of rock. Here they were supported by a single rope. The guides tried to find a way from the narrow ledge up the smooth slabs of rock. This effort was too much, for Furrer's frozen hands lost their grip. He fell back on Zurbriggen and Glynne Jones, thrusting them from the narrow ledge and dragging them, and Vuignier, down the precipice. The rope snapped, leaving Hill alone, alive and stunned, on the ledge. By a supreme effort he made his way to the summit, for he could neither help his comrades nor make his way down. On the top of the mountain he bivouaked in a howling storm. During the descent he twice lost himself, slept by the side of a torrent, and arrived at Zermatt completely exhausted 49 hours after starting the climb.

From Evolène there is a lovely view of the Dent Blanche, whose changing moods are reflected in the colour of the valley itself, and of the Glacier de Ferpècle. There is a noble path indeed beside the rushing Ferpècle torrent and then mounting to the Alpe Bricolla, some 8,000 feet high and the starting-point for many climbs, itself high above the glistening Ferpècle glacier. The ascent to the Col de Bricolla—the view from the nearby Pointe de Bricolla is exceptionally fine—is followed by the crossing of the Moiry glacier to the Col de la Lex and so via the Alp de la Lex to Zinal. A. W. Moore described the ice-fall of the Moiry glacier seen on the descent as 'of great height and very steep. The lower part of this extends completely from one side of the glacier to the other, but higher up, under the Pigne de la Lex, is a belt of smooth ice, which we had no doubt would give access to the field of nevé above the fall. Below this great cascade of séracs, the ice is as compact and level as above it is steep and dislocated.' The track towards the Ferpècle glacier and the Alpe de Bricolla turns towards the left at the little village of Les Haudères, the terminus of the bus route from Sion.

Les Haudères, like all the villages in the valleys, is an attractive huddle of timbered chalets, dark with age, with stone-shingled roofs and carved wooden balconies, often bright with window boxes of red geraniums. The valley is blocked here by the pyramidal Petite Dent de Veisivi which claimed the lives of the English scientist, John Hopkinson and his three children, Alice, Lina and John, on a fine summer day in 1898. The right-hand track, in process of becoming a road through the building operations in connection with the Great Dixence dam, climbs through woods, past the little hamlet of Le Goulet, to Arolla.

Arolla, so beloved by the great mountaineers of the Victorian age, is situated at the foot of Mont Collon and surrounded by woods of larch and the famed Arolla pine. It is deservedly one of the finest climbing centres in Switzerland. 'We got to the end of the world,' wrote Walter Larden on his first visit in 1882, 'and there saw an unfinished hotel sadly looking out on chaos. . . . We passed through a half-finished and most depressing

The Matterhorn, Valais

passage . . . and found three sad visitors, one being Dr. Hort of Cambridge, eating marmot by the light (and smell) of one paraffin lamp. They told us that nineteen people had just left, having believed themselves to have been poisoned by verdigris. . . . That night we fell asleep to the sound of driving rain and the ceaseless roar of the glacier stream.' The next day he 'looked out on a world . . . exquisite in colour, magnificent in form. . . . Above a sky of deep black-blue, sharply outlined against it the soaring outline of the Pigne d'Arolla, and the still more beautiful though less lofty Mont Collon. . . . Across the valley, a range of fantastic peaks, possessing, in spite of their fine-cut edges, the solid power of the mountains. At their feet, a picturesque wilderness of boulder and storm, not unmixed with fir-trees.' Sixteen years later he was still ecstatic in its praise. 'I have never felt the peace and beauty of Arolla more strongly than I did when I saw it next . . . through the open window there breathed the pure air of the mountain pine-wood; above the sunlight trees the Pigne lifted its summit to the sky. Not a sound but the distant voice of the stream. No hotels, no clatter of mules, no smells of the crowded village.' The scientist Thomas Huxley, who had found Evolène 'a dirty Swiss village . . . only redeemed by very good cooking' delighted in Arolla. This praise was, and is, in many ways deserved. The scenery is wild, but the bare slopes are set off by the pines, and Mont Collon gleams white against a blue sky. It has freshness and tranquillity, but there are none the less labourers' huts and the ugly impedimenta of an industrial world, arising from the scheme for building a tunnel to canalise the glacier waters into a reservoir in the Val des Dix, connected with the huge Grande Dixence hydro-electric project. When I was there in 1954 we decided that we would prefer to stay near rather than at Arolla.

In the event we turned back rather gloomily to the little hamlet of Le Goulet. At Evolène we had been unfortunate in our choice of hotel; a luncheon packet of dry bread and margarine and cold goat was hardly in accord with normal Swiss standards. An additional charge for an extra roll at breakfast had given the finishing touch. But the Pension du Lac Bleu was heaven, simplicity combined with cleanliness, food in lavish supply excellently cooked. We strolled to the icy Lac de Lucel and bathed our tired feet. It was June and there were no other visitors; but a local shepherd called for an evening drink, asked us tenderly about the health of Winston Churchill and speculated as to whether the Korean War was still on or not. He too, he said, had seen the world, for he had been sent on frontier duty during the World War, though which war seemed a little uncertain.

The next morning we left for the Val d'Anniviers, walking down to Les Haudères and then by way of the pretty little village of La Sage through the meadows and Alpine pastures, bright with flowers, to the Col de Torrent, 9,593 feet. The air was crystal clear, the views of the mountains from the

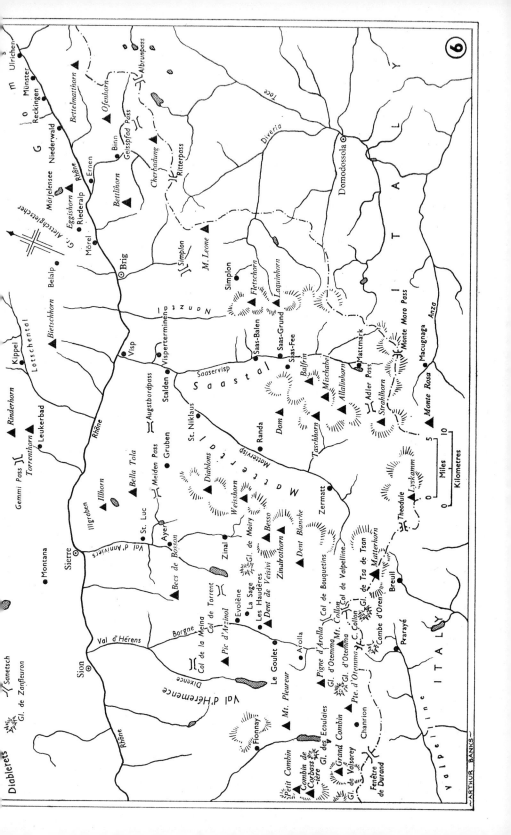

top of the ridge where the snow was still wet and patchy of bewildering splendour, including the Pigne d'Arolla and the Grand Cornier. Beyond the Col we glimpsed marmots sunning themselves; the silence was broken only by the thud of distant mountain avalanches. Nothing could be more perfect. It was therefore with a shock that on our way down to the Val Moiry a dark-haired workman appeared, shouting loudly. Equally suddenly there was a fierce explosion and as we threw ourselves behind a low rock, splinters of stone and clods of earth crashed around us. We were soon in the midst of new roads and blasting, all signs of the inevitable and heart-rending impact of industrial civilisation upon the wild Val de Moiry. Rose-coloured azaleas appeared through the broken rocks and twisted trees. It was wearily that we walked into the village of Grimentz, a place once as delightful as it was remote, and ate our steak at the Becs de Bosson.

Grimentz is situated on the western flank of the Val d'Anniviers which is still, I think, in spite of the reconstruction of the narrow, twisting road that mounts in hairpin bends from Sierre, skirting the Ravine de Pontis, the most beautiful of all the lateral valleys. 'I had formed high expectations of the scenery of the Val d'Anniviers,' A. W. Moore wrote after visiting it in 1864, 'and the reality far exceeded my ideal. Nothing is wanted to complete the effect, and rocks, woods and water combine to form a perfect picture.' The scenery is of unsurpassed grandeur; but unlike Saas-Fee it is not bare. There are fertile green meadows watered by the torrent Navizenche before it enters the deep ravine; and fir-clad slopes, villages of charm and character, perched on the hillsides. I have mentioned already the migratory habits of the peasants. The little villages of Glarcy and Villa, among others, are only fully inhabited for a part of each year. Marc Bourrit, who visited the valley at the end of the eighteenth century, believed that the natives were descended from a remnant of the Huns; but it is now thought their forebears were Celts. Some of the ancient customs are in all probability Celtic survivals. So each family may keep a barrel of wine which is preserved from generation to generation. When a member of the family dies, the mourners will knock on the coffin and toast the dead man or woman in this wine with the words 'au revoir.' In 1853 Alfred Wills held the people to be 'still more barbarous than the neighbouring valleys of Hérins and Hérémence. . . . Balmat told me that he once had occasion to penetrate a few miles up the Val d'Anniviers many years ago, and found the natives living in a state of nudity and filth, almost too gross and disgusting to relate.'

The Victorian mountaineers soon discovered that the village of Zinal at the end of the easternmost section of the valley was a perfect climbing centre. A little inn had just opened in 1859 where Joseph Fox was the first English guest; but the next year, the Cambridge geologist, Thomas Bonney, commented 'Found a newly-constructed "log-hut," with two little bedrooms, sweet with fresh pine-wood, no bigger than an ordinary ship's cabin, and a small salle à manger in which was a bed to hold a couple.' It was presumably in this latter room that Leslie Stephen stayed when he made the first ascent of the Zinal Rothorn in 1864. 'We followed the usual track for the Trift pass as far as the top of the great icefall of the Durand Glacier. Here we turned sharply to the left, and crossed the wilderness of decaying rock at the foot of Lo Besso. It is a strangely wild scene. The buttress-like mass of Lo Besso cut off our view of the lower country. Our path led across a mass of huge loose rocks, which I can only compare to a continuous series of the singular monuments known as rocking-stones.' Later they had to surmount three pinnacles. 'The pinnacle itself was . . . shaped like a tooth protruding from a jaw and exposed down to the sockets, and the two gullies afforded means of circumventing it. . . . The most ticklish part of the operation was in crossing to the other gully; a sheet of hard ice some two or three inches thick covered the steeply-inclined slabs. It was impossible to cut steps in it deep enough to afford secure foothold. . . . We crept along in as gingerly a fashion as might be, endeavouring to distribute our weight over the maximum number of insecure supports until one of the party had got sounder footing. . . . The second pinnacle demanded different tactics. . . . The rock was seamed by deep fissures approximately horizontal. . . . The hold was generally firm when the fissures were not filled with ice, and we gradually succeeded in outflanking the second hostile position. The third . . . was of far more threatening appearance than its predecessors. . . . The rock was so smooth and its edge so sharp, that as I crept along it, supported entirely on my hands, I was in momentary fear that a slip might send one-half of me to the Durand, and the other to the Hohlicht Glacier.' From the top of the third pinnacle, it was a comparatively easy climb to the summit.

The Zinal Rothorn, 13,856 feet, is only one of the cirque of great mountains, Lo Besso, 12,038 feet, Ober-Gabelhorn, 13,364 feet and Dent Blanche, a difficult climb from this side, which can be ascended from Zinal. Less demanding walks take the climber to the Pigne de la Lex with an opportunity to scramble along the ridge to the Bouquetin, with a fine point of view, and up to the Roc de la Vache, returning by way of the Arpietta Alp with glimpses of the Zinal Rothorn and Weisshorn. The best ascent for a view is the more isolated Diablons, 11,825 feet, which can be approached from Zinal by the hut on the Col de Tracuit. Finally Hubert Walker in his useful book *Walking in the Alps* recommends a night spent at the Mountet hut. 'The view thence is one of the most glorious in all the Alps, the amphitheatre enclosing the head of the valley being crowned with the Zinal Rothorn, the Gabelhorn, Dent Blanche and Grand Cornier. All these beautiful mountains present their steepest and most exciting faces in this direction,' and G. D. Abraham says, 'it is worth a king's ransom to wander up into that world of towering crag and eternal snow, and lunch in the sunshine with sight regaled meanwhile by an almost unsurpassed prospect of stupendous peak and glittering glacier. From the massive, monstrous form of the Dent Blanche, around the easterly ice-hung screen of peaks and over the tapering snow-cone of the Ober-Gabelhorn, to the graceful, bepinnacled crest of the Rothorn, the eye wanders untiringly.'

From Zinal a walk through the meadows and woods leads to the village of St. Luc, 5,390 feet high on a terrace above the valley. From Vissoie far below, the village with its brown chalets and white church gleams in the sun minute as a model; but no spot in the Val d'Anniviers provides such fine views both of the Rhone valley and the mountains of the Bernese Oberland beyond, and of the Pennine peaks. It has a multitude of beautiful walks. One track, now, alas, a road, leads through the woods to the high village of Chandolin. My visit here was separated by a gap of several years and yet on both occasions I found two young men of the village in stout mountain boots dancing with the waitress in the local café to the sound of an ancient gramophone; progress has by now substituted a juke-box. Beyond Chandolin a high path leads to a fantastic lesson in geology, the great yellow eroded sides of Illgraben forming a sheer precipice towards the Rhone valley, many thousand feet below. We came back to Chandolin to taste raclette, the traditional dish of the Valais. A slice from a giant cartwheel of cheese is slowly toasted over a wood fire, and the half-liquid mass is eaten on bread or potato with a dash of mustard.

There are innumerable high level walks from St. Luc to the alpine pastures and to the neighbouring peaks. On one such excursion to the Chalet Blanc below the Alpe de Tounot I saw the biggest herd of cows, short sturdy beasts, brownish-black in colour that I have ever seen. Even the cows of the Valais possess character. When they reach their summer pastures, they will not be content until they have found a leader. There are a series of cow contests, the cows fighting with each other in groups and pairs until one is clearly the victor. Henceforth until they descend to the valley this cow will be the acknowledged leader and all the herd will respect her authority. The cows were emerging from the cattle sheds where they had been milked. This milk is turned into cheese, and we saw the huge copper cauldron suspended over a fire into which the milk had been poured and rennet added. After the mixture had been stirred, the cauldron was swung away from the fire and the curds poured into a cheesecloth bag. This was squeezed to eliminate the whey and the resultant mass was deposited in the wooden cheese moulds.

There are three particularly fine points of view above St. Luc, the Illhorn, 8,938 feet, best ascended from Chandolin; the Hotel Weisshorn, 7,096 feet above the Alpe de Tounot on a spur of the Rochers de Nava, 9,090 feet, and

28 *The Grenz Glacier and the Lyskamm, Valais*

the easily surmounted Bella Tola, 9,935 feet. They provide a panoramic view of the Rhone valley and the distant Bernese Alps and the glittering coronet of the peaks of the Pennine Alps, among them the Matterhorn. It was with regret that I saw the thick mist suddenly descend as we clambered up the Bella Tola. We waited hopefully on the top, sitting on the rocks munching our lunch in the hope that it would clear, but a sudden peal of thunder in the very near vicinity forced a rapid retreat.

I always leave St. Luc with deep regret, and this in spite of breaking a bed at one hotel and enduring penurious housekeeping at another; the taste of potage de Grand-mère was not one of the pleasant memories that I shall take with me. The rebuilding of the narrow road up the valley, the construction of the dam in the Val de Moiry, the building of the road from St. Luc to Chandolin still sadden me. Indeed it was at St. Luc that I began writing a story of the bears who in company with Hans the woodcutter and a friendly bee stoutly resisted the attempts of Mr. Pampelmousse and his fellow capitalists from the city to destroy their freedom in the name of progress; but no publisher has ever thought it fit for publication. Yet in spite of all, the Val d'Anniviers is, I believe, the most beautiful of the lateral valleys of the great Pennine range.

It is possible to walk over the Meiden Pass to Gruben in the Turtmanntal. It was late June and while there was still snow about the new grass was carpeting the alpages and the rocks were ablaze with alpine rose and gentian. A multitude of star-shaped white flowers glittered by the small clear tarns. The immense snow-covered bulk of the Weisshorn, 14,804 feet, dominated the mountain scenery to the south. We did not meet a single person during the five hours' walk, but marmots scurried among the rocks. These delightful little animals live in burrows and warn each other of approaching danger by a whistling sound. In the autumn they collect grass for the period of winter hibernation. Fortunately they are protected—the use of steel traps is forbidden—from the greed and cruelty of men, save for three weeks of the hunting season. The peasants greatly appreciate the flesh of the marmot, but after seeing the animals enjoying their Alpine freedom I would not readily taste such a dish.

The path from the Meiden Pass leads steeply through woods to the little hamlet of Gruben in the Turmanntal. Although I believe that a road is projected from the Rhone valley, this is a deep glen which has so far preserved its freedom since it can be normally only reached from the Rhone valley by means of a bridle path, entailing a walk of some five hours. The scenery is lovely, the stream rushing down through rocks and woods from the Turtmann glacier at its head. 'We were in a little glade surrounded by pine forest,' Leslie Stephen wrote of his visit nearly a century ago, 'and with the Alpine rose clustering in full bloom round the scattered boulders. Above us rose the

Near Champex, Valais; the Grand Combin in the background
Medieval fortifications in the Rhone Valley: Saillon, Valais

Weisshorn in one of the most sublime aspects of that almost faultless mountain. The Turtmann Glacier, broad and white with deep, regular crevasses, formed a noble approach, like the staircase of some superb palace. Above this rose the huge mass of the mountain, firm and solid. . . . And, higher still, its lofty crest, jagged and apparently swaying from side to side, seemed to be tossed into the blue atmosphere far above the reach of mortal man.' This was an experience which could apply equally to more recent years. It was indeed ironical that in this most secluded and tranquil spot, so obviously free from all apparent noise, that I spent one of the most sleepless nights that I have ever had, owing to the combined efforts of the Swiss army on its manœuvres, engaging in noisy warfare throughout the night below the windows of the hotel, and the passage of the cows from the lowlands to the summer alps. What with the rattle of machine-guns and the continuous jangle of innumerable cow-bells, the local inn, the Schwarzhorn, was that night less quiet than a noisy hotel in a busy town.

From the Turtmanntal the Augstbord Pass, 9,490 feet, or, much rougher, the Jung Pass reached by scrambling up the Hüngerli Alp, leads after some six or seven hours' walking to St. Niklaus, and the most famous of all the Valaisan valleys with the summer and winter resort of Zermatt at its head. Zermatt was probably known to the Romans whose coins have been found on the near-by St. Théodule Pass, named after an early bishop of the Valais. The Pope, a local legend avers, offered a bell to Théodule, but there seemed no way of getting the bell from Rome to the Rhone valley. The Devil conveniently offered to convey both bishop and bell from Rome to Sion in a single night on condition that the bishop would surrender his see to him if he arrived within the city walls before the cock crew. It seemed as if Satan had a fair chance of victory when the bishop perceiving the walls coming close shouted out 'Coq, chante! Que tu chante! Oh que jamais plus tu ne chantes! (though presumably in Latin). At once every cock in the neighbourhood crowed lustily, and have gone on doing so ever since at an hour abnormally early even for cocks. Another legend asserts that Satan boasted to the bishop that he was more powerful. Théodule asked him to prove it and pointed to a great cauldron used by the shepherds for cheese-making. If Satan carried that on his shoulders across the pass as far as Pasquier, he, the bishop, would be his slave. The devil shouldered the cauldron, laboured up the glacier but near the top of the pass he slipped and rolled with his burden to the bottom of the valley.

Zermatt had to wait until the nineteenth century before it became widely known; though Aegidius Tschudi described the valley in 1538 and the Swiss botanists, Peter Thomas and his son, Abraham, made a stay there in 1765. Early travellers stayed here, as elsewhere, with the village priest, but in 1838 the cantonal government restricted the growing practice by forbidding parish priests from acting as hoteliers. The local doctor took the curé's place until Alexander Seiler purchased his chalet in 1855 and renamed it the Monte Rosa hotel.

A new and exciting chapter in Zermatt's history was about to begin with the conquest of the great peaks in its vicinity. The village is dominated by the Matterhorn, a mountain which has evoked a stream of similes. It has been likened to a ruined tower, an obelisk, a giant with tired shoulders, a rearing horse. 'Stronger minds,' Edward Whymper said, 'felt the influence of the wonderful form, and men who ordinarily spoke or wrote like rational beings, when they came under its power seemed to quit their sense, and ranted and rhapsodised, losing for a time all common forms of speech.' Whymper, whose name has been indelibly associated with the Matterhorn, the son of a wood-engraver, had been commissioned by the publisher, William Longman, to do illustrations for a book on the Alps. He crossed the Channel in 1860 and after visiting Kandersteg and walking over the Gemmi Pass to Leuk, he went on to Saas-Fee and Zermatt. There and then he set his heart on climbing the Matterhorn.

During the next four years he made seven unsuccessful climbs from Breuil on the Italian side. In 1865 he learned that some Italian climbers were about to make an attempt. 'Whymper had arrived two or three days before;' Giordano wrote to his friend, Sella, on July 11th from Breuil, 'as usual, he wished to make the ascent, and had engaged Carrel, who not having yet had my letters, had agreed, but for a few days only. Fortunately the weather turned bad. Whymper was unable to make his fresh attempt, and Carrel left him and came with me. . . . I have taken up my quarters at Breuil for the time being. The weather, the god whom we fear, and on whom all will depend, has been hitherto very changeable and rather bad. As late as yesterday it was snowing on the Matterhorn, but yesterday evening it cleared. In the night (10th–11th) the men started with the tents, and I hope that by this time they will have reached a great height, but the weather is turning misty again. . . . I have tried to keep everything secret, but that fellow, whose life seems to depend on the Matterhorn, is here suspiciously prying into everything. I have taken all the competent men away from him, and yet he is so enamoured of this mountain that he may go with others and make the ascent. He is here, in this hotel, and I try to avoid speaking to him.'

Whymper, aware of what was brewing, crossed the St. Théodule Pass and determined to try the climb from the Swiss side. At Zermatt he found the Chamonix guide, Michel Croz, with Lord Francis Douglas, who had just made the second ascent of the Ober-Gabelhorn, and with the Rev. Charles Hudson who proposed an ascent of the Matterhorn. Whymper and his new companions left Zermatt together on July 13th, 1865, and hurried on, fearful lest the Italians should get the lead; though in fact their fears were groundless. But, on their way down after a successful ascent, disaster over-took them. A little below the summit, Hudson's friend, Douglas Hadow, who had only recently left Harrow, slipped and fell on Croz. Croz, unprepared, also fell and pulled with him both Hudson and Douglas. On hearing Croz's shout, Whymper and the old Zermatt guide, Peter Taugwalder, clasped the rocks; but the rope broke. It was whispered later the rope was cut but there seems no real evidence for this suggestion. Whymper saw his companions slide down the slope and over the precipice. With the two local guides, the Taugwalders, he spent the night on the east face and then returned to Zermatt. The whole tragic episode gave rise to lengthy and acrimonious controversy. Whymper was indeed a vain and unreliable man, but he was an indomitable Alpinist and his *Scrambles in the Alps* must remain a mountaineering classic.

The conquest of the Matterhorn seemed to destroy its spirit, and although it continued to claim victims, it attracted an increasing number of moun-taineers. In 1878 it was climbed by a lady, Miss Lucy Walker:

A lady has clomb to the Matterhorn's summit
Which almost like a monument points to the sky;
Steep not very much less than the string of a plummet
Suspended, which nothing can scale but a fly.

No glacier can baffle, no precipice balk her,
No peak rise above her, however sublime,
Give three times three cheers for intrepid Miss Walker.
I say, my boys, doesn't she know how to climb.

Such was the tribute of *Punch*. Five years later its summit fell to amateurs climbing without guides. Later Lord Wentworth spent the night on the summit and remained there seventeen hours. In 1872 Mr. Jackson climbed from Breuil to the top and descended to Zermatt in a day of 18 hours. Ten years later Vittorio Sella made the first winter ascent. In 1902 the guides of Valtournanche took a cross to the top of the mountain and on September 24th the Abbé Carrel said Mass there. One fine summer day in 1892 there appeared to be as many as twenty-three people on the summit. The Matter-horn had become the fashionable mountain, but avalanches are still unleashed on its slopes and stones fall down its gullies.

Indeed the north face of the Matterhorn was not climbed until July 1931. Two brothers, Franz and Toni Schmid, who had bicycled from Munich to save the expense of the journey, pitched their tent on the Alpine meadows 3,000 feet below the Hörnli hut. They left their tent at midnight and by early morning had climbed the slopes of snow at the foot of the precipitous north face. The ice slope here is so steep that few climbers, even with the strongest crampons, would have attempted the ascent without cutting steps. But Toni and Frank thought that time was more important than safety. Toni led off up the ice to the end of the rope's length and drove in an ice piton to give security while Frank came up. In this way they managed to climb the great glazed slope. In its middle stretch there was a long gulley up which they crawled. The sun was setting as they passed out of the gulley by a difficult chimney and up a short ice-wall to the slabs above. They did not find it easy at 13,000 feet to discover a resting-place for the night and had to remain in an extremely uncomfortable, crouched position. The next morning they soon came to smooth slabs where there was no perceptible crevice into which a piton could be driven. They could only make headway by traversing a patch of snow. The weather had got much worse, and thunder and hail made their journey difficult, but at last they made the sum-mit. Toni Schmid was killed the next year, leading a difficult ice climb on the Gross Weissbachhorn.

If the Matterhorn is the pride of Zermatt, there are many other mountains to be climbed from here. The Weisshorn, first climbed by the English scientist, John Tyndall, in 1861, and the Dom, 14,942 feet and actually the highest mountain wholly in Swiss territory, usually approached from Randa, six miles north of Zermatt and first climbed by the Rev. J. L. Davies in 1858, are both within reach of Zermatt. So too are Monte Rosa, 15,217 feet, the Ober-Gabelhorn, the Lyskamm, the Strahlhorn and the Rimpfischhorn. The high Adler Pass, 12,461 feet, so-named by the Abbé Imseng, who discovered it, because an eagle flew over his party, is one way from Zermatt to Saas. Alfred Wills thought the view from the summit of 'inconceivable extent and magnificence. . . . Opposite to us, we behold the frowning precipices of the Allalinhorn, towering abruptly above the glacier. Then comes the wide, glittering expanse of the Fee, partly hidden by the chain of rugged heights which form the boundary wall of the Allalin glacier, and guarded by the majestic range of the Mischabel, whose black crags contrast finely with the broad fields of white in front. Further to the right, at a distance of thirty or forty miles but apparently quite near the whole range of Oberland lies unfolded . . . in one glorious line of mingled precipice and glacier. Not a cloud between us, and them, save one delicate wreath, which floats midway between the base and summit of the Jungfrau. . . . In the transparent atmosphere of this brilliant morning, distance is annihilated, and every glacier, every rock, every hollow and every gulley lies clearly and distinctly revealed to us . . . still more impressive and solemn, from the dimness of distance, are the colossal forms of the mountains of the Tyrol. . . . South of these, clad in a light blue haze which gives to them an indescribable charm . . . are the mountain chains which border on the lakes of Italy.'

Zermatt provides innumerable beautiful walks, among others one through the gorge of the Z'mutt to Staffel Alp, but more and more visitors go there simply to see the mountains and to use the rack-and-pinion railway built in 1898 to the Gornergrat, 10,134 feet high and the highest open-air terminus in the Alps. In nearly six miles of travelling it provides glorious prospects, especially after leaving Riffelberg. As a result of the massive invasion of tourists Zermatt, like Saas, is, as Guido Rey suggested, 'a discordant medley of the old and the new.' The vast hotels tend to dwarf the timbered chalets and the tranquillity of former days has disappeared. Between the seasons, however, repose returns to the valley. Then, to quote Rey again, 'in the village round about the smoke rises peacefully from the old chalets; down the narrow street pass the cows with their jangling bells, returning from the pastures; a sledge laden with hay slides silently down the hillside, and a little old woman, seated on a neighbouring knoll, and wearing the black headdress of the Valais, is watching two goats while she knits a stocking.'

Zermatt can only be reached by rail, for the road from Stalden ends after St. Niklaus. The left fork of the valley at Stalden ascends towards Saas-Fee, the most glacial of Alpine resorts. 'There is not a lovelier spot in Switzerland,' a traveller wrote in 1856, 'emerald meadows set in frosted silver; for the valley is almost encircled by a brilliant amphitheatre of glaciers descending from the Alphubel and the Mischabelhörner.' Saas is approached by a modern road through a valley containing a number of picturesque villages, and interesting churches. The best of these, at Saas Belen, has a circular nave and semi-circular tower, designed by J. J. Andermatten and built between 1809 and 1812. Though it is a nineteenth-century building it is an excellent example of late baroque style.

The village of Saas-Fee lies above the main valley at the foot of the glaciers. There is a path or pilgrim's way up the hillside provided with fifteen little chapels, each with its tableau of coloured wooden figures illustrating the story of the Redemption. The situation of the largest chapel, some half-way between Saas and Saas-Fee, dedicated to the Virgin was, in Samuel Butler's opinion, 'of such extreme beauty—the great Fee glaciers showing through the open portico—that it is in itself worth a pilgrimage.' This chapel was built in 1687 and enlarged in 1747. Many of the figurines, roughly carved yet vigorous and spirited, disclose genuine artistry. The chapels were probably built at the beginning of the eighteenth century, though Butler thought them of a much earlier date, to commemorate the placing of the valley, devastated by severe flooding, under the joint protection of St. Anthony of Padua, St. Francis Xavier and St. Nicholas.

The founder of Saas as a resort was the local parish priest from the neighbouring village of Saas-Grund, Joseph Imseng, an enthusiastic climber despite extreme short sight, who used to wear a very dilapidated cassock in his expeditions. This kindly, hospitable man, who was also a good Latin scholar, was much beloved by his people. 'If they thought he was going to leave them, *ils me déchireraient les culottes*,' he told Alfred Wills. He became the friend and adviser of all the climbers who visited Saas in the mid-nineteenth century. He accompanied Engelhardt, Wills and Ulrich to Zermatt across the great passes of the Mischabel range, the Adler, the Allalin and the Ried. He climbed the Nadelhorn alone but for his guide, the Allalin and the Fletschhorn with Ames and the Balfrin with Spence-Watson. In 1869 his body was found drowned in the grey mountain lake of the Mattmark.

Saas-Fee for long retained its isolation, only attracting a few climbers who gloried in the opportunities it presented to them. 'There were no disagreeables, no cliques,' Walter Larden wrote of the summer he spent there in 1886. 'The mountains and the love of the mountains seemed to dominate everything. . . . There were climbs in abundance, as serious work; and as a relaxation for off days, there were glacier expeditions made perhaps in company with eighteen others or so, with exciting step-cutting. The latter excursions usually wound up with tea, and cream, and jam at Clara's restaurant on the moraine, high up between the two glaciers. In the evening we had good music and once or twice Mr. Charles Dickens recited for us pieces out of his father's writings.' A traveller sixteen years previously found the local hotelier so pleased to have a guest that he laid on a dinner of ten courses: 'as to the nature of nine it was difficult to speak with any degree of certainty, but the tenth was apparently a blackbird that had perished of starvation and whose attenuated form the chef had bulged out with extraneous matter.' Modern Saas has protected itself against the motorist by insisting that all cars shall be parked before entry to the village. It is a pity that it could not also defend itself against the bazaars selling cheap souvenirs, cheap in taste rather than price, and the large hotels which here, as at Zermatt, overshadow the chalets of the village.

Saas is indeed a wonderful place for walks and climbs; and the amphitheatre of glaciers poised against the blue sky is impressive and beautiful. But Saas needs fine weather. In dull weather it is cold, gloomy and austere, though the sun immediately brings out the brilliance of colouring of rock, ice and pine. Its curious name is not derived from fairies but from the willow-tree the salix; *vallis solixa* is its name in a thirteenth-century text. A local tradition asserts that the people of the district are descended from Saracen invaders of the tenth century, and that this theory is supported by the evidence of local place-names, Monte Moro, Mischabel, and Allalin, which are clearly Arabic in origin. Mischabel, it is said, is derived from the Arabic for 'Lioness with her young.' The Saracens certainly invaded the Valais in 939, and were later employed by Hugo, king of Arles, to hold the Valaisan passes against his rival, king Berenger. It seems unlikely, however, that they should have bestowed names on mountains and glaciers which have survived the centuries. Mischabel, another scholar has stated, is simply a corruption of Mittlere Gabel or Middle Peak. Monte Moro may have been so entitled by the Valaisan invaders because of its association with the dusky intruders, but there seems comparatively little reason for believing that such place-names represent Saracenic influence. At a later date the Allalin glacier itself was the chief enemy of the people of Saas, for in its advance it broke the moraine barrier and so allowed the Mattmark lake to inundate the valley below.

Although I personally do not find Saas as attractive as St. Luc or as Evolène, it is infinitely grander and is the gateway to some of the greatest peaks of the Pennine range. It is worth taking the bridle path through the larch woods to Saas-Grund and following the main valley past the rushing Visp and the dreary glacial bed of the Mattmark lake, once an expanse of grey water at the foot of the Allalin and Schwarzenberg glaciers, to the Hotel Mattmark. Near here is the Blue Stone which played so large a part in the early researches on glaciers. Men had observed this huge block of stone as it was borne down by the glacier, emerging more and more from the ice until it eventually reached solid ground. The early Swiss glaciologist, Ignaz Venetz, a native of the Visp valley, deduced from his observations here that glaciers had once covered whole regions of the Alps. The same idea occurred to the naturalist Jean de Charpentier after he had talked with an observant chamois hunter, Jean-Pierre Perraudin, who lived in the Val de Bagnes. Perraudin noticed the shape of the rocks near his home and told Charpentier that 'Such things make me think that, a long time ago, a huge mass of ice filled the whole valley, and I can prove it, for those rocks are identical with others which are just now emerging from the ice.' The track goes past the Blue Stone to the stone chalets of the Distel Alp bored in the mountainside to permit the spring avalanches to pass by and thence by steps carved in the cliff overhanging the Talliboden. Finally a snow slope leads to the magnificent Monte Moro Pass, 9,390 feet, below the precipitous sides of Monte Rosa and to Macugnaga. The pass was used in the middle ages by Italians who settled near Saas and by German-speaking colonists who came to Macugnaga in the thirteenth century. Pilgrims and smugglers also made their way along the paved track through the waste of rock and snow. When the English traveller, T. W. Hinchliff, was on the pass in 1856, he met a stranger whom he invited to take a meal with him but, to Hinchliff's surprise, he refused. 'In a quarter of an hour the mystery was solved by the appearance of several men who had followed us, each of them carrying a large bale of goods on his back, and steadily following the course over the snow taken by the first man. Our porter explained that this was a party of smugglers working their way into Italy, the first man acting as a sort of pilot-fish to see whether the way was clear.'

31 *Looking from the Dufourspitze towards Mont Bla*

The Saas valley is the last of the southern lateral valleys branching from the Rhone valley itself. The next break in the mountain chain is the Simplon Pass beyond the summit of which the Valais and Switzerland terminate as the road goes down the savage gorge of Gondo towards Domodossola and the Italian lakes. The Rhone valley itself turns abruptly towards the north after Brig, following the course of the infant river, creating that great cleft in the Alps which provides the traveller with a series of mountain highways, leading to the Grimsel, Furka, Gotthard and Oberalp Passes.

The Gomstal or Vallée de Conches as this part of the Upper Valais is called provides scenery as fine as the valleys of the south. The villages with chalets darkened by weather and time but bright with flowers are as attractive. The orchards in autumn are as heavy with fruit. From Morel, four miles from Brig, a steep mule track leads to the high mountain resort of the Riederalp (with which it is also connected by chair lift). There are many fine walks, the loveliest probably that which traverses the Aletsch Glacier and leads to the Belalp.

The Belalp, approached usually by bus from Brig to Blatten and thence by bridle path, is 7,000 feet high and commands a splendid view of the Aletsch Glacier and the chain of the Pennine Alps. It is a wonderfully-situated high level resort much beloved by the Victorians, and a splendid centre for mountain excursions. Coolidge's aunt, Miss Brevoort, stayed there during the summer of 1876 and her letters well suggest the social milieu of the Belalp at that period. Among the guests were a government engineer from India and his wife, who regaled the earnest lady with information about Mount Everest (which she had an ambition to climb), the Dean of Canterbury who organised Spelling Bees to amuse his fellow guests and Oscar Browning, who had been recently dismissed from Eton for his too intimate friendship with the young Curzon, forever ready to talk scathingly about the headmaster, Dr. Hornby. 'He told me', Meta Brevoort wrote to her nephew, 'that Dr. Hornby's house is full of Swiss souvenirs. His wife is a little goose, who cannot even spell properly; pretty but vapid, and he fell in love with her and married her so quickly that he had to ask her Christian name when he was married.' A newly-wed couple on their honeymoon was the mountaineer and scientist John Tyndall and his young wife. 'She is very plain and thirty if a day old. He looks old and ghastly. The Klingelese had made a kind of triumphal arch ending in two tubs planted with small evergreens and flowers over the door of the salon, and strewn the threshold with flowers in patterns.' The Professor and his wife, who were obviously very much in love with each other, kept mostly to themselves; but Tyndall was ready to give some lectures on glaciers and their action to their fellow guests. Next year, Tyndall built himself a chalet at the Belalp:

157

Looking from the Simplon Pass towards the Bernese Alps

Sky-touching Simplon pass—
Flanked by the Lion Mountain to the left,
While to the right the mighty Fletschorn lifts
A beetling brow, and spreads abroad its snows.
Dom, Cervin—Weisshorn of the dazzling dazzling crown—
Ye splendours of the Alps! Can earth elsewhere
Bring forth a rival? . . .

It was shortly after his return from a visit to his beloved Belalp that Tyndall died. He was accidentally poisoned by his wife who gave him an overdose of chloral instead of the intended bicarbonate of soda. 'Oh, My Dear, I have given you chloral instead of your bicarbonate.' 'Yes, My Dear, I fear you have killed me.' Mrs. Tyndall long outlived her husband and did not die until 1940.

From Fiesch, ten miles from Brig in the main valley, there are innumerable high mountain excursions. One path ascends through pinewoods and meadows to the Eggishorn hotel, whence a steep track leads to the summit of the Eggishorn itself, only 9,626 feet high, but possessing one of the finest panoramic views in Europe, embracing the great Aletsch Glacier, some fifteen miles in length and two miles at its broadest width, with the snow peaks of the Aletschhorn and the Jungfrau behind it. Another path leads to the Märjelen See whose waters often contain floating ice. A crossing of the Aletsch Glacier brings the walker to the Concordia-Platz, so-called because in some curious fashion it is said to resemble the Place de la Concorde in Paris, a great cross-roads of mountain tracks, to the Jungfraujoch, the broad back of the Gross-Fiescherhorn and to the finely-shaped Finsteraarhorn, and to the Lötschen-Lücke, the mountain pass going from the Fafleralp to the Lötschental.

Another bridle path leads from Fiesch past Ernen with its painted houses and a memorable church, the choir and part of the tower of which were built by Schinner's architect, Ruffiner, and Mühlibach where the redoubtable Cardinal was born, to the Binnen-Tal. The village of Binn nestles among the mountains, a cluster of dark chalets. 'Binn in June was a revelation to me,' Walter Larden wrote in 1891. 'The trees, magnificent firs and larches, the flowers and ferns, and, above all, the beautiful stream formed a whole that was charming. There was a very fine fall above Heilig Kreuz; and above that, on the Ritter-Alp, a still more wonderful slide of water of great length and bewildering energy. And the stream that descends from the Geisspfad See well repays a day's ramble along its banks. The Ofenhorn crowns one valley, and the Hüllehorn shows above the trees up another. . . . Binn itself was a quaint village. It was very black and very dirty, and the "approach" to the

hotel lay between manure heaps.' Eight years later Oxford's future Public
Orator, the witty A. D. Godley, exclaimed:

Place me somewhere in the Valais, 'mid the mountains west of Binn,
West of Binn and east of Savoy, in a decent kind of inn,
With a peak or two for climbing, and a glacier to explore—
Any mountains will content me, though they've all been climbed before—
Yes! I care not any more
Though they've all been done before
And the names they keep in bottles may be numbered by the score.

The region is noted for the many crystals of uncommon minerals found
here as well as for its Alpine flowers. There are innumerable climbs, the
Eggerhorn, the Bettlihorn, the Ofenhorn, the Blindenhorn and the
Cherbadung, as well as walks over the passes in the direction of the Italian
frontier. Four hours of a beautiful mountain path trodden by centuries of
past travellers bring one to the top of the Albrun Pass, where the jagged
peaks of the mountains resemble the Dolomites and so down to the lovely
Tosa Falls. The Geisspfad Pass and a path 'which winds,' Hubert Walker
writes, 'as steeply as anywhere underneath jagged peaks and towering crags
on the Italian side' eventually reaches the Italian village of Devero. Yet a
third excursion over the Ritter Pass goes to the Veglia Alp.

So far, the villages and passes which I have mentioned lead from the
Gomstal itself. After Fiesch the Gomstal passes Niederwald, the birthplace of
the hotelier, César Ritz, Reckingen which has the finest Baroque church in
the Valais, built by the brother Pickel of the Vorarlberg between 1743 and
1745 (though its choir stalls were the work of a local craftsman, P. Lagger),
and possessing a spacious interior enriched by contemporary stucco and
frescoes, en route for the large village of Münster. This also has a noble
church, the choir late Gothic in design, the nave Renaissance and a high
altar, a masterly piece of work, from the hand of J. Keller of Lucerne.
Archdeacon Coxe, travelling in the eighteenth century, came from Oberwald,
which could not supply his needs, to Münster, walking there with a peasant
who talked most intelligently about the American War of Independence.
The next village up the valley, Ulrichen, was the site of two battles, in 1211
and in 1419, when the natives of the Upper Valais defeated the Bernese
who had invaded over the Grimsel Pass. The road towards Gletsch and the
Furka Pass diverges to the left at Ulrichen.

The right-hand track moves through the fields and larch woods of the
Eginen-Tal towards the summit of the Gries Pass, 8,089 feet, formed by the
lower extremity of the Gries Glacier, but smooth and easily traversed.
The path leads down steeply to the lovely Italian Val Formazza and the

foaming Tosa Falls, one of the finest waterfalls in the Alps. The district was colonised by Valaisans in the middle ages who came over the Gries or Albrun passes, and still bears characteristic signs of Valaisan culture. Many of the hamlets have German as well as Italian names, and German is spoken in the valley, at least down to Foppiano (or Unter Stalden), where the luxuriant vegetation of Italy replaces the sparser Alpine foliage. The Gries Pass, now comparatively little used, was once a significant thoroughfare from Italy to the Valais and central Switzerland.

Beyond Ulrichen on the main Furka road, the little village of Obergesteln, now stone-built, epitomises the fate that so many Swiss villages in the Alps have to a greater or lesser degree endured, a severe avalanche in 1720 which killed 88 people, and a fire which destroyed it completely in 1868. Four miles further on begins the final step or terrace of the valley down which the now infant Rhone flows in a glacial torrent, with a fine view of the Weisshorn to the south and in front the pyramidal Galenstock. The little village of Gletsch, the junction for the Grimsel and the Furka passes, is situated on the plateau which lies beyond this gorge. It consists of a few chalets and the Hotel du Glacier du Rhone, which was bought, enlarged and refurbished by Joseph Seiler. All round there is a bare waste of rock and mountain debris; the mountains, skirted by curving roads, tower threateningly against the blue sky. A little way from the hotel a stone marks the furthest point reached by the Rhone Glacier, now in rapid retreat, in the last century. A few miles away to the west and north the Bernese Oberland and the Forest Cantons begin.

The strategic and commercial importance of the Valais, indeed its place in Swiss and European history, resulted from the fact that it was a thorough-fare for the traffic passing over the Simplon into northern Italy. The Simplon road has had a long history. The original hospice on the summit, now a shepherd's shelter, was maintained by the Knights Hospitallers during the latter part of the middle ages; the square tower was added by the wealthy Brig merchant, Kaspar Stockalper in 1653. John Evelyn crossed over the pass in 1646 on his way from Milan to Geneva. He was depressed by its rugged nature (and so, I may add, was I when a front-wheel bearing of the car failed on the summit and forced us to descend at snail's pace to Brig again). Moreover his companion, Captain Wray's dog, chased and unfortunately killed one of a herd of goats. Evelyn was unimpressed by the accommodation of the hospice. 'Arriv'd at our cold harbour (tho' the house had a stove in every roome) and supping on cheese and milk with wretched wine, we went to bed in cupboards so high from the floore that we climb'd them by a ladder; we were covered with feathers, that is we lay between two ticks stuff'd with them, and all little enough to keep one warm.' He was the more disgusted the next morning when he found that he and his companion were locked in their room by a band of local peasants. After the latter returned from Mass they conducted Wray and Evelyn to a local magistrate who rebuked them for trying to run away and fined them for killing the goat.

The modern road in effect owes its existence to Napoleon. After his experience of the difficulties involved in conveying an army across the St. Bernard Pass, he began to build a highway, starting on the Italian side, immediately after his victory over the Austrians at Marengo. Before the road up the Simplon was finished, the only passes practicable for travellers in carriages had been the Brenner and the Tende passes. The road was finished in 1805, but the hospice was not completed until it was bought by the Augustinian canons of St. Bernard in 1825.

The Simplon Pass has been much apostrophised. 'Ascended the Simplon,' Thomas Moore wrote in 1819, 'which baffles all description. . . . Walked on by myself, and saw such a scene by sunset as I shall never forget. That mighty panorama of the Alps, whose summits there, indistinctly seen, looked like the top of gigantic waves, following close upon each other; the soft lights falling on those green spots which cultivation has conjured up in the midst of this wild scene; the pointed top of the Jungfrau [in all probability the Bietschhorn], whose snows were then pink with the setting sun; all was magnificent to a degree that quite overpowered me.' The Countess Spencer, who crossed the Simplon the same year, found that its austerities put the finishing touch to her dislike of mountain scenery. 'Oh, may I never see rock, torrent, cascade, or snow-topped mountain again.' In truth, the modern Simplon road, recently reconstructed, is straightforward, more or less bereft of hairpin bends on the Swiss side, but it ascends through fine scenery, with impressive backward glances at the giants of the Bernese Oberland. On its way down to Italy, it channels through the savage gorge of Gondo before it passes on its way to the warmth, colour and light of the Italian lakes.

7
THE TICINO

THE TICINO, the mountainous canton which fringes the Italian lakes, has long been associated with the Swiss Confederation. Yet Italian Switzerland, which it comprises, remains for the northerner a distinct entity, different in its customs as in its appearance from the Alpine regions of the north. Towards the end of the middle ages most of the area was ruled by the Duke of Milan; but the growing trade over the St. Gotthard Pass made the northern cantons eager to consolidate their control over this important highway by extending their influence to the south. In 1419 they purchased rights over the Val Leventina, the valley along which the St. Gotthard road runs towards Bellinzona and the lakes. The Milanese duke, Filippo Maria Visconti, challenged this action, claiming that the strategic centre of Bellinzona belonged to him.

Bellinzona, now the cantonal town,* was an important junction since it controlled the routes south from the St. Gotthard, from Chur along the valley of the Vorder Rhein and over the Lukmanier Pass, and the road up the Val Mesocco to the San Bernadino Pass. The three well-kept castles which still dominate the town are portentous reminders of Bellinzona's past importance. The Milanese mercenary leader, Carmagnola, however, defeated the undisciplined Confederate forces at Arbedo on June 30th, 1422, and harried them over the St. Gotthard Pass. The Duke decided to strengthen the defences of Bellinzona by a ring of fortifications, the design of which was approved by no less a person than Aristotile Fieraranti of Bologna, a military architect of considerable repute. At the end of the fifteenth century the duchy of Milan was claimed by the French king, Louis XII. To win Swiss support for this object Louis promised to cede Bellinzona and the surrounding area to the Confederates if he was successful. When, however, he actually got possession of Milan, he refused to carry out his promise, and once again the Confederate forces marched down the rocky Val Leventina, in 1503. Fearful of the effect of a Swiss advance in Lombardy, over which he had only a precarious control, the French king came to terms with the Swiss at the little town of Arona, at the far—Italian—end of lake Maggiore. Here

* It has only been the permanent centre since 1881. Until then Bellinzona, Lugano and Locarno, each took it in turn to be the cantonal capital, holding the position for six years.

he agreed to hand over Bellinzona and the Val Blenio to the joint control of Uri, Schwyz and Niedwalden. Thirteen years later the Swiss suffered a great defeat at the hands of Louis' successor, Francis I of France, on the battlefield of Marignano. Francis was, however, magnanimous, or discerning; in the hour of triumph and in return for the promise by the Swiss that they would not help his enemies he gave up his claims to Bellinzona, Lugano, Locarno, Mendrisio, Bormio, Chiavenna and the Valtelline. Although the region around the lake of Lugano and the eastern reaches of lake Maggiore and the hinterland behind them were now permanently under Swiss control, the Ticino did not yet receive full cantonal status. Twelve out of the thirteen *Orte* (or cantons), excepting Appenzell, jointly governed the Italian possessions, and it was not until 1803 that the Swiss, under pressure from Bonaparte, by the Act of Mediation admitted Ticino as a full canton. Later the Italian language was given equal status with German and French.

The countryside and people of the Ticino have a character of their own, visible as soon as the traveller has crossed the passes from the north, the Simplon and the St. Gotthard in particular, and dropped 2,000 or more feet down to the very different vegetation of the southern valleys. The climate is mild and sunny, but when the rains come they are often torrential. The warm wet winds from the Mediterranean are driven against the mountain wall which shields Ticino from the north—incidentally the canton includes both the highest and lowest points in Switzerland, the Dufourspitze, 15,217 feet, and lake Maggiore, 636 feet above sea-level—and release their rain over the lakes and the mountain valleys. In Faido in the Val Leventina eight and a half inches of rain have fallen in a day. Locarno has many more days of sun than Zürich and yet heavier rainfall. Almost dry river beds are filled by suddenly rising waters and the floods pour over the rocky beds, down the narrow gorges, into the wide lake deltas where they destroy crops and flood low-lying houses. The level of lake Maggiore into which the Maggia Ticino torrents flow has been known to rise as much as 26 feet, flooding the lakeside and causing the promenades of Locarno and Ascona to disappear temporarily under the deluge.

These differences in climate and height account in part for the particular character of the Ticinese countryside, the brilliance of its colouring, less delicate indeed than the pastel shades of Tuscany but with a radiance all its own. Although the mountains, less high than those in the Valais and the Bernese Oberland, are often free from snow in the summer months, the country is in many respects wilder and rougher. The granite peaks are jagged needles towering against a sky of Mediterranean blue. The valleys are deep and gorge-like and rise sheer from the cavernous channels through which for aeons past the floods have forced their way. The mountains, eroded of their soil by wind and rain as well as by disafforestation, stand above the luxuriant green of chestnut groves and fields of vegetable, maize and millet.

The spring comes earlier to the Ticino than anywhere else in Switzerland. The houses of the squat, primitive villages, seemingly hewn out of the countryside itself, are bright with mauve clusters of wistaria and the smoky green of young vines. Laburnum, golden-yellow, hangs over the flagged stone walls. The shrines along the roadside are encompassed by orchards of pear and cherry blossom. The Alpine meadows are sprinkled then with crocus and daphne, primulas, anemones and sweet-smelling narcissus. 'In this valley,' Douglas Freshfield wrote of the Valle Maggia, 'the strength of granite is clothed in the grace of southern foliage in a rich mantle of chestnuts and beeches, fringed with maize and vines, and embroidered about the skirts with delicate traceries of ferns and cyclamen.' Indeed the beauty of the Ticino arises from its contrasting quality, the fertility of its valleys and the bareness of the mountain rock, the aridity of the streams in summer and their torrential outpour in the wet seasons. 'Here the bold dark outlines of the granite precipices hanging over the luxuriant yet untamed loveliness of the valley appeal to our emotions with the strong power of contrast. . . .'

The roads up the valleys are narrow. That to Bosco Gurin is incredibly dusty and clings sinuously to the twisting slopes of the valley along which it runs. That to Mergoscia near Locarno follows a tortuous path through hamlets held, seemingly by divine providence rather than gravity, to foundations perhaps less precarious than they appear. In villages of great beauty the slim campanile of an Italianate church dominates the white houses clustered round it and all stand on green terraces high above the valleys under the shadow of the mountains.

The people who live here must be distinguished from the bourgeois inhabitants of the lakeside resorts. In appearance and manner they resemble their Italian neighbours, vivacious, passionate, positive, small and dark-skinned, men and women in youth possessing a grace and beauty denied to their northern compatriots. While the Ticino is Italianate it is, however, definitely not Italian. In general its people are perhaps less friendly and less gay than those of northern Italy, and its villages are better-ordered, cleaner, neater, more prosperous. The Ticinese, apart from the town-dwellers, are fundamentally an Alpine people. Their life is controlled by the terrain and, less than most of the inhabitants of Alpine Switzerland, is only very partially enriched or affected by the tourist. In many remote valleys he still appears an interloper, greeted with indifference and occasionally with hostility. At Bosco Gurin, an odd pocket of German-speaking peasants, the villagers chased with scythes a girl who offended their conservative susceptibilities by appearing in shorts.

33 *Above Lake Maggiore, near Ascona and Brissago, Ticino*

Yet these are not the things which ordinarily impress most of those who visit the Ticino. It stands for the majority of travellers for its lakeside towns, Lugano and Locarno in particular, and the smaller resorts which cluster around the Swiss parts of lakes Maggiore and Lugano. These provide a sophisticated holiday setting quite distinct from the hinterland. Lugano has a superb situation, facing the lake, framed between two small mountains, Salvatore and Monte Bré. The old town has winding streets and shaded arcades, a Franciscan church of Santa Maria degli Angioli with a wonderful fresco of the Crucifixion by Bernardino Luini and an early sixteenth-century cathedral dedicated to St. Lorenzo. In the main, however, Lugano is a holiday resort with a considerable German population, especially in the pleasant suburb of Castagnola. In the hot summer months when Lugano is best left to its visiting population, it caters for a more proletarian set of visitors from Great Britain. More even than Interlaken, Montreux and Lucerne, it appears then to become irretrievably Anglicised, and its inner charm is hard to discover amidst a welter of huge hotels and tea-shops. Lugano is also a resort much visited by the poorer Swiss, especially on their honeymoons. In spring and autumn it is, however, a very pleasant centre for excursions to the picturesque villages of the interior and the lake. Among the latter Gandria, with its fishing boats and its flowering pink and white oleanders and steep, narrow streets, and Morcote with a noble church tower, are particularly worth a visit, though they have not entirely escaped the mortal touch of touristic prosperity. There are also mountain excursions within easy reach of Lugano. The slopes of Monte Generoso are brilliant with Alpine flowers in spring and early summer. The summit, 5,581 feet, reached by rack-and-pinion railway from Capolago, provides a wonderful vista over the greater Alps, the peaks of the Ticino rising to the north with the Bernese Alps behind them, Monte Disgrazia to the north-east with the Bergamesque peaks further south. Monte Boglia, reached from the little village of Bré, near Lugano, Monte Tamaro, Monte Camoghe, the Denti della Vecchia and Monte Lema are other excursions from Lugano recommended by Hubert Walker in his *Walking in the Alps*, though I cannot speak with personal knowledge about them.

Locarno, at the head of lake Maggiore and perhaps best-known as the scene of the abortive peace conference of 1925, has initially less charm than Lugano, from which it is separated by the pleasing, wooded Monte Ceneri Pass; just as lake Maggiore may seem less attractive and less diversified than the lake of Lugano. Locarno has the appearance of a modern town, but the remains of an ancient castle and the beautiful church of Madonna del Sasso with its Franciscan monastery, founded in 1480 and built on a precipitous rock high above the town, suggest its earlier history. Yet if the town, apart from some pleasing arcades, appears somewhat characterless, it has

167

Camedo in the Centovalli, Ticino
Bignasco in the Val Maggia, Ticino

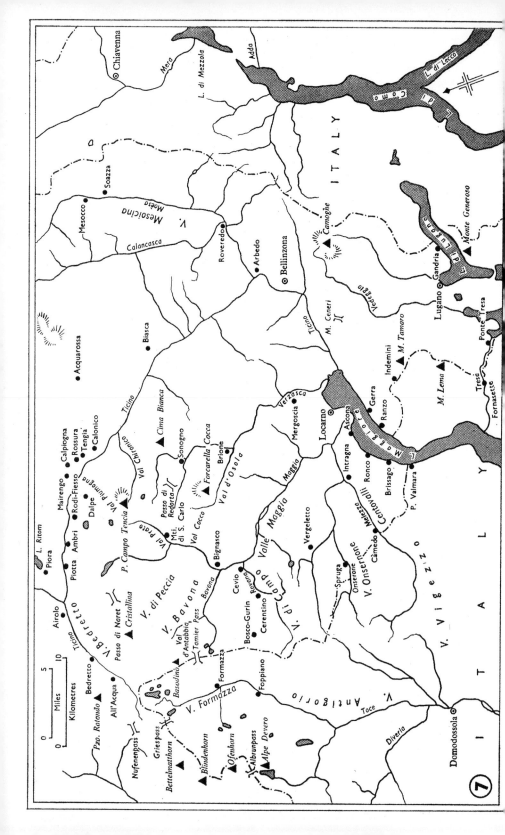

also a greater degree of provincial life than Lugano. It rarely appears dominated by its tourists, nor does it to any lavish extent seek to attract them. Locarno, less visited by the British, seems especially congenial to the Germans; I remember that President Adenauer had temporarily deserted the lake of Como to stay at the Park Hotel when I was in Locarno a few years ago.

Locarno's near-by neighbour, Ascona, has a more compelling charm. It has a leafy promenade bordering a small bay busy with sailing craft, and interesting old streets with some fine houses (and in Monte Verità an unusual hotel furnished with genuine works of art). The last Swiss village on the northern shore, Brissago, has much to commend it. The southern shore of the lake is the more attractive, made so by the poor surface of the road between Magadino and the Italian frontier. Its little villages, Magadino, Ranzo and Gerra, only visited infrequently, have that pleasing contrast of sun and shade which comes from high houses and narrow streets. The women scrub their laundry by the lakeside. Flowers embroider the fountain's edge in the little village square while a cat placidly washes itself in the open doorway through which come the strains of an ancient wireless. Here there is a timeless air.

Behind these villages on both the northern and southern shores soar steep wooded mountains up which narrow roads climb and twist to white-walled hamlets. On the southern shore there is a road from Vira up the slopes of Monte Tamaro to Indemini where Switzerland changes suddenly into Italy. While many of the Swiss villages are more prosperous than the Italian, they enjoy an air of picturesque dilapidation, perhaps nowhere more noticeable than at Arcegno, some two miles from Ascona, where granite cottages sleep peacefully in a narrow mountain rift. A road goes from Arcegno with wonderful prospect over the lake and the isles of Brissago and of shapely Monte Tamaro on the opposite shore, to the high village of Ronco.

A number of beautiful valleys have their starting point near the town of Locarno. The wide, stony delta of the Maggia, a mere stream trickling among white rocks in a dry summer, is near the opening of the Val Maggia, and of the district which because of the many streams which feed the torrent Melezza, a tributary of the Maggia, is known as the Centovalli or Hundred Valleys. The Val Maggia is broad and level, served by a little blue electric tram from Locarno, as far as Bignasco. Steep mountains surround it on every side. Grapes hang over trellises. The little white cottages sleep peacefully in the hot sun. Only the occasional lorries from the quarry at Rivio disturb its calm. At Cevio a high road ascends the Valle di Campo to Cimalmotto, the starting point of many mountain passes. At Cerentino, a village four miles from Cevio at the mouth of the Valle di Bosco, a track winds in a series of narrow zig-zags to the German-speaking village of Bosco Gurin.

The scenery of the Val Maggia grows grander after Cevio. 'The landscape,' Douglas Freshfield wrote in his book on the *Italian Alps*, 'takes a more romantic character. The valley-walls close in and bend, and huge knobs of ruddy-grey rock thrust themselves forward. The river, confined to a narrow bed, alternately lies still in pools, whose depth of blue no comparison can express, or rushes off over the white boulders in a clear sparkling dance. Chestnut-trees hang from the crags overhead; higher on the hills every hedge is a stripe of verdure fringed with the delicate shapes of the birch and larch.' Bignasco is beautifully situated where the Val Bavona and the Val Lavizzara converge to form the Val Maggia. The white steeple of its church stands silhouetted against the grey precipices and snow caps of Mount Basodino and the heights of Campo Tencia. Works concerned with the construction of a dam momentarily marred the scenery but the waters of the Maggia are again limpid. Bignasco, where the Hotel Post is an admirable small hotel, is a starting point for innumerable excursions into the remote mountains. 'As we draw near the first scattered houses of Bignasco,' Douglas Freshfield wrote, 'the mountains suddenly break open, and reveal a vision of the most exquisite and harmonious beauty, one of those masterpieces of nature which defy the efforts of the subtlest word-painters. . . . The waters at our feet are transparent depths of a colour, half sapphire and half emerald. . . . In the foreground on the bank of the stream are frescoed walls and mossy house-roofs, beyond a summerhouse supported by pillars, and a heavily-laden peach orchard lit with a blaze of sunflowers. At the gate of the Val Bavona a white village (Cavergno) glistens from amidst its vineyards. Sheer above it two bold granite walls rise out of the verdure, and form the entrance to a long avenue of great mountain slopes. Behind these foremost masses the hills fall valleywards in noble and perfectly harmonious lines. Each upper cliff flows down into a slope of chestnut-muffled boulders in a curve, the classical beauty of which is repeated by the vine-tendrils at its feet. In the distance the snows of the Basodino seen through the sunny haze gleam, like a golden halo, on the far-off head of the mountain.'

The Val Bavona opens to the left of the village. It is a deep and narrow valley up which a track wanders through chestnut woods between the mountains to the little village of San Carlo at its head. San Carlo is at the opening of the severe Val Antabbia, giving the most rapid approach to the highest of the surrounding mountains, the 10,750-foot Basodino, from the summit of which a panorama of the Bernese and Ticinese peaks opens in magnificent fashion. 'The ascent,' Freshfield wrote, 'is simple and not at all tedious; a steep path up a moist flower-sprinkled cliff, rolling alps commanding views of the red mountains of the Gries, then steep banks of frozen snow and a short exciting scramble up the highest rocks.' Several high passes lead from the Val Bavona into other Alpine valleys, more especially the Val

36 *View of the Lake of Lugano from Monte Generoso, Ticin*

Formazza, and to the Tosa Falls; the Tamier Pass, the Passo d'Antabbia between the Basodino and the Tamierhorn involving a relatively easy crossing of the Antabbia Glacier, the Halbihoren Pass and the Forcla di Cristallina over the ridge to the Val Bedretto. Yet when I think of the Val Bavona it is of the little stone villages situated amidst tangled vines and walnut-trees rather than of the jagged heights and, such is the way that memory works, of the time when I tried to replenish a lighted spirit stove and the mild explosion that followed scattered burning methylated around to the detriment of the new and expensive nylon shirt of a dozing friend. He was a scientist and his indignation was combined with astonishment that anyone could be so foolish as not to foresee the inevitable result of so imprudent an action.

The Val Lavizzara opens steeply to the right of Bignasco, and from it many minor valleys diverge, the Val Cocco, the Val Peccia, the Val Prato and the Val Sambuco. The Val Cocco provides an interesting ascent to the Forcarella Cocca, the 7,000-foot pass dividing the Val Cocco from the dreary Val d'Ossola. The Val Prato provides access to the Pizzo Campo Tencia, the 'three-domed snow-crest which dominates the eastern range,' and to the Monte di San Carlo which Mr. Walker has described as 'one of the loveliest alps I know.' 'The alp occupies an angle between two tremendous waterfalls and from its green lawns whichever way you look you see glittering cascades backed by forests of chestnuts and ringed round by graceful peaks.' The way up the Val di Prato takes the walker through a gorge, up a steep stairway to a plateau closed by the Pizzo Campo Tencia, 10,089 feet high with magnificent views and the most exhilarating of walks along the ridge of peaks.

The village of Fusio lies at the head of the Val Lavizzara. The two valleys which branch to the right before it is reached are also gateways to mountain walks. From the Passo di Naret at the head of the Val Peccia a track leads to Ossaco in the Val Bedretto. The Val Sambuco also leads to the Passo di Naret and gives the opportunity to climb Mount Cristallina. The near-by Lago di Naret is beautiful and isolated. When J. V. Widmann visited Fusio in 1892 he found that the innkeeper purposely had no signs or inscriptions so, he told his guest, that 'you need not expect to have any demands met other than those that I choose to grant.' Nearly thirty years earlier, Douglas Freshfield with his two companions, arrived unexpectedly there. The innkeeper and his wife were without resources; but they knew that the parish priest was to have a fowl for his dinner that day. 'The good dame hurried off to the parsonage, and like David robbed the priest.' Fusio is still remote from tourism, but the postal bus from Bignasco has its terminus there, and it is no longer out of touch with the outside world.

The principal valley, parallel to the Val Maggia to the east, is the Val Verzasca which opens near the village of Gordola, three miles from Locarno.

37 *The road to Palagnedra in the Centovalli, Ticino*

It is joined with the Val Maggia by mountain passes, for the Alpine geography of the Ticinese Alps is bewilderingly complex and labyrinthine. In its early stages the valley is a deep and narrow gorge down which the brawling Verzasca torrent tumbles. Brione, the principal village, is at the opening of the wild Val d'Ossola, with a connecting pass to the Val Maggia. A way from the last village in the valley, Sonogno, leads westwards over the Passo di Redorta to the Val Pertusio and Prato, whence commented Freshfield, 'the eye ranges over the wilderness of its mountain-ridges, a savage expanse of ruined gneiss naked of snow and void of prominent peaks or bristling ridges.' Another route skirts the Bocchetta di Cima Bianca, descends past a little lakelet and proceeds through the Val Chironico to Giornico in the Val Leventina.

The Val Maggia debouches from the Centovalli at Ponte Brolla. The road and the fascinating tram-train go up the valley to the Swiss–Italian frontier at Camedo and eventually to Domodossola where they join the route from the Simplon. There are some interesting villages, among them Intragna where the family of the French statesman, Gambetta originated, and, on the Swiss side, two typically picturesque valleys, the Valle Onsernone down which the Isorno flows, and up which a narrow road twists to the villages of Russo and Spruga; and the Valle Vergeletto leading to the little village of that name located amidst wooded hills of every shade of green.

The Val Leventina which stretches from Airolo at the foot of the St. Gotthard Pass to Bellinzona and the Monte Ceneri Pass, which divides the canton into two distinct parts carries the main road and railway. The nine-mile railway tunnel from Göschenen emerges at Airolo, and the road over the pass, having swept down 48 magnificent hairpin bends, reaches the floor of the Val Leventina in the green basin in which Airolo is situated.

Above Airolo to the left of the St. Gotthard road as it comes down the mountainside the bleak Val Bedretto, down which the river Ticino flows from its source, has its opening. There are here a number of poorish villages inhabited by peasants, some of whom are French speaking, nomadic in character. The valley is subject to regular and tragic visitations by avalanches, and the village church of Bedretto is protected by a specially-constructed buttress. Passes lead from the Val Bedretto into the Rhone valley and other parts of the Ticino. From the hamlet of All'Acqua a steepish path leads through rhododendrons and larch woods towards the stony alps and the little chapel of San Giacomo, 7,370 feet, two hundred feet below the summit of the San Giacomo Pass, the frontier of Italy and Switzerland, from which there are excellent views of the snow peaks of the Oberland and neighbouring mountains; the path descends eventually to the Tosa Falls and the Val Formazza. A track from the Rhone valley crosses the Gries Pass, 8,070 feet, between the Bettelmatthorn and the Grieshorn, which also marks the Swiss–

Italian frontier, and joins the Val Bedretto at the chalets of Gruina, at the foot of the Val Corno. The path at the head of the valley mounts stonily to the grassy ridge of the Nufenen Pass, where the snow lies late, between the Pizzo Gallino and the Nufenenstock. There is a fine retrospect of the white peaks around the Aletsch Glacier. The Nufenen Pass marks the boundary of the cantons of Valais and Ticino.

The St. Gotthard road and railway move downwards in the valley of the river Ticino, pushing its way over huge boulders and between deep ravines. The problem confronting Favre in building the railway was how to lower the line in the fifteen miles between Rodi-Fiesso and Giornico. He solved it as he had done in the Reuss valley by spiral tunnels. These enabled him to take the trains down some 2,785 feet in the 28½ miles between Airolo and Biasca without difficulty.

From Ambri-Piotta near Airolo where there is the huge electric power-station of the Swiss Federal Railways, the steepest funicular in Switzerland ascends to the Sanatorio del San Gottardo and thence to the picturesque village of Piora at the end of the little lake Ritom, well stocked with fine trout. 'A fine breezing open upland valley of singular beauty,' so Samuel Butler described it, 'and with a sweet atmosphere of cow about it; it is rich in rhododendrons, and all manner of Alpine flowers, just a trifle bleak, but as bracing as the Engadine itself. The first night I was ever in Piora there was a brilliant moon, and the unruffled surfaces of the lake took the reflection of the mountains. I could see the cattle a mile off, and hear the tinkling of their bells which danced multitudinously before the ear as fire flies come and go before the eyes; for all through a fine summer's night the cattle will feed as though it were day. A little above the lake I came upon a man in a cave before a furnace, burning lime, and he sat looking into the fire with his back to the moonlight. He was a quiet, moody man, and I am afraid I bored him. So after a while I left him with his face burnished as with gold from the fire, and his back silver with the moonbeams; behind him were the pastures and the reflections in the lake and the mountains; and the distant cowbells were ringing.'

The Val Leventina road below, which carries an immense amount of traffic, is itself impressive but less interesting. It is sometimes wreathed in a thin layer of haze, especially in its lower reaches where a cement works funnels its smoke into the atmosphere. Faido, 13 miles below Airolo, is a pleasant little town with some good sixteenth-century houses. The great granite mountains, stretching 5,000 to 6,000 feet above the valley, are indented with deep ravines, and small villages reached by narrow dusty roads, looking from below like the headquarters of brigands, are lodged precariously on their slopes. Samuel Butler, who was much attached to this region, has described his wanderings among them in his *Alps and Sanctuaries*, of how he went to Mairengo where there is the oldest church in the valley with two high altars side by side (whether this is still so, I do not know), to Dalpe on the southern side of the valley, overshadowed by pines, cliffs and the Dalpe glacier and Calpioguia. Above Dalpe a path goes to the untamed valley of the Piumogna, reached also by a road from Rodi Fiesso, which leads to the glacier whence the river comes. Another track leads to Campolungo and Fusio. Of Rossura on the northern slopes he noted, 'I know few things more touching in their way than the porch of Rossura Church; it is dated early in the last century (viz. the eighteenth), and is absolutely without ornament; the flight of steps inside it lead to the level of the floor of the church. One lovely summer Sunday morning, passing the church betimes, I saw people kneeling upon these steps, the church within being crammed. In the darker light of the porch, they told out against the sky that showed through the open arch beyond them; far away the eye rested on the mountain—deep blue, save where the snow still lingered. I never saw anything more beautiful. . . .' At Calonico near the graceful Gribbiasca waterfall the church had been built on the edge of the cliff. 'The curate of Calonico was very kind to me. We had long talks together. I could see it pained him that I was not a Catholic. He could never quite get over this, but he was very good and tolerant. He was anxious to be assured that I was not one of those English who went about distributing tracts, and trying to convert people. . . .' Even in the mid twentieth century few tourists leave their cars or trains to burrow in these forbidding regions.

At Biasca, which has a much-restored Romanesque church, the St. Gotthard road is joined by the traffic which comes down the Val Blenio from the Lukmanier Pass and the Vorder Rhein. The lower stretches of the valley are still marred by the debris of the great landslide of 1512 which destroyed many villages hereabout. Later the Val Blenio combines the attractiveness of the high Alps with the luxuriance of Italian vegetation. Acquarossa, as its name implies, is a small spa, visited for its lithium ferrous springs and its 'red fango' mud baths. Olivone, the last village of any size, is picturesquely situated beneath the granite bulk of Mount Sosto.

The road from Thusis and the Hinter Rhein, which comes over the San Bernardino Pass, enters the Val Leventina shortly before Bellinzona. The Val Mesocco through which it winds its way, besides the Moësa river, is not spectacular but is very attractive. Mesocco itself, the terminus of the little railway from Bellinzona, is dominated by the finely situated remains of the castle of Misox, the home of the counts of Misox until they sold it to the Trivulzi of Milan in 1483, which was destroyed by the Grey Confederates in 1526. The near-by church of Santa Maria di Castella has some fifteenth-century wall paintings. Water cascades down the mountains; the Buffaflora

38   *Soglio in the Val Bregaglia, looking towards the Val Bondasca and the Sciora peaks*

near Soazza is a particularly fine fall. Walnut-trees, chestnuts and figs grow abundantly. It was at Roveredo, the chief town of the district, that agents of Carlo Borremeo, whose gentle piety earned him eventual sanctification, brought to the stake the Prior and eleven old women in 1583 on charges of witchcraft.

Roveredo is seven miles from Bellinzona. Shortly the St. Gotthard road goes over the Monte Ceneri Pass in the direction of Lugano and the plains of Lombardy. The traveller who wishes to remain in Switzerland may well prefer to follow the road along the lake of Lugano, past the Italian frontier near Gandria, touching the lake of Como at Menaggio, and then turning north towards Chiavenna and the Italo–Swiss frontier at Castesegna in the Val Bregaglia. This furnishes a lovely opening to the Maloja Pass and the Engadine, with an abrupt and striking return to Alpine scenery.

It is perhaps difficult to say what constitutes the charm of the Ticino. Mainly, I think, it is the contrasts it provides. The mountains are stark granite, reflecting each change of light, glowing violet, grey, green, rose; but the vegetation of the valley is profuse. Almonds, figs, peaches, pomegranates, vines, medlars and mulberries grow without difficulty. In the spring and summer the gardens are full of colour, of oleanders, azaleas, camellias and magnolias. The leaves of the trees are of every shade of green while the grass may be burnished brown or vivid emerald. The rivers are clear and limpid rather than glacial. Chapels, often crowded with faded frescoes, crucifixes and shrines stand by the dusty, white roads. The countryside is both wild and ornamented. 'As the sun neared the horizon,' the Ticinese, Lavizzari, wrote of the shades of evening near Gandria on the lake of Lugano, 'it painted a scene of incomparable beauty, sweetly moving. Lit with purple and gold, the clouds formed a radiant crown for the sinking orb. The outlines of the lake and hillsides were gilded, and the mountain tops, soon to be shrouded in the black veil of night, were aflame. The pyramid of the Salvatore rose solitarily above the glittering mirror of the lake, flinging far its long shadows, as if to bring the matchless day to a solemn ceremonial close.' Emil Egli, from whose book on *Swiss Life and Landscape* I have taken Lavizzari's quotation, summed up the scenery of the Ticino by saying that it 'has the sharp clarity of a wood engraving.'

39 *Soglio in the Val Bregaglia*

8

THE ENGADINE

THE ENGADINE, the valley of the Inn or En, reached from the Ticino by way of the Val Bregaglia and the Maloja Pass or by the San Bernardino and Splugen passes, is rich in scenery and interest. The valley down which the infant river runs limpid and clear as a Hampshire trout stream is a mile broad with high mountains, averaging 9,000 to 10,000 feet on either side, though they seem less high than they actually are because the valley is itself more than 5,000 feet above sea level. The summits of the mountains are flecked with snow, even in summer. Up the lateral valleys, especially that in which Pontresina lies, there are glimpses of glaciers and white peaks. Because of the height and the atmosphere the colouring is peculiarly vivid. The little chain of lakes through which the Inn flows from its source in the Piz Lunghin towards St. Moritz are brilliant blue-green, and set within a frame of pine and larch and grassy slopes. In winter everything sparkles with frost and light; even the squat ugliness of the great hotels is at least partially redeemed by the snow. The Engadine's supremacy as a winter resort passes unchallenged, for the cool wind—the *Thalwind* (which, it must be admitted, sometimes blows too freely in other months down the main valley)—keeps the snow crisp and the sun exhilarates.

The small villages have considerable charm; their churches with slim towers and spires, or Italian campaniles and cupolas, albeit Protestant and usually locked, stand amidst stuccoed houses with shingled roofs. There are ancient mansions, some once in the possession of the princely families of the Engadine like the Plantas, which have been fortunate to escape the ravages of the fires which have destroyed so many an Engadine village. The houses are often decorated with graffiti and enriched by vaulted porticoes; the windows are often protected by finely-designed wrought-iron railings so characteristic of this region. On the walls there may be inscriptions in Romansch, the lettering sometimes of singular beauty. Of the 125,000 people of the canton of Grisons or Graubünden, in which the Engadine is situated, 40,000 still speak Romansch. Most places have two names, Schuls or Scuol, Susch or Süs, Martinsbrück or Martina, but except for Samaden (which has become Samedan) and Bevers (which has become Bever), the well-known resorts retain their familiar names, St. Moritz rather than San Murezzan, Pontresina instead of Puntraschigna and Sils rather than Segl. The streets are often narrow and redolent sometimes with hay, sometimes with the pungent scent of goats, but flowers border the running fountains where the cows drink and the women do their washing. Beneath the veneer of tourism, as in all Swiss valleys, the life of the people threads its even way among the vicissitudes of wind and weather, and of the changing seasons.

The Engadine is usually divided into two parts, Upper and Lower, the Upper Engadine, about 25 miles long, extending from the Maloja Pass to the Punt'Ota between Scanfs and Zernez, and the lower, about 37 miles in length, stretching to the Swiss–Austrian frontier at Martina. The Upper Engadine can be entered from the other part of the Grisons by the Julier Pass the road from which debouches at Silvaplana or by rail through, or road over, the Albula Pass which brings the traveller to the chief town of the district, Samedan, a quiet little place with some fine houses, among them one where the hero of the Grisons, Jürg Jenatsch, was born. Yet world-famous as is this region of the Upper Engadine which includes Samedan, Celerina and St. Moritz, I find the scenery dull, even dreary, for its vast caravanserais are an inevitable reminder that this is in winter the world of those who long to find themselves figuring in the *Tatler* as well as the paradise of the winter sports enthusiast. Its quilt of snow may transform St. Moritz, providing the beauty which in summer it certainly lacks, but its architecture is ponderous and its prices probably higher than anywhere else in Switzerland; even the public lavatories seem to be more expensive. It caters essentially for the tourist, and few pastries please the palate more than Hanselmann's. Hot chocolate and whipped cream may indeed help to diminish the ennui that St. Moritz awakens in unsympathetic travellers.

St. Moritz, however, is no Victorian spa, though its hotels make it plain that the latter part of the nineteenth century was its heyday. The Romans knew that its waters had therapeutic properties. The sixteenth-century physician, Paracelsus, himself of Swiss birth, affirmed in 1539 that 'of all the mineral springs in Europe known to me, I give preference to that which I found in the Engadine at St. Moritz, the water of which is in August acid like vinegar. He who takes this water medicinally regains his health, and will never be troubled by stone or gravel, gout or arthritis. It strengthens the stomach so that it can digest tartar even as an ostrich digests iron and a blackbird sand.' Leslie Stephen came there in 1869 and found the presence of royalty and tourists equally disagreeable, but confessed that St. Moritz 'acts like one of those flytraps to be seen in old-fashioned inns, which do not indeed diminish the swarm of intrusive insects, but profess at least to confine them to one spot.' He continued: 'The upper valley of the Inn is one of the very few Alpine districts which may almost be called ugly. The high bleak level tract, with monotonous ranges of pine forests at a uniform slope, has as little of the picturesque as can well be contrived in the mountains.'

Yet within a few miles of St. Moritz in the direction of the Maloja Pass the beauty of the mountains, of the Piz Margna, its dark rocks streaked with snow, and of the little lakes of Campfèr, Silvaplana and Sils, can rarely be surpassed. The rocky slopes here are clothed with the dark green of the pines. The woodland paths are brilliant with flowers in early summer, and burnished with the red berries of the rowan tree in autumn. All this, and much more, can be seen from the top of the Muottas Muragl funicular, 8,060 feet, close both to St. Moritz and Pontresina. The most delightful village in these parts is certainly Sils-Maria, partly because it is a little way off the main road which goes through neighbouring Sils-Baselgia but mainly because of the innumerable opportunities for the lovely walks it affords and its own intrinsic charm, marred but not lost by the Scottish baronial style of the Hotel Waldhaus. 'Of all places that I know,' Walter Larden wrote in 1899, 'Sils–Maria—unless it has changed—is the most perfect spot to make a long stay at, provided that one does not require to be within easy reach of many high climbs. . . . At Sils–Maria you can walk, in delightful air, under fir-trees along the margin of the purest of mountain lakes.' The philosopher, Friedrich Nietzsche, found consolation in his surroundings at Sils for the spiritual poverty of his fellow-men and a stone in his memory stands on the promontory of Chasté by the lake.

The lakes of Sils and Silvaplana, both within easy reach of the village, reflect the light and colour of the Upper Engadine. Even when mist veils the Piz Lunghin and twirling over the waters announces the coming of bad weather, they are not devoid of beauty. A little path through the woods passing the cluster of dark chalets at the hamlet of Isola at the foot of the wild Val Fedoz leads to the Maloja Pass. 'I have just returned from a three days' holiday,' Oscar Browning wrote to his mother on August 4th, 1879. 'I left this Saturday morning at 4.30 with Trench, the son of the Archbishop of Dublin, Mr. Wainwright and his brother-in-law. We went up the Roseg Valley and over the shoulder of the Capuchin to Sils Maria; the descent was very steep, and we had some capital glissades. I was dreadfully tired in the evening. When I had reposed myself I walked with Trench along the Silser Lake to the Maloja Hospice. The evening was perfect, and I do not think I ever saw anything more beautiful.'

The loveliest of the easy walks is undoubtedly that up the Val Fex, which opens between the Piz Corvatsch and the Piz Margna. The footpath crosses the river Laret at Sils and leads by the chalets of Platta to the Hotel Sonne and the little whitewashed church of Crasta, standing in late spring amidst fields of crocus and silhouetted against the surrounding mountain peaks. The track ascends through woods, where I saw the only snake I have ever come across in the Alps, above the rushing stream to the barns of Curtins and the Hotel Fex. The clangour of cow bells, friendly grey beasts only too willing to nuzzle wetly for apples and pears in a coat pocket, shows that the summer pastures have been reached. The remains of an old moraine, the Mott Selvas, provides a view of the lower end of the Fex Glacier. It was near here, sitting in the shelter of a cow shed, that I had a delicious but simple al fresco meal; the light however, was so strong, reflecting the snows of the mountains at the head of the glacier, Il Chapütschin, La Muongla, Piz Glüschaint, Piz Tremoggia, Piz Fora and Piz Gutz, that I much regretted that I had not brought dark glasses. It was odd to find near here a little hut entitled *dogana*, but the Swiss customs house shows that the pass over the Fex Glacier has long been used, sometimes by smugglers from Italy. From the Tremoggia Pass at the top of the glacier there is a wonderful view of the Monte della Disgrazia, 12,068 feet. 'The noble mass,' so Douglas Freshfield described it from Monte Sissone, '. . . rose tier upon tier out of the great glacier which extended to our feet; its rocky ribs protruded sternly out of their shimmering ice-mail, and the cloud banner which was now flung out from the crowning ridge augured no good to its assailants.' The path leads down to Chiesa in the Italian Val Malenco but if he wishes the energetic walker can turn south by Chiareggio and walk over the Muretto Pass along the Val Muretto to Maloja.

Maloja, the little hamlet above the pass of that name which leads down in a series of well-engineered curves which seem, for some reason, steeper than they are, to the Val Bregaglia, a few miles from Sils-Maria by a road which skirts the lake of Sils, is itself a fine excursion centre, but it has an air of fallen greatness. This is partly the result of a curious whim on the part of a rich Belgian, Baron Renesse, who began building but left incomplete a mock medieval castle overlooking the valley far below. It is also evoked by a vast edifice, the Palace Hotel, which has stood mournfully empty since the economic crisis of 1931. There is, I need hardly add, a little English church near the hotel, also closed. For Maloja was a happy hunting ground of the socially distinguished and the mountaineering dons of Victorian England. The shuttered rooms and grass-strewn terraces seem inhabited by their ghosts; when Sir Richard Burton was there in 1890 he and his wife were pleased to find among their fellow-guests Dean Carington, Dr. Welldon, Sir John and Lady Hawkins, the Duchess of Leinster and Lady Maud Fitzgerald, Lord Elcho, Lord Dunraven and Mr. and Mrs. Bancroft as well as the inimitable if sycophantic Oscar Browning who had become self-appointed 'boss' of the hotel. Thomas Huxley, commemorated by a stone beside the lake, was another of its devotees; 'I have,' he wrote, 'nothing but praise for this place—the air is splendid, excellent walks for invalids, capital drainage. . . .' The Duchess of Teck stayed here and was pleased to let Dr. Huxley take her arm; later she stayed at St. Moritz and visited Maloja when recuperating from the Golden Jubilee of 1897. Four years previously she had accompanied

Dr. Welldon to see the glacier-mills which had been recently excavated, and which were named in her honour the 'Princess Mary Adelaide mills.' These mills, great concavities ground out of the rock in strangely regular fashion by boulders harder than themselves, swirled by the floods of long ago, situated on the belvedere at the ridge of the pass, are worth visiting, not for themselves as much as because they link the historic present with the Ice Age, nearly half a million years ago. The Engadine was then covered by an enormous glacier which swept down into the Val Bregaglia as far as and beyond the lake of Como. When this great stream of ice melted, water poured over the crest of the modern pass towards the valley below, so starting the process which brought into the being the glacier-mills.

It is, however, easy to escape from Maloja's past. Even in 1886, John Addington Symonds, somewhat put out of his stride by meeting no less than 17 acquaintances at Maloja, 'broke away from these for a seven hours' walk up the sublime Murettothal and on the Forno Glacier.' Symonds' choice was a wise one, for the valley passes the attractive Lago di Cavloccio en route for the Muretto Pass, leading to Chiesa in Italy, and the Forno Glacier, surrounded by a glorious group of mountain peaks, the Cima di Castello, the Monte Sissone and the Cima di Rosso. The Piz Lunghin, 9,120 feet on the western side of Maloja, the mountain where the Inn has its source (and in the near vicinity of which the Mera and the Rhine also rise), provides splendid views. The path past the dark little Lej dal Lunghin (from which the Inn flows) goes to the summit of the Septimer Pass, 7,582 feet, once much-frequented by travellers, which descends to Bivio in the Julier Pass road or to the Aversertal.

The famous painter of the Engadine mountains, Giovanni Segantini, who died of pneumonia in a little hut on the Schaffberg overlooking the Inn valley in 1899 was buried in the cemetery at Maloja. Few artists have ever successfully been able to depict mountains or mountain scenery, but Segantini had realised that light was as significant as colour. 'I studied the men, the animals, the country and the earth,' he wrote, 'in the innermost valleys of the Grisons, and settled in Savognin where I stayed for eight years. Many a summer have I spent in the high valleys, and winters in the chalets of those Alps. There it was that I turned my eyes particularly to the sun, by whose rays I lived, and which I wished to master. It was there that I studied nature in its most living form and brightest colours.' No one has ever painted the mountain peaks of the Upper Engadine and Val Bregaglia better. There is a Segantini Museum at St. Moritz, where many of his pictures are housed.

The Maloja is not a pass in the accepted sense of the word, for on its northern side, the high valley of the Inn runs without much appreciable difference in height for many miles, but the southern side is a steep mountain slope which leads to the sub-Alpine valley along which the river Mera

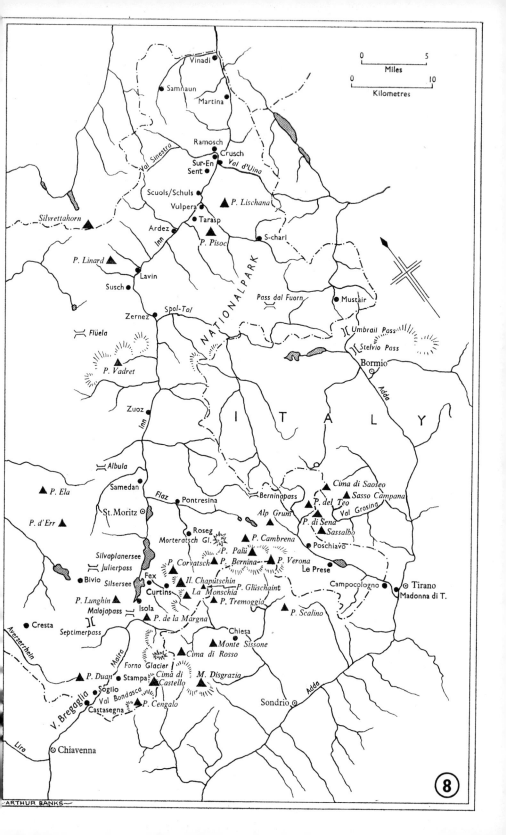

Vinadi
Samnaun
Martina
Ramosch
Crusch
Sur-En
Sent
Val d'Uina
Val Sinestra
Scuols/Schuls
Vulpera
▲ P. Lischana
Ardez
Tarasp
S-charl
Inn
P. Pisoc
Silvrettahorn ▲
P. Linard ▲
Lavin
Susch
Zernez
Spol-Tal
Pass dal Fuorn
Mustair
N A T I O N A L P A R K
⊃⊂ *Flüela*
Umbrail Pass
Stelvio Pass
▲ P. Vadret
Bormio
⊙
Adda
Zuoz
Inn
I T A L Y
⊃⊂ *Albula*
Samedan
Flaz
Pontresina
Cima di Saoseo
P. del Teo ▲
▲ Sasso Campana
▲ P. Ela
St.Moritz ⊙
⊃⊂ Berninapass
Alp Grüm
P. di Sena
Val Grosina
P. d'Err ▲
Roseg
Morteratsch Gl.
▲ P. Cambrena
Sassalbo
Silvaplanersee
⊃⊂ *Julierpass*
P. Palü ▲
Poschiavo
P Corvatsch ▲
▲ P. Bernina
▲ P. Verona
Bivio
Silsersee
Fex
Le Prese
P. Lunghin ▲
Curtins
Il. Chapütschin
P. Glüschaint
Campocologno
⊙ Tirano
Malojapass
Isola
La Monschia
Madonna di T.
⊃⊂
P. de la Margna ▲
▲ P. Tremoggia
Cresta
Septimerpass
⊃⊂
Maira
Chiesa
P. Scalino
Aversserrhein
▲ Monte Sissone
Forno Glacier
▲ Cima di Rosso
P. Duan ▲
Stampa
Cima di
Castello
M. Disgrazia
Adda
Soglio
Val Bondasca
Sondrio ⊙
Castasegna
▲ P. Cengalo
Liro
V. Bregaglia
⊙ Chiavenna

0 _____ 5
Miles
0 _____ 10
Kilometres

⑧

ARTHUR BANKS

rushes towards the lake of Como. The watershed is a precipitous, narrow escarpment down which the road curvets. 'So steep is the slope, so thick the wood,' Lord Schuster commented in his *Peaks and Pleasant Pastures*, 'that, whether you look from above or below, a passage seems impossible, and . . . Italy is cut from you by an impassable chasm. Deep down are the white houses of Casaccia, and beyond them still the road winds down through forest into a gorge that ever narrows, hung round with the blue mystery of the South, and lost at last in the shadow of mountains that stand round about the Lombard Plain.'

In the world of the Val Bregaglia, nearly 2,000 feet below, the little white houses nestle amidst chestnut and walnut-trees under a warm sun. The air on the Maloja is colder, the light more brilliant, less golden. The scene changes dramatically. The Val Bregaglia, so different from the Upper Engadine, is yet one of the loveliest valleys in the Swiss Alps. The road descends amidst forests of pine, beech and chestnut, through green meadows and fields of maize towards the Italian frontier and Chiavenna. The Maloja Pass is some 5,955 feet high. The first village in the valley, Casaccia, stands at 4,183 feet. Vicosoprano is 3,501 feet. The frontier village, Castasegna, is 2,283 feet and Chiavenna is 1,083 feet. The mountains on the left-hand side, the Bregaglia Alps, and the high green hills on the right-hand side enclose the valley steeply. The jagged, needle-like peaks, streaked with snow, seem to soar to a staggering height, 'cascading,' as Hubert Walker has phrased it, 'sheer descent of turret on turret of rock.' Their spires, so appropriate a name, composed of tough porphyritic granite, stand stark against the blue sky, haloed by shafts of golden light in early evening.

The villages of the Val Bregaglia have their own beauty. While the style of architecture is reminiscent of Italy, they are free of the poverty and the meanness so often typical of Italian villages only redeemed from sordidness by the brilliance of the sunlight. The streets are narrow and cobbled, with deep gutters at the sides down which cool water splashes. The houses are tightly packed together, bright with coloured wash, their wooden balconies gay with flowers, their windows protected by the lovely curved iron grilles typical of the Engadine. The very names, Casaccia, Vicosoprano, Stampa, Promontogno and Castasegna, are singularly mellifluous. Vicosoprano, the diminutive capital of the district, has a fine town-hall (with a useful torture-chamber) as well as some attractive houses. Although the churches of the valley are Italianate in appearance, the region is Protestant and the interiors are depressingly bare (when one can get in to see them), the frontier at Castasegna constituting a religious as well as a political boundary.

The mountain peaks, sculptured of granite, provide a range of wonderful ascents, more especially for rock-climbers. The 'great mountain-mass glowed in the afternoon sunshine,' Douglas Freshfield wrote in the *Italian*

Alps. 'Its base was wrapped in chestnut woods, its middle girt with a belt of pines, above spread a mantle of the eternal snow. The sky-line was formed by a coronet of domes and massive pinnacles, carved out of grey rocks, whose jagged yet stubborn forms revealed the presence of granite full in front, the curving glacier of Val Bondasca filled the space beneath the smooth cliff faces.' Two ravine-like valleys, the Albigna, opening north-east of Vicosoprano, and the Bondasca, south of Promontogno, give access to the glaciers, peaks and passes of the range the principal ridge of which constitutes the Swiss–Italian frontier. The gorge-like Albigna valley, full of savage beauty, down which a fine waterfall with 'clouds of sunbeam-painted foam' cascades, leads to the Albigna glacier and the Cacciabella Pass.

The Val Bondasca opens shortly after the pleasant village of Promontogno where incidentally Samuel Butler met the lady with sixteen parrots who appeared in his essay, *Ramblings in Cheapside*. 'I met a lady one year . . . who had some parrots that always travelled with her and were the idols of her life. These parrots would not let anyone read aloud in their presence, unless they heard their own names introduced from time to time. "And have you divined," I asked, "to which side they incline in politics?" "They do not like Mr. Gladstone," was the somewhat freezing answer, "this is the only point on which we disagree, for I adore him."' The narrow road passes over a bridge crossing the Mera torrent to the peaceful hamlet of Bondo where there is a finely-proportioned palace belonging to the English branch of the de Salis family, who once ruled the valley and played so important a part in the history of the Grisons. Bondo is free from travellers and a perfect place for a picnic. It is at the opening of the wild Val Bondasca at the head of which stand, like mighty sentinels, the splintered Sciora peaks, the jagged Cengalo and the precipitous cliffs of the Piz Badile, the north-east face of which was not climbed until 1938, with the Bondasca glacier at their base. The walker can cross from the head of the valley towards the Passo di Cacciabella and descend the rocky slopes to the Val Albigna and Vicosoprano. A more arduous climb leads to the opening of the Val Trubinasca and the Alpe de Sassfora, going eventually to the frontier at Passo di Trubinasca. There are two mountain passes from the Bondasca Glacier to Italy, the Passo di Bondo, 10,204 feet, and the Passo del Ferro, 10,509 feet, leading down to the Italian Val Masino.

The Bondasca spires, the valley beneath them, and the great forested hills which stand guard in front of them are best seen from the village of Soglio, reached by a narrow, twisting road from Promontogno, and lodged on a terrace of the high green hills the other side of the Val Bregaglia. Soglio is an entrancing place, more especially after the tourists have taken their cars away and the only foreigners left are those staying at the Hotel Willy. The hotel is one of five palaces originally in the possession of the de Salis family,

The Morteratsch Glacier, near Pontresina, Upper Engadine

which had its headquarters here from the fourteenth century, though the chief palace was fired by the Spaniards during one of the more complex campaigns of the Thirty Years War. The hotel Willy, built in the seventeenth century, still houses many interesting pieces of furniture and amply repays a visit, if only for a slice of the walnut cake made here; but it is better to stay a few days to sample the cooking supervised by Madame Christine Willy. It is then possible to feel the atmosphere of the real Soglio which seems so little changed from the sixteenth century and to understand why Segantini, who loved to paint here, played on its name and called it 'La Soglia del Paradiso,' the threshold of Paradise, or why the poet Rilke found peace here after the turbulence of war-weary Germany. 'I was curious,' he wrote before he eventually settled near Sierre, 'to see if Switzerland will be able to arrange once more for the kind of conditions in Soglio; everything there was like a promise of future events, like the pattern of material which will provide me later with a white dress, a cloak and hood of invisibility.'

Soglio is situated on a shelf amidst fields. A track goes past the Caroggia fall through glades of chestnut-trees to Castasegna, and another rocky path goes down to the village of Stampa. Mountain walkers may attempt the passage of the Duana Pass, or even the fine view-point of the Piz Duan, 10,279 feet, which lies north-west of the village; a good pass goes over the Forcella di Prassignola to the Madriserthal and the high village of Avers-Cresta. Yet I think it is better to sit simply, as do the village elders, on the stone seats outside the ancient palaces and absorb the miraculous changes of light and shade as the sun strikes the splintered pinnacles of the Bondasca spires. The luminous light of evening is nowhere more beautiful than in Soglio. Indeed when Johann Scheuchzer visited Soglio in 1703, he found that the villagers used the peaks of the range of mountains to the south as a sort of natural sundial, to gauge the position of the sun and to discover the time of day. For this reason the peaks bore such names as Piz della Nuove, Piz delle Dieci and so on. Soon after dawn the alpenhorn summons the goats of Soglio to their pastures in the mountains. Within minutes they emerge in the public square from the different alley-ways. They return as the sun sets, receiving a warm welcome from the villagers, as they pause to take a drink at the local fountain before they separate to their various homes. Outside the Hotel Willy one of the maids sweeps away with sedulous broom any droppings that may have fallen. No scene, simple yet moving, has left so indelible an impression on my memory, not even a magnificent display of lightning on the distant peaks the other side of the valley. I have indeed so far refrained from returning to Soglio for fear that the spell it has once cast may disappear at the touch of a second visit.

The peasants of the Val Bregaglia, and of Soglio, appear aloof and sometimes unfriendly; and their interests do not coincide with those of the

190

42 *Tarasp and its castle, Lower Engadine*

tourist. The old peasant woman with her wicker basket on her back, full of hay, potatoes, or chestnuts; the farmer driving his oxen cart; live in a milieu wide apart from those of the summer visitors. The manageress of the tea-shop at Sils-Maria, hearing that I was to visit Soglio, stressed the independence of the people who lived there—they spoke only Ladin, a dialect of Romansch —and were wholly un-Swiss. 'Our soldiers', she said, 'when they go there on manœuvres hardly feel they are on Swiss territory.' Fundamentally their attitude is one of detachment rather than hostility. Soglio has a transcendent beauty. Its great and exciting days have long passed into history, together with the story of the de Salis family; but it is a community rooted in the centuries and privileged to look out upon one of the most resplendent views in all the world.

The Val Bregaglia has taken us out of the Engadine, and without crossing the frontier into Italy at Castasegna, we must move back, up the Maloja Pass, skirting the little lakes, through St. Moritz to Samedan and thence turn south-east towards the most attractive of the larger resorts of the Upper Engadine, Pontresina. Except for its lake Pontresina has nearly all the features of St. Moritz, luxury shops, attractive cafés, good hotels and even a bandstand in the Tais woods as well as mountain excursions of unsurpassed grandeur; but it seems also to possess a life more intimately associated with the countryside around it. It is still essentially a country town elevated by tourism into a popular resort. Since the middle of the nineteenth century it has indeed attracted a stream of visitors. A traveller in 1856 commented on the difficulty of obtaining accommodation and the activity shown in building new hotels. In 1878 Mrs. Squire Bancroft 'repeated her reading of the death of Jo from *Bleak House*; the result was very gratifying, and allows her to think in many a walk . . . how much she helped to make them.' The inevitable English church was consecrated by the Bishops of Gloucester and Bedford in 1882; the Bancrofts gave the bell and a stained-glass window. 'Between two and three hundred people join at table d'hôte in the middle of the season at each of these hotels [Kronenhof and Roseg] and half at least are English,' a visitor commented the same year.

Pontresina's popularity is hardly surprising. The monotony characteristic of the landscape of the Upper Engadine in the vicinity of St. Moritz has been replaced by infinite variety. From Pontresina the mountains of the Inn valley catch the light of the sun, appearing mauve, grey, blue, rose, while to the south the great ice peaks of the Bernina range dominate the scene. When E. S. Kennedy made the first ascent of the Piz Bernina in 1861 the President of the Ober-Engadin presented him with a bouquet and the band from Pontresina played 'God save the Queen.' The village situated above the Flaz and Bernina torrents faces the charming Tais woods and the Roseg valley. The path leads through the forest towards the hotel Roseggletscher at its

Alp Grüm; the Palü Glacier
In the Upper Engadine

head, standing amidst green meadows surrounded by great mountains, Rosatch, Chalchagn, Misaun, Tschierva, Roseg, Sella, Glüschaint, Chapütschin, Corvatsch, Surlej. 'This is what I wanted to see once more in my life,' wrote Wilhelm Röntgen, the discoverer of X-rays. 'This roaring stream is for me the symbol of potential power. . . . This morning we walked for quite a distance through the forest and along the roaring glacier water in the really very beautiful Rosegg valley.' Above the hotel a path leads up the east side of the valley to the lower end of the Tschierva glacier. After crossing this there is an ascent to the green alp of the Aguagliouls, 9,078 feet, situated on a promontory between the two glaciers. The view from the near-by Piz Aguagliouls, 10,256 feet, of the great peaks and glaciers of the Bernina Alps is exceptionally fine. North of the hotel a stony path winds steeply up the Fuorcla Surlej, 9,042 feet, another marvellous point of view, which goes over to the main Engadine Valley. The mountaineer may use the inn at the top of the pass to ascend the Piz Surlej, 10,472 feet, and the Piz Corvatsch, 11,346 feet, both comparatively easy mountains to climb. A walk through the forest goes from Pontresina to the Morteratsch glacier where the ice is encircled, as it appears from the road, in a frame of Arolla pines and snow peaks.

The road which passes the Morteratsch leads out of the Engadine to another beautiful enclave of the Swiss Alps. It needs only some 1,700 feet to reach the summit of the pass, but the scenery, embracing the frozen river of the Morteratsch, and the glittering ice of Piz Palü is of the finest order. 'This outstandingly beautiful mountain,' Mr. Walker has written in his notable guide to mountain walks, *Walking in the Alps*, 'gave me a day of perfect pleasure and 15 hours of continuous walking. We started from the Diavolezza shortly after 2 a.m., were on the first peak of Piz Palü just after sunrise, and continued to walk along its ridge from peak to peak bathed in golden sunshine. Meanwhile great galleons of cloud rose up like curtains from the valleys far below and filled them up until we were walking on glittering islands in a gentle billowing sea. We reached the Fuorcla Bellavista, descended to the Loch under the Fortezza rocks, crossed the Morteratsch glacier and came to the Boval hut. . . . We walked on down to Pontresina and reached it hot, tired and exceedingly happy.' At Bernina Hauser, 6,720 feet, a path to the left goes up the Val de Foin, a haunt of marmots who seem exceptionally tame here and of Alpine flowers, while to the right a track (and a cable railway) bends towards the wonderful belvedere of the Diavolezza hut, 9,700 feet. The summit of the Bernina Pass is 7,649 feet and somewhat bare and desolate. Beyond its three small lakes there may be glimpsed the Cambrena Glacier and the snow-capped Cambrena and Piz Canale. A railway, built between 1906 and 1910, ascends the Bernina Pass and because of its few tunnels provides even better views than the road. Except for a small section of the Jungfrau railway, it is the highest adhesion railway in the Alps. At the station of Alp Grüm, the glistening ice of the Palü glacier appears on the right while far below the valley of Poschiavo and its little lake glitter in the sunlight.

The Val Poschiavo, Italian in architecture, vegetation and appearance, has been in fact a part of the Grisons since 1486. Indeed it was once a centre of Protestant culture; the two earliest books printed in Ladin were published in Poschiavo in 1522 and 1560. For over half a century, from 1549 to 1615, its Landolfi press turned out Protestant literature. The Protestant church was built between 1642 and 1649. But here, unlike the Val Bregaglia, Catholicism has regained its sway. Poschiavo is a pleasant little town, full of interesting old houses and the ancient abbey of San Vittore. Remote from tourism, the mountains which gird the valley present an immense variety of high walks, along the ridges, the Pizzo del Teo, the Pizzo di Sena and the Pizzo Sassalbo, all over 10,000 feet, to the east, or from the Pizzo di Verona to the Pizzo Scalino to the west; and over the passes, to the Val Grosina, to the Val Malenco and the Val Fontana.

The lake which bears the name of Poschiavo is two and a half miles away from the town. Indeed I can think of few places where I would more gladly spend a rest-cure than at the hotel at Le Prese where the water laps gently at the foot of the high mountains under the golden warmth of the sun. Four miles further on the frontier with Italy brings the road close to Tirano, somewhat strangely a place in the eighteenth century where men were recruited for service in the Prussian army. An even more curious form of recruitment was being carried out towards the end of the same century when it was discovered that a highly respected lady of the district was engaged in the business of supplying village girls for the delectation of the priests serving the Madonna di Tirano, a great church, built between 1504–33 and an important place of pilgrimage. For some obscure reason this is said to have been one of the causes of the revolt of the Valtelline which, with Bormio and Chiavenna, passed then from the control of the Grisons to Napoleon's newly-created Cisalpine Republic.

The road up the Upper Engadine which we left to visit Pontresina follows the river Inn through a number of attractive villages, Ponte where the Albula road linking the Engadine with Chur, Davos and Klosters joins the main highway; Madulain; Zuoz, once the chief place of the Engadine and still possessing some fine sixteenth-century houses and the ancestral tower of the Planta family; and Scanfs to Zernez and the Lower Engadine. The scenery of the Lower Engadine is in many ways more spectacular than that of the upper part of the valley. The character of the country changes from a wide and comparatively level plain to narrow gorges banked by forests, through which the Inn flows in a turbulence. The villages are perched on the lofty terraced hillsides. This part of the Engadine has suffered severely from avalanches.

Zernez has a fine church rebuilt in 1607 by Rudolf von Planta, and a castle where the Planta family lived from 1400 to the middle of the nineteenth century. It is also the starting point for the Swiss National Park and the Ofen Pass road which runs through it. The former was established as a nature reserve in 1909 and covers an area of fifty square miles. Mountainous —there are some 110 summits between 9,000 and 10,000 feet in its area—and criss-crossed by streams and thick woods, it is a perfect sanctuary for beasts and flowers. All hunting, the picking of flowers and indeed all human activity is forbidden in the interests of the chamois and the ibex or bouquetins (which having become extinct were reintroduced into Switzerland in 1920), red deer, roes, marmots, foxes, martens and many species of birds. The flowers include some of the rarest of Alpine plants. Special Park guards prevent any breach of the regulations and visitors are asked to keep to the paths which thread the unspoiled landscape.

The National Park is crossed from east to west by the Ofen Pass road. It follows the Spöl-Tal, beside a rushing stream, emerges in the valley of Champsech and after traversing the National Park ascends the lengthy Val del Fuorn through woods of larch, spruce and fir, with rocky pinnacles in the background to the summit, some 7,070 feet. The name, Ofen or Fuorn, is said to be derived from a foundry worked here in the seventeenth century. Although the scenery is fine, it is a trifle monotonous, and I would not rank the road as one of the more interesting of Alpine passes. At the summit, however, there is a goodly array of the Engadine peaks to the north and south-west, and towards the west many of the snow-covered crests of the majestic Ortler range come into view.

The Val Müstair or Münstertal into which the road drops is yet another of the Alpine enclaves which have become Swiss by accident rather than by design. The people speak Romansch. The climate is mild, so that fruit and cereals grow at an unusual height. Santa Maria is a quiet and pleasant holiday resort, and modern travellers are unlikely to suffer the inconvenience, as John Addington Symonds did in 1885, of removing the hens who were roosting under the bed in which he slept. A century earlier Archdeacon Coxe had left Santa Maria to cross the Umbrail Pass to Bormio where he commented that it was 'no bad remark of my servant, that the villages looked as if the inhabitants were mostly dead, and the place deserted.' The Umbrail Pass, the road to which ascends some 4,000 feet in five miles by means of 36 hairpin bends, is one of the highest in Switzerland, 8,212 feet. There is an exciting view of the Ortler mountains and their glaciers before the road descends to the Italian customs house and links up with the even higher Stelvio Pass. Müstair or Münster, two miles further down the Val Müstair, is the last village in the Grisons. Unlike the other villages in the valley, its people are Catholic and the place takes its name from a Benedictine convent, founded, so it is alleged, by Charlemagne in the early ninth century.

The main road down the Lower Engadine makes its way through gorge and forest above the Inn towards Schuls-Tarasp. The mountains slope precipitously towards the valley and the villages are poised on terraces above it, the slender church towers silhouetted against the sky. The road over the Flüela Pass joins the Lower Engadine at Susch. From the little village of Lavin, much exposed to avalanches, it is possible to ascend the Piz Linard, 11,200 feet, after rough going over scree and snow. The view from this mountain, the highest peak of the Silvretta Alps, embraces the Bernese, Bernina, Ortler and Pennine chains as well as the lake of Constance. The scenery of the valley, the river rushing through a chasm far below, is so superb, so wild and so romantic that the hotels of Schuls (or Scuol to use the Romansch), Tarasp and Vulpera come as something of a shock.

The chief town of the Lower Engadine, as Schuls-Tarasp is entitled to be called, is in fact a conglomeration of villages, though a health-resort of international reputation. Its alkaline springs are said to be particularly good for dietary and gastric troubles. The vast hotels of Vulpera, on the terrace above the river on its eastern bank, with their elegant lounges, tennis courts, brilliant and well-kept flower gardens, surrounded by dark pine woods, provide an unwanted element of sophistication in a situation of undimmed beauty. Schuls must be one of the last Swiss resorts to publish a weekly list of its guests; and the reading is at least significant of modern society. Indeed Schuls-Tarasp has something of the provincial magnificence of the capital of a small nineteenth-century German state. It seems appropriate that the lovely castle of Tarasp, a medieval building but recently restored, which crowns a hill-top in a fashion both dramatic and romantic, should have been bequeathed to the former Grand Duke of Hesse, by the German manufacturer responsible for its restoration. Tarasp did not in fact become a part of the Grisons until 1809. Purchased by the Hapsburg family in 1464, it came into the hands of the princely Dietrichsteins who held it until Austria yielded it to France in 1801. The lower town of Schuls with its old houses and market-place overlooked by the high mountains, Piz Lischanna with its silvery peak, and Piz Pisoc, is a reminder that the real life of Schuls is divorced from the wealthy Americans, Germans and Egyptians who patronise its pretentious hotels.

Schuls is none the less a most attractive centre for the exploration of remote and beautiful country. The Inn flows under old wooden-covered bridges over great boulders and rocks, plunging through ravines and wooded clefts, towards the Austrian frontier. The mountains are superbly shaped. On the western side the heights and ski-slopes of the Silvretta range overlook the valley, the hillsides bright with flowers and sprinkled with high villages. Shortly after the hamlet of Crutsch, a little road ascends towards the neat village of Sent, destroyed by fire in 1921, to the wooded Val Sinestra, watered by the Lavancra torrent and surrounded by the Silvretta Alps. To the south and east there are grand views of the Piz Lischanna and the Piz Pisoc. The latter is difficult to climb but the summit of the Piz Lischanna, reached by way of the Val Lischanna, has a panorama embracing the Ortler and Bernina Alps and in the distance the steeples and spires of the Dolomite range. The Clemgia gorge, with waterfalls and rocky glades, in the valley of S-charl with its fragrant cedar wood of Tamangur, pierces the mountain range between the Piz Lischanna and the Piz Pisoc.

Shortly after leaving Schuls in the direction of Austria a road or track swerves to the right, descending to the Inn which it crosses by a timbered bridge, the central pillar of which is an immense boulder, to the little hamlet of Sur-En. This is, as I can vouch personally, an excellent place for a picnic lunch. A path through the woods brings the walker easily back to Schuls. Alternatively, and more arduously, it is possible to take the rough track past the scattered chalets of Uina Dadora and Uina Dadaint in the Val d'Uina and so through the savage ravine of Il Quar which closes the valley. Steps blasted in the cliff-side lead high above the gorge amidst magnificent scenery to the Grosslager Alp and the Schlinig Pass, 7,539 feet, and so into Italian territory.

Beyond Schuls towards Austria the Alpine scene is of unsurpassed grandeur, for the valley of the Inn becomes steeper, the sides of the mountains close in, the villages, Remus, Tschlin, are primitive and picturesque, the road is still fortunately at the time of writing narrow and gravelled. The Swiss customs are at Martina (or Martinsbrück), though the actual frontier is at the Inn bridge by Weinberg or Vinadi, nearly four miles on, thus enabling the last segment of Swiss territory, the Samnaun valley, well worth a visit, to be customs free. When Archdeacon Coxe crossed into the Tyrol from the Lower Engadine in 1779, he found that the Austrian garrison there consisted of a single soldier. Nearly two hundred years later, there is still a slightly comic opera air about the frontier here, a tribute, perhaps, to the theatrical beauty of the scene. There is no lovelier way of leaving Switzerland for Austria than by the Inn valley.

9

THE GRISONS

THE ENGADINE and the Val Bregaglia form part of the Grisons, the largest canton in Switzerland, though in population it ranks thirteenth. It is in fact a state in miniature. Its name, more accurately represented by the German title for the canton, Graubünden, means the 'league of the Greys' and it is primarily a confederation of diverse communities rather than a distinctive unity. Geographically it consists of a series of mountain valleys, some, like the Engadine, with a plateau 5,000 to 6,000 feet in height. The high Alps which separate them have done much to condition the character of the people as well as their political and religious features.

The Grisons are divided linguistically. A seventh of the population speaks Italian and half German. The remainder, some 40,000, speak Romansch which originated as a *lingua rustica* of the Roman Empire. In recent years, as I have mentioned earlier, the retention of Romansch has tended to become a rallying call for patriotic Graubünders. Societies have been established to encourage its use and to promote its rather meagre literature, mainly lyric poetry. Time alone will show whether this will be an effective action; nor, in fact, is there much to be said for its survival if it is contrived artificially. Actually Romansch consists of two dialects, Ladin spoken in the Engadine and Rhaeto-Romansch in the Rhine valley and neighbouring regions. The first book in Ladin was published at Poschiavo in 1560 and that in Rhaeto-Romansch at Lindau in 1601. The first complete translation of the Bible, which appeared at Chur in 1718, was dedicated to the Prince of Wales, the future George II; he acknowledged the compliment with a gift of fifty guineas. The indefatigable Archdeacon Coxe, who was interested in the language, learned much about it from a M. Aporta whom he met at Scanfs in the Engadine, and at Ilanz in the Vorder Rhein valley he bought a number of books written in Romansch 'which have so considerably swelled my travelling library, that if I continue to increase the collection, I must hire an additional horse for the purpose of carrying my baggage of information.' Romansch was indeed recognised as one of the four official languages of Switzerland as a result of a referendum held on February 20th, 1938; though it is the principal language of only just over 1% of the population.

Such unity as the Grisons possess arises from the past history of its Alpine valleys. During the latter part of the middle ages they were in continuous conflict with their ecclesiastical and temporal overlords, more especially the Bishop of Chur. To bargain the more effectively the various communities came together into leagues, the League of the House of God (or Lia de Ca De) in 1367, the Upper or Grey League (Lia Grischa) in 1395, representing the districts on the Upper Rhine, and the League of the Ten Jurisdictions (Lia dellas Desch Dretturas or Zehn gerichten Bund) in 1436. The communes had not been at first concerned with the movement towards autonomy and confederation gathering momentum in central Switzerland; though representatives of the leagues are said to have come together at Vazerol in 1471 to form the Triple Perpetual League. But as the frontiers of the Grisons were contiguous to the domains of the Hapsburg Emperor, Maximilian, the friendship of the other Swiss cantons was of some importance to their eastern neighbours. At the end of the fifteenth century the Emperor Maximilian made a final effort to bring the Swiss more definitely under his rule. An isolated attack by Imperial troops on the Benedictine convent of Münster or Müstair in the Val Müstair, on the very fringe of the Grisons, brought the league to its defence and prepared the way for a more definitive alliance with the other Swiss cantons. The hardy Swiss soldiers, men of the mountains, won victory after victory, though the warrior leader from the Grisons, Fontana, was killed in battle by the river Calven. The subsequent treaty signed at Basle on September 22nd, 1499, confirmed the practical independence of the Swiss Confederation and its allied territories.

Henceforth the fortunes of the Grisons were to be very closely bound up with those of the Confederation, though they continued to be an allied state, not a member canton. Indeed full membership did not come until 1803. The leagues constituting the Grisons came closer together at a meeting at Ilanz in 1524 and subsequently overthrew the remaining feudal magnates and destroyed their castles. The Protestant religion also seeped into the territory, though the final religious pattern was a complicated patchwork. The most powerful factor in promoting the reformed faith was opposition to the Bishop of Chur, and between 1521 and 1524 preachers carried it to the villages of Fläsch, St. Antönien, Igis, Malans and Davos. It was eventually decided at Ilanz in 1526 that each commune should decide for itself the faith it wished to follow, but the second article of Ilanz accepted six months later led to the virtual repudiation of Roman Catholicism. The evangelisation of the Grisons by Protestant preachers was, however, only partially effective, and historically accidental. When, for instance, the people of Pontresina wanted a new parish priest in November 1549, the village elders chose the Italian Paolo Vergerio, once a papal nuncio, who had accepted the reformed faith and fleeing from the wrath of the Italian Inquisition over the Bernina Pass had recently arrived at Pontresina. Under his lead, Protestantism became the order of the day.

45   *Steep wooded slopes in the Samnaun Valley, Lower Engadi*

The geographical position of the Grisons placed them in a difficult and serious position, and in the first half of the seventeenth century their freedom and independence were very much at stake. Their western frontiers were secure, but as neighbours they had to the north the Austrian Hapsburgs, to the west Venice, and to the south, Milan, all Roman Catholic powers. Moreover the drift of European politics had brought about a close alliance between the Spanish and the Imperial Hapsburgs which was knit, in terms of communication, not merely by the Brenner Pass but by the valley parallel to the Engadine, known as the Valtelline which the Grisons had acquired in 1512, as also by the Engadine itself.* The French who had been the chief power intent on curbing Spanish-Imperial ambitions were actively engaged in using the Grisons to this end. The natives of the Grisons themselves were split by religious, political and family differences. The powerful Planta family of the Engadine were Roman Catholic and pro-Spanish. The de Salis of the Val Bregaglia were pro-French. There were reasons for believing that in the ensuing crisis of the years 1620–39 the Grisons might lose their hard-won independence.

This complex story is worth mentioning, if only because it forms the setting of Jürg Jenatsch, the hero of C. F. Meyer's famous novel, who played so prominent a part in the history of the Grisons. Jenatsch, who was born at Samedan in the Engadine, was an intriguer and amoral warrior in whom, however, as in his contemporary Wallenstein, there also appeared occasional streaks of idealism, and Jenatsch certainly had a genuine concern for the future of the Grisons. The frontiers of the Grisons marched, as I mentioned a little earlier, with Venice on the west and with Milan, then under Spanish rule, to the south. Spain was above all concerned with preventing an alliance of the Grisons with Venice, for while Venice was a Roman Catholic power, she was also anti-papal and pro-French in her sympathies. Venetian wealth was used to grease the palms of the great men of the Grisons to such good effect that a treaty was negotiated in 1603, but it was not renewed in 1613 because the Protestant pastors feared that Roman Catholic influence was increasing as a result of the Venetian connection. Protestant intrigues can also be detected in the revolt against the Plantas in the Engadine in 1618, which served to unite once more the Plantas with their former enemies, the Hapsburgs. Two years later the Catholics of the Valtelline threw out their Protestant overlords and appealed to Spain who repulsed the Swiss Protestants at Tirano; while the Catholic cantons, and the Catholic Upper League of the Grisons, showed overt sympathy with their co-religionists.

It was at this juncture that Jenatsch made his appearance. In 1618 he had

* The control of the Valtelline was important to the Imperialists because of Spanish interests in northern Italy.

Near Landquart in the Grisons

been an evangelical pastor of 22. Championing the cause of the Protestant Grisons he had sacked Rudolf Planta's castle at Zernez, obliging Planta to take refuge in the Tyrol. Subsequently he induced a tribunal at Thusis to outlaw Rudolf and his brother, Pompeius, and to torture and execute Nicholas Rusca, the archpriest of Sondrio. Jenatsch and his wife, Anna, were in the Valtelline at the time of the Catholic rising of 1620 but they managed to escape up the Val Muretto to Maloja. Next year he rode with a group of followers from Grüsch in the Prättigau, having learned that the Plantas were plotting to get rid of him, through Chur to the castle of Rietburg. Here he surprised Pompeius Planta in his bedroom, and butchered him to death with an axe in his daughter's presence, an episode that the lady with some justification neither forgot nor forgave.

In spite of Jenatsch's forays against the Catholics and the Spaniards, the outlook for the Grisons remained grave. The Austrians occupied the Prättigau and the Lower Engadine as far as Zernez, and advancing over the Scaletta Pass threatened Davos, Klosters, Landquart and Chur. Jenatsch escaped over the Panixer Pass to Glarus and Zürich, and for a time joined Mansfield's Protestant army in Germany. The Protestants of the Grisons resisted stoutly, especially after a command that they should attend the Mass on April 24th, 1622. Led by their local pastors and by Rudolf de Salis, the men of the Prättigau threw out the Austrians. Jenatsch himself returned to help them and eventually forced the Austrian commander, Baldiron, to retreat from Chur. The respite was, however, temporary, and the odds were still heavily against the Grisons. The Austrians returned in force and by 1623 were exerting effective control over the Val Müstair, the Lower Engadine, the territory of the League of God's House and most of that of the League of the Ten Jurisdictions. The terms of the treaty of Lindau amounted to a virtual repudiation of the Grisons' independence.

Meanwhile the French and the Venetians had been trying in company with Savoy to thwart the plans of the Imperialists and Spaniards. Under the direction of Cardinal Richelieu, who was now in power in France, a confederate army under the command of the Marquis de Coevres, which included men from Berne, Zürich, the Valais and the Grisons (under Rudolf de Salis and Jenatsch) invaded the Engadine over the Albula Pass and, pushing on over the winter snows of the Bernina Pass, captured Tirano. By the beginning of the spring of 1625, Chiavenna and Bormio had been freed of Spanish and Papal troops. Subsequently the Valtelline was, by the terms of the treaty of Monzon in 1626, placed under papal protection and given practical autonomy, provided it paid tribute to the Grisons. This was much less than the Grisons had wanted, but it was better than nothing.

Three years later war again broke out between France and Spain over the succession to the duchy of Mantua, which Richelieu had claimed on behalf

of a French prince, the duke of Nevers. The Austrian soldiers marched through the Grisons to help their allies, the Spaniards, in northern Italy. Once more the Grisons turned to Richelieu who allowed Henry, duke of Rohan, the Protestant leader, to go to their aid with French troops. Richelieu was, however, simply treating the Grisons as a pawn in his complicated diplomatic game. By the terms of the treaty of Cherasco, which ended the war of the Mantuan succession, Hapsburg soldiers were to be withdrawn from Grisons territory, and French and Grisons garrisons were to hold the Valtelline, Bormio and Chiavenna. This was again a disappointment for the Grisons, being much less than they had hoped for.

Richelieu was, however, losing interest in the problem of the Valtelline and ordered Rohan to return home. The way in which the situation had developed explains the curious moves that Jenatsch was now making. He had been in Venice in 1629 and subsequently in touch with his arch foe the Spaniards; in 1633 he stayed with the Capuchin friars at Rapperswil. He seems to have become convinced that the future of his country could be best assured by a political and religious volte-face. Accordingly, in 1635, the former Protestant pastor was received into the Roman Church, and made overtures to the Spaniards. In a tortuous sort of way he had come to realise that dependence on France was a less secure way of ensuring the independence of the Grisons than an agreement negotiated with the Spaniards and the Austrians. As governor of Chiavenna, he concluded the articles of Milan with Spain, by which the Grisons' control over the coveted Valtelline was recognised, providing that the Roman Catholic faith was alone allowed there and that Spanish troops were given free passage through it. Jenatsch did not live to see the confirmation of the peace. He was murdered on January 24th, 1639, whilst drinking wine with his fellow officers in a tavern at Chur. The peace was ratified in September 1639, and ten years later Austrian claims over the Val Müstair and the Lower Engadine were redeemed by a cash payment. The independence of the Grisons was secured.

This historical excursus is more relevant than may at first appear for an understanding of the modern Grisons, suggesting as it does both the internal divisions which separated and the underlying patriotism which united them. The Grisons retain their definite character. While the canton contains resorts of world-wide reputation attracting an international clientele like St. Moritz, Arosa, Davos, Klosters, Lenzerheide and Flims, there are many villages and valleys remote from the tourist area and mountains that seldom see a climber. The Grisons has been opened up far less than have the Bernese Oberland and the Valais. The surface of many of the roads is abominable (and for some reasons may it long remain so); in particular there are execrable patches from the top of the Oberalp Pass to Ilanz, between Thusis and Tiefencastel through the exciting Schyn ravine and over the superb bridge at

A crocus field on the Wiesen Alp near Davos, Grisons

Solis, and from Schuls to the Swiss–Austrian frontier. There are small villages with small hotels, running streams, mountains and meadows where the tourist agent has not penetrated. The deep-rooted life of the peasant is little affected by the summer and winter tourist invasions but moves to the age-long rhythms set by the four seasons. The Grisons are a mountainous land, only 30% of which is at all productive, and the peasant has a hard task to exact his tribute from the soil. The foreigner does not find him easy to know or to understand. In some ways Llewellyn Powys, who spent his earlier and declining years at Davos, managed to penetrate the veil in his beautifully-written *Swiss Essays*. As John Russell commented in his book on *Switzerland*, we are there suddenly reminded of things which the ordinary guide books never mention: the peasants' 'passion for night-long dancing on wedding-days, the tiny aperture, or soul-window, carved above the ordinary windows in order that, after death, the soul may slip through unhindered on its way to heaven; and crueller customs, such as that of strewing autumn crocuses before the house of a girl suspected of unchastity.' Llewellyn Powys, with the eye of a trained observer, noted the beautiful woodwork of the chalets, built of fir and larch while the Arolla pine, the solitary tree of the mountain heights, resisting the tough challenge of the winter blizzard, supplied the material for interior panelling and furniture. He described also the changing scenery of the mountain year, the vast blue forests so thick that shafts of sunlight only penetrate here and there, while squirrels scramble up the trunk and on the branches and lichen festoons the firs with grey-green tracery; the fresh sprouting grass of spring, the tinkle of the goats' bells as the animals make for the high pastures, the ceaseless roaring of the river, the red berries of the mountain ash supplying food for deer and birds, the uncanny silence of the winter snows.

The valleys down which the rivers plunge under the shadow of the mountains provide the key to the geography of the Grisons. The Vorder Rhein has its source in the neighbourhood of the Oberalp Pass and is steadily reinforced by streams flowing down the tributary valleys, the Medelserrhein and the Rabuisa, until it is joined at Reichenau by the Hinter Rhein. The Hinter Rhein starts near the San Bernardino Pass and its waters are further increased by tributary streams, the Averserrhein, flowing down the Val Ferrera from Avers Cresta, and the Albula. The united stream, now the river Rhine, flows swiftly down a widening valley to Chur, the cantonal town, through Landquart where it is joined by the stream from Klosters; it then leaves the territory of the Grisons and turning north eventually enters the lake of Constance. The Engadine is watered, as we have seen, by the Inn, which rises on the Piz Lunghin near the Maloja Pass and later absorbs the Flaz which flows past Pontresina, the Spöl at Zernez as well as other rushing torrents. The Mera which surges down the Val Bregaglia makes its way to

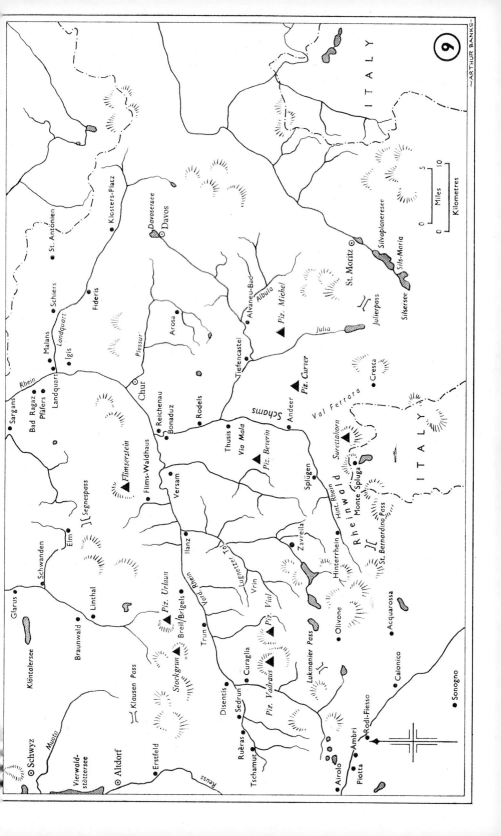

the lake of Como. Thus the rivers which rise in the Grisons at long last reach the North Sea, the Mediterranean and the Black Sea.

The Rhine valley as it becomes a part of the Grisons is broad and fertile and the mountains which slope towards it are shapely rather than awe-inspiring. Farms, cattle and fruit trees abound, and the villages which chequer the valley are pleasant. The towns contain many old houses and ancient monuments. Bad Ragaz, at the mouth of the wild Tamina gorge, became a fashionable spa after the thermal waters of Pfäfers had been conveyed by a four-mile conduit to the growing village. A monk of the monastery at Pfäfers, said to have been founded by St. Pirminus in 740, discovered these waters when out hunting; the Hof Ragaz Hotel was originally a residence of the Benedictine abbot of Pfäfers. The monastery was suppressed in 1838 and is now a mental hospital. The parish church of Pfäfers, designed by Ulrich Lang, is a fine building, notable for the frescoes of Francesco Giorgioli (1694) and the stucco work of the Ticinese artists Betini and Peri. A bathhouse was built as early as 1242. In 1451 the cure was described as a stay of some six to seven days in the water, the guests actually sleeping and eating in the baths because the ladders leading out of the ravine in which the baths were situated were of such an alarming steepness. These conditions were later improved and an artificial channel leading to a new bathhouse was constructed in 1630. The early seventeenth-century regulations, quoted by Sir Gavin de Beer in his entertaining book *Early Travellers in the Alps*, forbade brawling at the baths 'nor may anyone do violence to another by splashing, ducking or throwing into the water. No one may pledge another with drink, lest from fullness with wine accidents might happen. . . . Those who subscribe to the new faith must keep it to themselves, and the singing of psalms in German is expressly forbidden on payment of a fine. Those, however, who feel an irresistible need to sing in their bath, may sing other holy or at least reputable songs, provided that the baths be not filled with din. . . .' Modern Bad Ragaz, with its trim public gardens, its Kursaal and Neubad, and its covered thermal swimming bath, seems far removed from those days, but a visit to the narrow Tamina valley with its cliffs towering over the road as far as Bad Pfäfers and thence to the Tamina Gorge brings the visitor not merely to the hot springs which gush from the rock but also to traces of the old gangway by which the early patients went to their primitive accommodation, huts supported by beams projecting from the cliff, before they were lowered by hanging ropes into the warm waters.

Chur or Coire, which is the cantonal town of the Grisons, is pleasantly situated on the river Plessur before it joins the Rhine. It has still a number of relics of ancient history, for it was from 452 the seat of a bishop who became a prince of the Holy Roman Empire. The towns-people, however, resented his rule and as early as 1464 rejected it and later accepted the Protestant faith.

The cathedral, where Jürg Jenatsch was buried, was built between 1150 and 1265 on the site of an earlier church, parts of which may have been incorporated into the new building. It is a mixture of many styles. The chapel of St. Lawrence was added to the south aisle in the fifteenth century. The high altar, by Jacob Russ, is of the same period and impressively rich. The cathedral is dedicated to St. Lucius, said by an early legend to have been the first Christian king of Britain, who entered the Grisons over the Luziensteig Pass between Vaduz in Liechtenstein and Maienfeld. The Romans executed him at Chur, together with his sister, Emerita, who was burned there. When Gilbert Burnet, later bishop of Salisbury, visited Chur in 1685, he told the then bishop that he could prove that the story of Lucius was 'a fable in all parts of it. . . . This signified nothing to the bishop, who assured me that they had a tradition of that in their church, and it was inserted in their breviary, which he firmly believed.' The bishop showed Burnet a relic of St. Emerita's veil. 'I confess,' said Burnet, 'I never saw a relique so ill-disguised, for it is a piece of worn linnen cloath lately washt, and the burning did not seem to be above a month old.' The stout Protestant was certainly correct in his judgement of the legend of Lucius. Bede indeed mentioned the conversion of Lucius, the king of Britain, at the king's request by emissaries of Pope Eleutherus; but he, like others of later date, was misled by a scribal error. The word used for Britain actually referred to Britium, and Lucius, the king of Britain and patron saint of Chur, was really, it seems, Lucius Abgarus IX, king of Britium, near Edessa, in Mesopotamia. Be that as it may, the cathedral, the fifteenth-century Protestant Martinskirche, the narrow streets with their sixteenth-century houses, make Chur a graceful place, though industrialised on its outskirts.

It is not indeed a town in which visitors to Switzerland linger overlong. They will be heading for the Engadine, Davos or Arosa, or for Flims and the passes beyond. The route to Klosters and Davos forks at Landquart. Klosters is situated at the upper end of the beautifully wooded Prättigau, separated from the Vorarlberg and the very delightful valley of Montafon in Austria by the Rhätikon range. At the little village church of Schiers in this valley the women have the right to receive the sacrament before their menfolk in commemoration of the part they played in the rising against the Austrians in 1622. For the Prättigau, like so many of the other valleys in the Grisons, is still redolent of its past. It was from Grüsch, imposingly situated above the Taschinesbach, that Jenatsch rode to kill Pompeius Planta. At Seewis, high above the valley, the Protestants in 1622 slew the Capuchin friar, Fidelis, still reputed a martyr and saint in the district. At Fideris Bad Jenatsch took the waters in 1627. At Castels there are the remains of a fortress held by the Austrians which the peasants seized in 1622 armed only with cudgels. At Küblis the pleasant Schanielen valley leads to the skiing resort of St. Antönien, one of the first villages in the Grisons to accept the Protestant faith. Klosters itself, nearly 4,000 feet high, is an admirable centre for walks and climbs besides being a famed winter-sports centre.

The road and the railway mount steeply from Klosters to Davos, located in a mountain valley a thousand feet higher than Klosters, watered by the Landwasser and a miniature lake, 'a long straight reach of valley,' as Robert Louis Stevenson described it, 'wall-like mountains upon either hand that rise higher and higher and shoot up new summits the higher you climb, a few noble peaks seen even from the valley; a village of hotels, a world of black and white—black pinewoods, clinging to the sides of the valley, and white snow flouring it, and papering it between the pinewoods, and covering all the mountains with a dazzling curd.' Davos is a winter-sports resort of the first rank, more especially for skaters and skiers; the Schatalp provides one of the finest Swiss bobsleigh runs. The mountain panorama is superb. Yet the sanatoria for consumptives stand first in the mind. The brilliant sunshine and clear atmosphere made Davos, together with Montana and Leysin above the Rhone valley, one of the most highly reputed resorts for the treatment of phthisical patients until modern drugs became more effective weapons in helping recovery than the bolstering of the patients' resistance by rest, sunlight and sterile air. Dr. Alexander Spengler was the first to make use of this treatment in 1865. John Addington Symonds lived there from 1877 to 1893. 'Many as are the drawbacks of spending one's life at Davos,' he commented in 1889, 'it has, aesthetically and sensually, the greatest pleasures which an epicure can hope for. All the Apennines, from Consuma to La Vernia, through Rieti, Aquila, Sulmona, Tivoli, have not a single line of beauty in them equal to what lies above us everywhere in this region. The beauty here, of line and profile, is so overwhelmingly rich, that artists cannot deal with it.' Here there burgeoned that overwhelming passion for the Swiss Alps which some have found so strange a characteristic of the historian of the Italian Renaissance. 'Neither Rome nor the Riviera wins our hearts like Switzerland. We do not lie awake in London thinking of them; we do not long so intensely, as the year comes round to revisit them.' It was at Davos that Llewellyn Powys found the spiritual tranquillity which is revealed so sensitively in his *Swiss Essays*. On a more worldly plane it may be mentioned that Conan Doyle was responsible for laying out the golf course. The road from Davos ascends the stony, bare and rather uninteresting Flüela Pass and by numerous loops reaches Susch in the Lower Engadine.

Arosa is another mountain resort, some 16 miles from Chur up the Plessur valley where the scenery is of striking beauty, and the railway there another illustration of Swiss engineering skill. Some 6,000 feet high and encompassed by pinewoods and high mountains, the village clusters around the deep blue waters of the Ober-See and Unter-See as lovely in winter as in summer.

The road and railway which go down the Rhine valley towards its source from the direction of Chur pass the old castle of Reichenau which formerly belonged to the Planta family. At this village for a short while in 1793 the future king of the French, Louis-Philippe, stayed as a refugee, teaching mathematics at a local school as Monsieur Chabot and employing his spare time by seducing the cook, Marianne Banzori. He came of a family not distinguished by moral restraint: even so he seems to have been singularly careless of the obligations of a refugee to respect the standards of the countries in which he sought retreat. In 1804 he was quick to realise the implications for his own safety of the judicial murder by Napoleon of his Condé cousin, the Duc d'Enghien, and fled into the wilds of Norway; but, even there, lost little time in selecting, a trifle tactlessly, the daughter of a Lutheran pastor as the object of his light but successful addresses. Reichenau-Tamins stands in my memory chiefly as a railway junction where we fed the chickens under a blazing sun while waiting for the train to Andermatt, for it is here that one line branches to St. Moritz and the other to Disentis, Andermatt, Gletsch and Brig.

It is at Reichenau that the two valleys of the Vorder Rhein and the Hinter Rhein separate. The valley of the Vorder Rhein is singularly attractive, its small villages and towns compact and interesting, its valleys comparatively untouched by the tourist. The only well-known resort is Flims-Waldhaus where the Swiss traveller Johann Scheuchzer sought out his compatriot, Sir Gaudentius de Capel who had been knighted by William III. It is a tranquil spot, girdled by woods of larch and beech through which many miles of smooth and mossy paths twist and turn, none more attractive than the Cauma See. There are fine views from the near-by mountains, especially the Flimserstein and from the Segnes Pass which goes over to Elm; the track over the pass is not especially difficult, though Scheuchzer urged that persons liable to attacks of dizziness should go another way. Near the top of the pass he saw the great natural arch, 65 feet long, of the Martinsloch through which the sun's rays shine once every spring and once every autumn on the church of Elm. A walk through the woods from Flims to the chalets of Conn brings an impressive view of the extraordinary gorge of the Vorder Rhein at Versamm, a precipitous cleft in the rocks, through which the river thunders, 'rent and ploughed with ravines as by the malice of some other spirit.' Flims is certainly a charming village with one of the most attractive post offices in Switzerland, a diminutive chalet surrounded by flowers.

The chief town of the Vorder Rhein valley is Ilanz, with a fine view of the mountains above Breil. Its history goes back to the eighth century and it was the meeting place of important conferences in the early sixteenth century. Its churches and gabled houses, the latter built in the seventeenth century by men who had made money in foreign service, as well as the sparse remains of its former fortifications bear witness to its earlier importance. It is situated at the entrance of the Lungnez valley, one of the most beautiful in the region, especially when the cherry trees are in flower. The valley down which the river Glenner foams is narrow and romantic; one part of it, the Valser Rhein, mounts to the superbly-situated hamlet of Zervreila, while the parallel valley, the Rein de Vrin, ascends to Vrin. At Villa the 'valley expands, yielding a vast prospect over the mountain passes which lead to Splügen and to Olivone—a wilderness of craggy peaks and billowy snow-fields, all smoothed and softened with clear sunshine and blue shadows.' From both places there are innumerable high walks and climbs.

The Vorder Rhein valley mounts slowly from Ilanz to Disentis. Its lateral valleys bring many glimpses of glaciers and snow mountains. Villages and churches are perched on the high hills surrounded by woods; below, meadows and orchards border the river. At Truns a maple tree is said to be a descendant of that under which the abbot of Disentis administered the oath to the Vorder Rhein group of communes who formed the Grey League. Disentis itself is a quiet spa with a radio-active iron spring. It also possesses an impressive abbey church, an offshoot of the Benedictine monasteries of Reichenau and Pfäfers, the latter the oldest Benedictine house in Switzerland, which was founded in the eighth century. During the middle ages it ranked as an imperial abbey and its abbots were princes of the Holy Roman Empire. In the seventeenth century it was associated with Pfäfers, Engelberg, St. Gall and Einsiedeln in a reformed congregation; and the present church was built to the design of Caspar Moosbrugger, possibly assisted by Franz Beer. Among its inmates was Placidus a Spescha who was sent to the hospice maintained by the abbey on the Lukmanier Pass in 1781. He started collecting crystals, began reading about geology, and subsequently explored the country-side around Disentis. With single-minded persistence he overcame the many difficulties which faced him. The French troops pillaged and burned much of the monastery in 1799. Placidus' collection was destroyed and he himself was made a prisoner by the Austrians. Yet he managed to climb the Piz Walhrein, the Piz Urlaun, the Stockgrun, the Oberalpstock and, at the age of 72, the Tödi. In the nineteenth century the abbey fell on evil days and by 1879 there were only four monks in residence. Its revival was largely a result of the stimulus provided by the other Swiss Benedictines, and especially by Benoit Prevost who came from Muri Gries to preside over its destinies from 1880 to 1916. It is now a school. Its modest splendour has survived the unfortunate restorations of the twentieth century. The little town faces the Medel glacier and the high peaks of the Piz Valdraus and the Piz Vial. The valley is here far from narrow, and there is a feeling of light and freedom, as the rising hills recede into the distant landscape.

Disentis is the junction of two pass roads, the Lukmanier and the Oberalp.

49 Ruèras, on the Oberalp P

The Lukmanier traverses a narrow ravine, ascends in zig-zags to the hamlet of Curaglia, becoming steadily wilder and more austere until it reaches the eighteenth-century hospice of Santa Maria, founded by Abbot John III of Disentis in 1374. It then climbs to the 6,000-foot summit before it descends rather more gently to join the St. Gotthard road at Biasca. The pass, which presents every variety of Alpine scenery, was once an important commercial route, traversed also by emperors, prelates and statesmen. At one time the abbey of Disentis maintained six hospices along the road.

The Oberalp Pass, which also starts from Disentis, has long been used and is still a highly-significant factor in Swiss military defence. The road is itself easily negotiable but the surface is gravelled. At first it passes through the green meadows of the Val Tavetsch to Sedrun where there is an interesting church with a carved wooden altar. The little village of Ruèras beyond, where I have stayed in a spotlessly clean pension, provides a wonderful view of the Val Tavetsch as of the valleys and mountains beyond, receding into the blue haze. Some of the cornfields here are among the highest in Switzerland; the corn is stacked on high racks, known as histen, to help the process of ripening. Tschamut is the last hamlet before the summit of the Oberalp. The scenery has by now changed to a desolate treeless area which with its browns and greens, greys and purples, is reminiscent of some of the wilder parts of the Scottish Highlands. The top of the Oberalp, with its little trout lake, its drab barracks, its fortifications, its avalanche tunnel (for the railway) and its low grassy escarpment, is bleak and dreary but the view looking towards the Val Urseren and the peaks beyond the St. Gotthard and Furka passes is impressive. The summit of the pass marks the boundary of the Grisons and the canton of Uri.

The Hinter Rhein, which we left at Reichenau, provides scenery of a different character, if equally fine. The Domleschg valley, narrow and fertile, is notable for the many castles which guard its heights. A few of these, such as the castles of Rhäzüns and Ortenstein, have been preserved or restored, but most are in a ruinous condition, a reminder of the insurrections which overthrew the feudal barons towards the close of the middle ages. It was at Rietberg Castle, which dominates the village of Rodels that Jenatsch murdered Pompeius Planta. Perhaps the most impressive ruin is that of the Hohen-Rhätien, perched impressively 3,000 feet high on a rock at the mouth of the Via Mala above the Hinter Rhein, near the pleasing market-town of Thusis.

Thusis is the starting point for two Alpine passes, the Splügen and the San Bernardino, both of which follow the same road for some miles. The construction of these highways throws some light on the political relations of the Grisons with their neighbours at the beginning of the nineteenth century. The building of the San Bernadino road which started in 1818 and 1824 resulted from an agreement between the canton, which contributed 60,000 francs towards its cost, and the King of Sardinia who gave 395,000 francs and agreed to allow the annual transit, free of duty, of 30,000 quintals of grain and rice. The Ticino had also been interested in the projected road but had been persuaded from giving help by the Austrians who thought that the opening of the pass would be detrimental to their own commerce. To counter the advantages of the new road over the San Bernardino, they sponsored the rebuilding of the road over the Splügen in the hope that the Grisons would complete it on their side of the territory. The Grisons had, however, spent all their money on building the San Bernardino and the Austrians had eventually to pay for the completion of the Splügen themselves.

After leaving Thusis, the San Bernardino and Splügen road enters the grim Via Mala, perhaps the most impressive road gorge in Switzerland, which travellers had to skirt until 1473. Nearly four miles long, its precipitous limestone cliffs rise to a height of 1,600 feet, and in places are not much more than 30 feet apart; at its bottom the Hinter Rhein rushes in a wild torrent. There are places where the road had to be carried along a shelf blasted out of the rock of the precipice itself. The gorge opens to the valley of Schams encircled by mountains, Piz Curver, Piz Beverin, Pizzo Tambo and the Surettahorn. The village church of Zillis, some five and a half miles from Thusis along this road, has some interesting and unusually complete early medieval ceiling paintings of curious design. At Andeer, the next village, there are Romansch inscriptions over many of the doorways.

Andeer is at the entrance to the wild Val de Ferrera, leading to the village of Avers-Cresta which has, so it is said, the only parish church in Switzerland where services are held at a height of 6,400 feet, every Sunday of the year. 'I have never,' exclaimed J. A. Symonds of a visit made to the valley in 1887, 'seen anything in the way of high river scenery to equal this. . . .' The Averser Rhein, he said, 'has a tremendous volume of the clearest azure water, which sometimes hides in obscure caverns and cambra-tufted gorges; sometimes swims through grassy meadows with wide swishing curves that hollow out the turfy margin to their liking; sometimes carves a monumental way through cliffs of pure white marble . . . sometimes falls thundering in cataracts arched with changeful rainbows; sometimes glides deep and solemn, in dark pools that make the spirit dream of death, and long to dive in them and pluck the heart out of their mystery.' The mountains are split by gorges down which the water runs 'for mile after mile . . . leaps and roars between masses of marble crags tinted with lichens, and clasped about by huge pine-roots.' High passes lead from the Val de Ferrera to Soglio in the Val Bregaglia.

At Roffla, where the old road came up from Thusis before the Via Mala was pierced, the valley of Schams, once a lake, is closed by yet another

ravine. Splügen is at the parting of the passes. The one which bears this hamlet's name curves in zig-zags to a bleak summit, 6,946 feet high. The limestone mountains of the Splügen Kalkberge come into view and to the east appears the glacier-girt Surettahorn. To the west, the snows of the Pizzo Tambo are visible. The Italian customs house is a little below the summit at Monte Spluga. When William Brockendon crossed the frontier in 1825, this territory was under Austrian rule. 'At the Austro-Lombard customs-house,' he wrote, 'a crowd of ill-paid officials are always ready to increase their pittance by pouncing upon any unfortunate wight who happens to pass that way. A bribe with an Austrian douanier is always a matter of course and crudely solicited.' The road soon, however, leaves its somewhat desolate neighbourhood for the lush vegetation of Chiavenna and Italy.

The San Bernardino, over which the Emperor Sigismund rode into Lombardy in 1414 to summon the fathers of the Church to the Council of Constance, ascends the Rheinwaldtal to Hinterrhein, with the Zapport glacier in full view. It mounts in a series of hairpin bends, presenting a fine panorama of the head of the Hinter Rhein valley and the glaciers of the Adula. The summit is less bleak than the tops of some passes, the little lago Moesola relieving the varied mountain scenery. The pass, known previously as the Vogelberg (Mons Avium) or Passo Ucello, was apparently re-named after the great fifteenth-century preacher, St. Bernardino of Siena. Peter Lindeberg wrote rhetorically of a journey in 1596; 'Sleepless, we tire with our weary feet at some distance from great Mount San Bernardino, its peaks surrounded by the highest vaults of heaven, congealed with cold and covered with white frost which neither the course of the fiery Apollo, nor high summer, nor the burning Dog-star can touch, but only cold and the Boreal wind. . . .' The road winds down to the varied beauty of the Val Mesocco in the Ticino.

The main road through Thusis follows high above the Albula torrent through the narrow Schyn gorge to Tiefencastel, a picturesque village situated at the confluence of the Albula and the Julier, the streams which bear the same names as the passes over which the roads go into the Engadine. The railway and the road to the Albula pass proceed along the valley through Bad Alvaneu and Filisur to the attractive resort of Bergün, which possesses a twelfth-century church with a slender tower. The villagers, who speak a sub-dialect of Ladin, are for the most part Protestant. 'From Chur we had ten hours to Borgon,' wrote Sir John Reresby in 1656, 'where we rather chose to lie upon benches than in nasty beds.' The Albula pass, reconstructed between 1853 and 1866, climbs to 7,600 feet, descending through forest to Ponte in the Engadine. The railway which goes through the Albula tunnel is a triumph of engineering skill. It was built between 1898 and 1903 and entailed the construction of some 40 tunnels, including the three and half miles of the

52 *In the Toggenburg; the Churfirsten in the background*

Albula. Moreover the track rises some 3,580 feet between Thusis and Preda, a distance of 27 miles. In the steepest section there is a difference in level of 1,365 feet in the four miles between Bergün and Preda. The engineers had to employ a number of interesting expedients. After leaving Bad Alvaneu the railway is carried along the hillside high above the valley to the ravine down which the river Landwasser flows from Davos to join the Albula. The opposite side of the ravine is a sheer precipice. The engineers met this problem by building a viaduct, of 330 feet radius and 230 feet high, which runs directly into a tunnel in the face of a cliff, the final arch of the viaduct being sprung direct from the cliff wall itself. To keep the gradient within permissible limits the device of spiral tunnels, already used for the St. Gotthard and Lötschberg railways, was repeated.

The Julier Pass road, which was much used by the Romans as the traces of the ruts of chariots in the rock still indicate and by Venetian merchants during the middle ages, mounts steeply from Tiefencastel through woods and rock galleries to the little resort of Savognin, backed by the craggy walls of the Piz Michel, the Tinzenhorn and the Piz d'Acla. Further on it skirts the artificial lake supplying Zürich with water, below which lies the drowned village of Marmorera. It then rises to the little village of Bivio. This is where the mule track emerges from the Septimer Pass which took travellers from the Val Bregaglia to the Julier road. There are fine views of the mountains at the summit of the Julier, to the north the Piz d'Err and to the south the Bernina with the Bianco ridge. The Julier road soon descends 2,000 feet to Silvaplana and long before the village has been reached, the deep blue of the lakes in the Upper Engadine appear in the setting of meadow and larch against the mighty bulk of the Piz Margna.

10

THE ALPS OF NORTH-EAST SWITZERLAND

THE MOUNTAINOUS AREA of north-east Switzerland, contiguous to the Grisons, is little visited by the tourist, and even the climber might find it difficult to name a peak in the district, apart, possibly, from the Säntis. Although there is no mountain of more than 10,000 feet, many of these massive heights have a discernible character of their own, more especially the Säntis, the Glärnisch and the Churfirsten. The attractive German town of Lindau on the lake of Constance, still reminiscent of a medieval German city, looks towards an impressively Alpine country in Appenzell. Further south a walk along the lake-front of the equally fascinating town of Rapperswil on the lake of Zürich provides on a clear day a fine view of the mountains to the east and south.

The natives of this region have their own particular characteristics. A strongly imbedded democratic tradition flourishes in Glarus and Appenzell, both cantons, like Unterwalden, where the male population meets every year in an assembly to elect the magistracy. This is a form of democracy of which Jean-Jacques Rosseau would have approved, and I have wondered if such assemblies as these gave him his notion of the *general will*. The countryside where the foothills slope gently towards the rocky mountains is verdant with undulating meadows, in which chalets seem planted in a haphazard yet artistic fashion as in some wonderous toy garden. It is soothing rather than savage, well-cultivated, and if mountainous, yet less arduous than the more familiar Alpine districts.

The traveller by train from Zürich reaches the little junction of Ziegelbrücke. By now the flat reedy marshes of the upper end of the lake of Zürich have given way to alpine scenery. Ziegelbrücke is the junction for Glarus, the chief town of one of the smaller of the Swiss cantons which consists in the main of the valley watered by the river Linth, separated from its neighbours by high peaks. The Linthal is not merely pastoral. It has its industries, more especially cotton spinning and textile printing, both of which need its abundant water supply. This combination of agriculture and small industry, typical of many of the communities in this region, testifies to the way in which the people have taken advantage of their opportunities.

Glarus is predominantly an Alpine canton. It has been associated with the Confederation since 1388 after the Swiss had defeated a superior Austrian force at the little town of Näfels near by. Its people are independent and resolute. The men meet on the first Sunday in May in the *Landsgemeinde* to choose the magistrates. The government of the canton consists of a parliament or *Landrat* which is elected for four years, and an executive body or *Regierungsrat* which is appointed every three years by universal suffrage. The cantonal assembly votes for the members of the *Regierungsrat* and selects the judical officers. The *Landrat*, which has no legislative power, presents proposals to the assembly, the *Landsgemeinde*, for the latter to accept or reject. The proceedings are colourful but not merely archaic. The officials go in procession to the public square of Glarus, headed by ushers in red medieval costume. The *Landammann* carries a sword, symbolising popular sovereignty. After the assembly has taken the oath to the constitution, it gets down to its business. This fascinating Arcadian republic seems more reminiscent of a Greek city state than of twentieth-century Switzerland, but it is still an effective instrument of government and regarded proudly by the individualist and independent-minded people of the canton.

Glarus is unique in another way. Its people had early accepted the Protestant faith. Indeed, Ulrich Zwingli was for a short time here. But in 1683 Protestantism and Roman Catholicism were placed on an equal footing, and henceforth pastors and priests sat side by side in the *Landsgemeinde*. Archdeacon Coxe, whose Whig sentiments were stirred by the republican simplicity of Glarus, was equally pleased by its religious tolerance. 'In several parts of this canton,' he noted, 'the Protestants and Catholics successively perform service in the same church, and all the offices of state are amicably administered by the two parties.' The Protestants and Roman Catholics still make common use of the parish church of Glarus, a practice which the English naturalist, John Ray, had noticed during his visit to Switzerland at the end of the seventeenth century.

The life of the canton appeared particularly pleasant to Coxe in the eighteenth century. In some ways, he said, its scenery reminded him of the English Peak district but the river Linth was broader and faster than the Derwent, and the hillocks of the Peak were molehills by comparison with the alps of Glarus. Its rich meadows produced delicious milk and butter 'and the honey of these mountainous countries is most exquisite.' He might have mentioned the special green Schabzeiger cheese, manufactured from skimmed milk and coloured with the blue melilot, which is a speciality of the region. He found the chalets clean and simple, affording 'a most pleasing conviction of the peasant's happiness. If I had never seen these little democratical states, I could have formed no idea of the general equality and indistinction that prevails among the inhabitants.' It is, perhaps, a pity to mar this happy picture by recalling that in 1782, within a few years of Coxe's visit, a young servant girl was sentenced to death on a charge of witchcraft, the last capital sentence of this sort in European history.

His tribute was, and is, however, not wholly undeserved. The Linthal valley combines industrial efficiency and pastoral economy within a framework of mountain scenery. The chief town, Glarus, was burned down in 1861, as a result of the föhn which blows ferociously down the valley, and has no ancient buildings. It is situated at the foot of the massive Vorder–Glärnisch with the Glärnisch rising behind it; in spite of the fact that this mountain is less than 10,000 feet high, a glacier lies between its two peaks. From Glarus a road leads up the narrow Klön-Tal where there is a serene little lake, now a reservoir for the Löntsch power works, at the foot of the sombre precipices of the Glärnisch. At the end of the road, a track goes to the summit of the dreary Pragel Pass over which the Russian soldiers under Suvorov tramped in the autumn of 1799 during their retreat from the Muotathal.

Higher up the Linthal itself, the village of Schwanden marks the beginning of the Sernf Tal which leads to the Alpine village of Elm, at the foot of the Piz Segnes. Elm is a centre for some comparatively easy mountain climbs, to the Martinsloch en route for the Segnes Pass and Flims, the Kärpfstock and the Hausstock. Suvorov's Russians came this way over the Panixer Pass to Ilanz after they crossed the Pragel. The Freiberge above Schwanden was made a Chamois reserve as early as 1569, less to preserve the animals than to ensure that each man of Glarus should have the two beasts to which he was entitled at his marriage. It is, perhaps, worth adding that a man from Schwanden was the first to bring potatoes from Ireland to Switzerland in 1697.

There is another resort on the shelf above the valley, the charmingly located village of Braunwald. This looks towards the massive Tödi, Clariden and Hausstock mountains, and is the starting point for a number of ascents, up the neighbouring peaks, over the rough Kisten Pass to Briel (or Brigels) or across the Clariden Pass to Amsteg in the Reuss valley. From the Linthal itself a long excursion leads through woods and gorges to Alpine pastures and wild rocky heights before reaching the Ober-Sand Alp at the foot of the Tödi. The Sand-Alp Pass, some three or four hours further on, 9,120 feet high, situated between the Tödi and the Catscharauls, affords a splendid prospect and descends by a steep and stony track to Disentis. The canton of Glarus ends as the road up the Linthal climbs the Klausen Pass towards the Reuss valley and the lake of Lucerne.

The river Linth, which used formerly to rush in full flood to the lake of Zürich, was diverted between 1807 and 1827 by a skilful piece of engineering on the part of Conrad Escher, into the Walen-See, a noble piece of water, some nine miles long and one and a quarter miles broad. It lies at the foot of

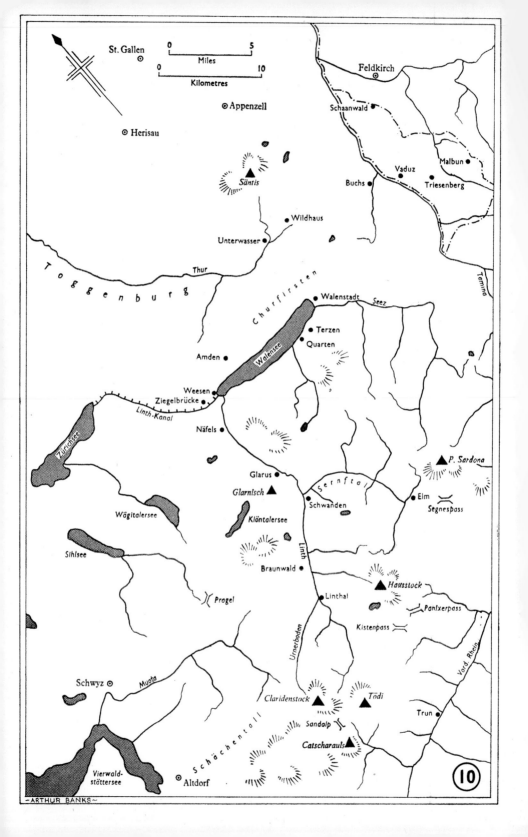

St. Gallen ⊙

Miles
0   5
Kilometres
0   10

⊙ Appenzell

⊙ Herisau

Feldkirch ⊙

Schaanwald

Säntis ▲

Vaduz   Malbun

Buchs   Triesenberg

Wildhaus

Unterwasser

T o g g e n b u r g

Thur

Tamina

C h u r f i r s t e n

Walenstadt   Seez

Terzen
Quarten

Amden

Walensee

Weesen
Ziegelbrücke
Linth-Kanal

Näfels

P. Sardona ▲

Zürichsee

Glarus
Glarnisch ▲

S e r n f t a l

Elm
Segnespass

Wägitalersee

Klöntalersee

Schwanden

Sihlsee

L i n t h

Braunwald

Hausstock ▲

Panixerpass

Pragel

Linthal

Kistenpass

Vord. Rhein

Schwyz ⊙   Muota

Urnerboden

Schächentall

Claridenstock ▲   Tödi ▲

Trun

Sandalp

Catscharauls ▲

Vierwald-
stättersee

⊙ Altdorf

⑩

~ARTHUR BANKS~

the precipitous cliffs of the Churfirsten range of mountains, mistakenly believed to have been so named after the seven princely electors of the Holy Roman Empire. These great grey ramparts descend so steeply towards the waters of the lake that there are only two hamlets on its northern shore. The little village at the western end of the lake is a pleasing place to spend a quiet holiday, as is also Amden, a group of houses surrounded by pastures on the slopes of the Churfirsten, reached by a narrow road from Weesen. The villages along the shores of the Walen-See bear names which in all probability commemorate the numbering of medieval pasture lands, Quinten, Unterterzen, Quarten, Prumsch and Siguns. Murg leads to a picturesque valley, with little lakes and high alps.

The Walen-See which Coxe described as 'uncommonly wild and picturesque' and affording 'a perpetual variety of beautiful and romantic scenes' terminates at the little town of Wallenstadt, once busy with traders passing from Germany through the Grisons to Italy, but now a provincial backwater. In the early sixteenth century, Benvenuto Cellini, who had just crossed the still snow-covered Bernina and Albula passes, had a dangerous passage of the lake after leaving Wallenstadt. The ferry was peculiarly primitive and a sudden storm arose—'sometimes,' as Coxe wrote later, 'a violent north wind rushes down from the mountains, and renders the navigation dangerous.' Cellini and his fellow-travellers prepared to hang on to their horses in the hope that if the ferry sank, as there seemed every likelihood of its doing, the horses would swim to the shore. Cellini, it should be added, was wearing a coat of mail and heavy boots. Fortunately, before they had to put this to the test, they were able to scramble on to a small promontory jutting into the water and make their way along the shore to Weesen.

The country north of the Walen-See, from which it is separated by the Churfirsten, partly Appenzell and partly St. Gall, is very attractive. The valley of the Toggenburg at the head of which rise the Churfirsten and the Säntis range consists of meadows and rich farming land, topped by fir-clad slopes. The many shades of green blend with the timbered chalets, to provide an unforgettable pastoral picture. The region was originally governed by its own counts, but when the line became extinct in 1436, the cantons of Zürich and Schwyz battled for possession. Subsequently it fell into the hands of the abbot of the rich monastery of St. Gall, but his overlordship was much resented by a population which was largely Protestant and resulted in constant conflict, more especially the Toggenburg war of 1712. The great Swiss reformer, Ulrich Zwingli, was himself a native of these valleys and was born at the little village of Wildhaus where his reputed house can still be seen. Here he was brought up by his uncle, Bartholomew, who was rural dean of Weesen.

Wildhaus, which is some 3,600 feet high, is at the foot of the Schafberg,

7,822 feet, and two miles from the little village of Unterwasser, which is well-suited for making the ascent of the Sieben Churfirsten and of the Säntis. It is more probable, however, that the traveller will reach the top of the Säntis, 8,215 feet high, and the highest peak in the Appenzell range, by the very remarkable Schwebebahn, an aerial railway which has been described as 'one of the most daring conceptions of its kind in the Alps.' The cars are lifted on cables up the rocky cliffs of the Säntis, rising some 3,677 feet in 12 minutes. The view from the summit as a result of the mountain's isolated position embraces not merely the lake of Constance, the plains and mountains of Bavaria but the Grisons and the Bernese Alps.

The Appenzellers, like the men of Glarus, realise that the price of liberty is eternal watchfulness, as the record of constant disputes with their spiritual and temporal overlord, the abbot of St. Gall, shows. One part of the canton, the Inner Rhoden, has remained mainly Roman Catholic in religion, while the other, the Ausser Rhoden, accepted Protestantism. They remain loyal to their past traditions, to the meeting of the people in full assembly, and more than many other Swiss, like to wear their lovely peasant costume. 'The country,' Coxe wrote in the eighteenth century, 'is singularly wild and romantic; consisting of a continued series of hills and dales, vallies and mountains, the tops of which are crowned with most luxuriant pastures . . . the hills and vales being strewed thickly with hamlets, scattered at a small distance from each other, and exactly placed in the very spots which a man of taste would have chosen.' The railway train and the motor car have contributed an inevitable element of sophistication. There is a certain amount of village industry. But in general Coxe's picture of this little-visited Alpine region remains true.

The furthest corner of the Swiss Alps is separated from the mountains of Appenzell by the broad and fertile valley through which the river Rhine flows on its way to the lake of Constance. It constitutes the minute and fascinating principality of Liechtenstein, joined to Switzerland by a customs union since 1920. It consisted in the middle ages of two fiefs of the Holy Roman Empire, the county of Vaduz, including the mountainous region and the southern part of the Rhine valley, and the lordship of Schellenberg, comprising the northern part of the valley. These passed through various lords, the counts of Montfort, the barons of Brandis, the counts of Sulz and the counts of Hohenems, until James Hannibal III, count of Hohenems, in desperate need of money sold Schellenberg in 1699 to Prince John Adam of Liechtenstein, head of a noble Austrian house. Thirteen years later he added the county of Vaduz to his possessions. The prince was thus able to convert his titular royalty into an imperial fief. The Emperor Charles VI created the principality of Liechtenstein in 1719 and gave its ruler a seat in the Imperial College of princes.

53 *The countryside in Appenzell; the Santis in the background*

The princes for the most part continued to live in Vienna where they amassed great wealth and a wonderful collection of pictures. Prince Joseph Wenzel was one of Maria Teresa's marshals in the Seven Years' War. Prince John I commanded the Austrian armies in the war against Napoleon. Prince Aloysius I was a patron of the arts. His successor, John II, ruled over his small state for seventy-one years from 1858 to 1929 and outlived a series of European revolutions. He had seen his state engaged in war against Prussia as a member of the German Confederation in 1866 and yet survive the Confederation's dissolution. The First World War had brought the Imperial house of Austria into penurious exile. The little state, which had abolished compulsory military service in 1868, escaped the troubles of the youthful Austrian republic, and the prince found that Vaduz was a more secure home than his lovely palace in *Vienna infelix*. He had had the fortunate notion of transferring much of his world-famous art treasures there too. The Liechtensteiners, more fortunate than their neighbours in the Vorarlberg, applied for and were admitted into a customs union with Switzerland in 1920.

Liechtenstein may be regarded as a part of the Swiss Alps. Yet no one who visits this lovely little land can neglect its past history. Its national colours, of blue and red, and its dynastic colours, of red and white, are everywhere. Picture postcards of the prince, Francis Joseph II who has been ruling since 1938, and his wife, appear in nearly every shop. The complicated royal coat of arms surmounts the royal pew in the choir of the parish church and appears on the façade of the government building. Liechtenstein is perhaps best known to the outside world by reason of the frequent issue of new stamps of high aesthetic quality, the sale of which greatly assists the revenues of the state. The prince, who had a few years ago to restore from his own pocket the defalcation of an official, has done what he can to encourage the finances of the state by attracting and sponsoring light industries. The chief minister may sometimes be seen in the Café Real in Vaduz, drinking his evening coffee and smoking his pipe. When a small group of Nazi sympathisers tried to force an *anschluss* with Austria shortly before the Second World War, the attempt was frustrated by the local priest and some Boy Scouts. As there was no gaol in Liechtenstein, the prisoners were incarcerated at St. Gall. The taxes are so light that a very large number of companies are registered here; but it is expensive to become a naturalised subject of this last surviving member of the Holy Roman Empire and the German Confederation.

This minute state, where the cows are said to outnumber the inhabitants, is a mountain land, sloping down to the river Rhine by the side of which grow the grapes from which pleasing table wines are made. The little capital is dominated by its castle, much restored in the early twentieth century, which

54 *Wildhaus in the Toggenburg; the Santis in the background*
55 *Elm, Glarus*

is lodged imposingly on a rock overlooking the roofs of the town. There are many mountain walks in the country behind the Rhine valley; but I must add that in damp weather I have encountered as venomous horse flies in the woods here as anywhere else in Switzerland. We were staying at a little hotel outside the town. I can always enjoy an odd half-hour, especially in wet weather, skimming the visitors' book of those lesser hotels whose owners encourage their guests to contribute prose, verse and even illustrations laudatory of the hotel itself and of the beauties of the surrounding country. In the book of my Liechtenstein hotel a Yorkshire lady delighted me by writing that the dramatic and splendid view over the Rhine valley to the mountains beyond reminded her very forcibly of the charms of Ilkley Moor. If to discover the similar in dissimilarities is always a sign of genius this lady must take a lofty seat in the hierarchy of the elect. Above Vaduz winding roads meander to small mountain resorts, Triesenberg, which boasts a modern church of some distinction, Silum, Sücca and Malbun, all centres from which there is a number of attractive mountain walks.

Liechtenstein is in some respects the last outpost of the Swiss Alps; but the Alps do not properly belong to Switzerland alone. They extend into France, Italy and Austria; but Switzerland contains their heart just as the Alps have themselves been the nucleus of the Swiss state. No cursory survey of the Swiss Alps can do justice either to their beauty or their history. The writer, like the summer or winter visitor, is an ephemeral traveller in a land which he only superficially understands. All he can do is to point to certain features which have caught his attention and impart this information to others. He may incidentally help them to comprehend the nature of the country through which they travel or which they have visited. For the rest he realises to what small extent he would be in a position even at the end of a lifetime spent among the mountains to describe their beauty or the lives of the people who live under their shade. He can only declare with the seventeenth-century writer, Robert Burton: 'peregrination charms our senses with such unspeakable and sweet variety, that some count him unhappy that never travelled, a kind of prisoner, and pity his case, that from his cradle to his old age beholds the same still.'

INDEX